They said to him, "Tell us who you are so that we may believe you."

He said to them, "You read the face of the sky and earth and he was in your presence then but now that he is before you you do not know how to read him."

THE FACE OF THE

SKY AND **EARTH**

MEDITATIONS ON THE

GOSPEL OF THOMAS

THE FACE OF
THE SKY
AND EARTH

Meditations on the *Gospel of Thomas*

Bro. Jeremy Puma

First published on *Fantastic Planet* in 2003-2005

By Bro. Jeremy Puma

Minister, Palm Tree Garden Gnostic Community

Copyright 2007 Palm Tree Garden Publications

ISBN: 978-0-6151-4274-6

A Note on Translation

As a practicing Gnostic, it struck me as unfortunate that the extant translations of *The Gospel of Thomas* were limited to those performed by members of the scholastic community, who, generally speaking, are not adherents of the religious tradition in question. *Thomas* represents a living, breathing collection of information, and in the interest of allowing that information to break free of the realms of scholasticism, I determined to learn enough about the Coptic language to attempt my own translation from the perspective of a student of Gnosticism. Although I am in no way fluent, I amassed a small collection of textbooks and glossaries and set about translating the *Gospel* word-by-word. The translation of each Saying in this collection is the result of this endeavour. Although the informed reader will no doubt note many similarities between my translation and those of my predecessors, it is my sincere desire that the serious student of the Gnostic Way will also find a notable number of differences.

I am greatly indebted to the following Coptic resources, to which I constantly referred during the composition of this text:

- *Introduction to Sahidic Coptic* by Thomas O. Lambdin
- *Coptic Gnostic Chrestomathy: A Selection of Coptic Texts with Grammatical Analysis and Glossary* by Bentley Layton
- *A Concise Coptic-English Lexicon, 2nd. Ed* by Richard Smith

Unless otherwise noted, all excerpts from the New Testament were taken from *The Unvarnished New Testament*, a translation from the original Greek by Andy Gaus, and all excerpts from Gnostic texts (barring *Thomas*) from *The Nag Hammadi Library in English*, edited by James A. Robinson.

Introduction and Apologia

1. From Blog to Book

This commentary on *The Gospel of Thomas* originally appeared—in a much-truncated form—between and November of 2003 and March of 2005, on the "Fantastic Planet" weblog. Composed as an attempt to provide a cohesive collection of thoughts and meditations on that most prevalent of Gnostic scriptures, I wanted to produce something that would be useful instead of merely interesting, something that addressed modern concerns within a Gnostic context, by a Gnostic, for people interested in Gnosticism.

Since this commentary originally appeared on a website, and was composed over the period of a year and a half, I make no apologies for differences in tone, style and focus from Saying to Saying. Some are downright scholarly, some conversational. Since one of my major goals was to present the text as a living document, writing within each moment, I actually embrace these variations, and look to them to provide the reader with what I consider an illustration of Gnostic exegesis.

There are naughty words in here. A sense of humour helps.

While composing this commentary, I attempted to ask myself two questions. First, regardless of whether the source material is "officially Gnostic," it is beyond doubt that the work was valued in the original communities of Christians who would one day be labeled as such. So, what would these words have meant to those original communities, and to the individuals who utilized *Thomas* in the specific, textual context represented by the collection of Gnostic material uncovered at Nag Hammadi, Egypt in 1945. In other words, *Thomas* has never existed in a void. How does it look in relation to Gnosticism in general?

The second question, in many ways more difficult, essentially boils down to *gnosis*. Gnosis is the recognition that each of us contains a part of the divine, a part which is at odds with the limitations of reality as we perceive it. It is a revelation that cannot be described, and it is like knowing someone personally, being acquainted with someone, rather than like knowing the contents of a book or the definition of a word. Gnosis can hit one expectedly or unexpectedly, but usually the latter. It can be as immediate as a slap in the face, or as slow and gradual as an accumulation of snow. The experience is like diving into an infinitely cold swimming pool for an infinitely small period of time and seeing something infinitely large and glorious, only to be pulled out again almost immediately. Gnosis is a direct and specific knowledge of, not faith in, God. So, the second question becomes, "Where is the *gnosis* in *Thomas*, and how can we apply it to our lives in the modern world?"

To elaborate, most Gnostics discuss gnosis in terms of sleep versus wakefulness. When one has had gnosis, one is said to have 'awakened from sleep.' In *The Secret Book of John*, for example, Jesus says **"He who hears, let him get up from the deep sleep."** When one has had gnosis, one has awakened from a bad dream. Like waking from sleep, gnosis is a natural experience, available to anyone and everyone. Of course, those who are more open to it are more likely to find it, but it can nonetheless strike anyone, anywhere, any time. This, in essence, is Jesus' message in *Thomas*: that in spite of the worries of life, divinity can, and does, break into all of us. We just have to recognize it for what it is.

2. The Pleroma vs. The World of Forms

Within any discussion on gnosis, one would do well to include the idea that the Gnostics called *Pleroma*. Pleroma, which translates literally into 'fullness,' is to the whole of sensible human reality, or the *"World of Forms,"* what gnosis is to the individual. It is the filling of the macrocosm with God, the gradual process of the Kingdom of Heaven unrolling across the whole of existence. The World of Forms, imperfect, needs to be made perfect by God, so it is slowly but certainly filling with spirit and divinity. Pleroma is used to describe the Spirit of God, the Kingdom of Heaven, God itself, or the Ideal Realms, all of which "fill" the World of Forms. The Pleroma is also often referred to as a place— an indwelling of spirit— and various levels of reality came to be known in Gnostic literature as "the Pleromas," each a living, active sphere.

As an analogy, think of the World of Forms as a hollow sphere, and God as a sort of pinkish gas. Once a gas is put into an empty container, it expands to fill that same container. When a gas is spread out enough, one may not even be able to see the gas within the container, but it is certainly present. In this way, God fills the World, is present in everything, refines and is expanding into everything. Since God is in everything, one only has to seek to find it. God is his own Kingdom, and the Kingdom is already here, making itself stronger. Each person who attains to gnosis helps the process, and each person who wants to make things 'good' allows the forces of imperfection to weaken, enabling God to fill the universe even sooner.

Someday, the World of Forms will be so full of God that it will begin to become more and more perfect. The perfection will overwhelm the imperfection, and the World will be absorbed into the Pleroma. At this point, there will be no difference between the World and God. There will only be God. And, if we all work on filling the Universe with God, with spirit, then of course the Kingdom will be here on Earth: Earth and the Kingdom will be the same. It is spreading out all around us, but we do not see it happening. This is the central result of the Pleroma teaching: the rectification of the World of Forms. This is the message of the *Gospel of Thomas*, a message that appears clearly and distinctly only if read contextually.

Gnosis and pleroma existed, as ideas, for centuries before the birth of Jesus in Palestine, and can be found in most cultural mythologies, in some way or another. Everyone talks of the inbreaking of the divine into our world, the happiness that results from being possessed by God, and that, although we do not currently exist in paradise, we eventually will, either as a people or each of us individually. Unfortunately, human society somehow managed to forget this fact. Like the children's game 'telephone,' in which a message is passed from person to person and eventually becomes vastly different from the original, the information that man receives from the pleroma is often mutated after time, until it is once again able to break into someone who is in a position to spread the idea. Nonetheless, it often does reach into people who can spread the idea, and since everyone is different, everyone has a different gnosis.

As a Christian Gnostic, I see the sort of ultimate experiencer and exemplar of the Gnostic experience, the mythological epistemology by which I try to lead my meagre existence, as the Jesus of *Thomas*, who, as a recipient of living information, 'saved mankind,' as God, and as the Messiah, by reminding us that the world is filled with God, you just have to use your ears to hear him. Jesus was a man who was possessed by the same divine spirit that had possessed other great teachers of the past. The Christos, or Holy Spirit, had descended into Jesus the Man. Jesus understood this inbreaking as gnosis, and, when he did, recognized the divinity in everything and everyone, including himself. Thus, he preached that everyone should be loved and respected, and should try to do good, because divinity is everywhere, but we, as imperfect humans, are unable to experience it directly.

Jesus was possessed by the Christos, the Gnostic Holy Spirit. Most Canonical Christians would understand the Gnostic Christos as the Logos, described in the first chapter of the *Gospel of John*. This was Jesus' own, individual gnosis; it was the Word of God, spoken directly to Jesus, which filled him, and which he subsequently became. For this reason, Jesus is said to have been the 'Only Begotten Son of God.' Also, as the Christos played an important role in the Gnostic creations myths, and literally became one with Jesus, it can be said that Jesus was present at the proverbial 'In the Beginning,' as well as, in most cases, the Garden of Eden. The redemption of the entire universe is represented by Jesus' gnosis. Just as the universe is filling with God, so did God, through the medium of the Christos, fill the essential being of Jesus, literally transforming him into God incarnate. *The Tripartite Tractate*, a Valentinian work, has this to say on the subject of the Logos and its relation to Jesus:

> The Logos uses him as a hand, to beautify and work on the things below, and he uses him as a mouth, to say the things which will be prophesied.

To even near the highest realms, one must achieve at least a sense of understanding, or gnosis. After all, did not Socrates derive inspiration from the famous words "Know Thyself," "Gnôthi Sauton," over the temple at Delphi? Gnosis is "Know Thyself FOR Thyself."

Goodwill and love are the natural result of the experience of gnosis and the resultant freedom. In the *Dialogue of the Saviour*, perhaps a preparatory text for Gnostic Christians who are about to be baptized, Jesus expounds upon the path, or "Way," to the Kingdom of Heaven. In one section, Judas (Iscariot? Thomas? It does not specify) says to Jesus, **"Tell me, Lord, what the beginning of the path is."** Jesus replied, **"Love and goodness. For if one of these existed among the Archons, wickedness would never have come into existence."**

Since the coming of the Kingdom of Heaven is the Parousia, so can each person, through the medium of gnosis, have an individual Parousia, an individual resurrection or anastasis, even before death. When the spirit becomes one with the Kingdom of Heaven before death, it can never again be turned away from that Kingdom. Thus, after death, the Gnostic spirit is assumed by God in an ultimate anastasis.

3. Philip K. Dick: Modern Gnostic Prophet

Modern society is witnessing a revival of Gnostic thought within popular culture. Nothing is more illustrative of this than the popularity of the writings and ideas of Gnostic visionary and Science-Fiction Author Philip K. Dick (1928-1982 CE). Besides being a prolific sci-fi author whose stories and novels have been made into films like "Bladerunner," "Total Recall," "Minority

Report" and "A Scanner Darkly"—not to mention the obvious influence of his work on films like "The Matrix" Triolgy and "Waking Life"— Phil compiled his most essential spiritual questions in an eight-thousand page *Exegesis*. As such, "Phildickian" Gnosticism has a definite "database" of symbolic language and images, and a definite mythic structure. For instance, "The Black Iron Prison" describes the control system of the Archons. "Plasmate" refers to the living information in which the Logos resides. "The Palm Tree Garden" represents paradise, the Reality underneath the layer of Maya.

Phildickian Gnostics also attempt to find God within what he referred to as "the trash strata," the discarded items for which the Illusion usually has no use. This includes conspiracy theory, occultism, pop tabloid culture, etc. Nothing is so outlandish that it should not be investigated. If someone says that giant reptilian overlords live underground and sacrifice virgins to the Queen of England, we take a look! We might find something of value, because God hides in what has been discarded.

Phildickian Gnosticism also looks at everything in the spirit of FUN! Gnosticism and spirituality never have to be drab and joyless, centered on sentimentalised theological texts full of abstract terminology. Gnosticism can be described in terms of NeoPlatonic analysis of a Kentucky Fried Chicken Commercial, or it can be described in terms of Superman Comics, or it can even be described in the terms used by the original Gnostics. Phildickian Gnostics see the entire World of Forms as a playground of symbols, behind any one of which God could be hiding.

More than anything else, however, Phildickian Gnosticism requires constant inquiry, a hyperactive investigatory spirit that is willing to change its mind (or, in Phildickian terms, find a different expression of Nous) whenever necessary. This is an essential aspect of the spirit in which this commentary was composed.

4. The *Gospel of Thomas* and You

The most important lesson of Gnosticism as illustrated in the *Gospel of Thomas* is the pursuit of the Divine by the individual. The expression of this Divine within each individual manifests based on that individual's experience. In other words, you might disagree with much of what I have to say in this commentary. In some ways, it is better if you do, because these are **my** conclusions to which I arrived after thought and meditation and prayer. But, if you disagree with something in these pages, or are put off, or hate hate hate something you read, fine!

The important thing is simply sharing some thoughts with people who are interested in Gnosticism. Although I have attempted to construct these commentaries in a way that will be accessible to the layman, I have also assumed that those perusing a commentary on a Gnostic Gospel will be interesting, intelligent people who can figure out difficult stuff.

THANK YOU

I am profoundly indebted to the following individuals, in no particular order, who all helped inspire this work in too many ways to count:

The Apostle Judas Thomas, Emily, Brett Hamil, Reverend Sam Osborne+, Father Jordan Stratford+, Tim Boucher, Ran Prieur, Joel Gazis-SAX, Kenneth Patchen, Nikos Kazantzakis, Doug and Anna Dalrymple, Philip K. Dick, Dogen Zenji, Antonio de Nicolas, Maria Colavito, Dr. Robin King, Plato, George Herriman, Kobe Louise the Libertarian Dog, all of the wonderful, amazing readers of "fantastic planet," all of those individuals throughout my life who had occasion to shake their heads thinking "there he goes again with that danged Gnostic stuff," and, of course, the Holy and Divine Mother Sophia, without whom literally nothing would be possible.

❧THE SAYINGS❧

ONE

These are the secret Sayings that Jesus, who lives, spoke, and Didymos Judas Thomas wrote down. And he said, "Whoever falls onto the meaning of these words will not taste death."

This introductory passage explains itself rather well. The introduction makes reference to "Jesus, who lives," which points out the fact that whenever the passage is read, Jesus is alive to both scribe and the reader.

"Didymos" and "*Thomas*" both translate to "Twin." There was a long-standing tradition in certain circles that Jesus had a twin brother named Judas, who was called "Judas *Thomas*" ("Judas the Twin") to distinguish him from that other famous Judas. The concept of *Thomas* as Jesus's twin occurs frequently in Gnostic literature, usually related to the idea that each one of us has a perfect Ideal Twin. The *Pistis Sophia* expresses this concept in direct relation to Jesus through a tale from Jesus's childhood, told by his mother Mary:

> When thou wast small, before the Spirit came upon thee, while thou wast in a vineyard with Joseph, the Spirit came forth from the height, he came to me into my house, he resembled thee. And I did not recognize him and I thought that he was thou. And the Spirit said to me: 'Where is Jesus, my brother, that I meet him?' And when he said these things to me, I was confused and I thought that he was a phantom to tempt me. But I took him, I bound him to the leg of the bed in my house, until I came out to you in the field, thou and Joseph, and I found you in the vineyard, as Joseph was hedging the vineyard with reeds. Now it happened, when thou didst hear me speaking the word to Joseph, thou didst understand the word and thou didst rejoice. And thou didst say: 'Where is he that I may see him? Or else I await him in this place'. But it happened when Joseph heard thee Saying these words, he was agitated and we came up at the same time, we went into the house. We found the Spirit bound to the bed. And we looked at

thee with him, we found thee like him. And he that was bound to the bed was released, he embraced thee, he kissed thee. And thou also, thou didst kiss him and you became one.[i]

This meeting between Jesus and his divine Twin, after which they merged into a single being, contains ideas that we find throughout the *Gospel of Thomas*, and to which we will be returning. Jesus, as the perfected Human, mirrors each of us in our encounter with our own Divine Twins.

The first Saying encourages the reader/listener not only to read the Sayings, but to *understand* them, thus the term "meaning," which we might also translate as "gets." The "words" that follow have deeper meanings than appear at the surface. The phrase in the original Coptic, **"falls onto the meaning of"** the Saying, implies a far more radical process of uncovering the meaning of the Saying than simple reading and interpretation based on book knowledge. Study of the Sayings in the *Gospel of Thomas* can never be a truly intellectual exercise; rather, it is a matter of moving forward and falling into meaning as though falling off of a cliff.

Although not obvious from this Saying alone, those who truly understand the meanings behind the Sayings will, according to the teachings of Jesus, not be affected by death. This is not to say that understanding these Sayings will keep one's physical body alive throughout eternity; what is meant by "death" in this context will be illustrated as we go along. Suffice to say that the Sayings have to be understood at a deep, personal level— they cannot just be recited and memorized by rote.

TWO

Jesus said, "One who seeks should not stop seeking until one finds what one is seeking. When they find what they are seeking, they will be troubled. When they are troubled, they will be amazed, and will become king over the All."

Jesus warns the listener not to expect an experience like any other experience he or she has ever had when following his Way. The Gnostic Jesus points his listeners towards *gnosis*, direct and personal acquaintance with the fullness of divinity that resides within the World of Forms. Gnosis is similar to the concept of Zen enlightenment or satori, as described by famous Zen teacher D.T. Suzuki:

> Satori may be defined as an intuitive looking into the nature of things in contradistinction to the analytical or logical understanding of it. Practically, it means the unfolding of a new world hitherto unperceived in the confusion of a dualistically-trained mind. . . . Logically stated, all [the World's] opposites and contradictions are united and harmonized into a consistent organic whole. . . . Satori can thus be had only through our once personally experiencing it.

> Its semblance or analogy in a more or less feeble or fragmentary way is gained when a difficult mathematical problem is solved, or when a great discovery is made, or when a sudden means of escape is realized in the midst of most desperate complications; in short, when one exclaims "Eureka! Eureka!"[ii]

Gnosis is literally a surprise—it hits its recipient over the head like an archetypal flowerpot fallen from a brownstone's windowsill! When one has had the Gnostic experience—not limited to followers of the Gnostic path, but available to anyone—one is indeed amazed, and comes away with the all-encompassing feeling that one knows the entire Universe and, indeed, that everything is new.

The Sayings in the *Gospel of Thomas* are Gnostic Christian *koans*, seemingly absurd riddles designed to lead the seeker to enlightenment, similar to the old Zen question, "What is the sound of one hand clapping?" Each Saying can lead the contemplator to the experience of gnosis. This idea also sheds more light on Saying One, wherein Jesus exhorts his listeners not just to listen or read, but to understand, to "get" the meaning of his words. One falls onto the meaning and shouts "Eureka! I see!"

Another important feature of gnosis is that it can only be experienced on a personal, individual level. There is no such thing as group gnosis; what brings me to the understanding might be completely different than what brings you to a similar conclusion. By extension, my experience of gnosis may lead me to completely different conclusions than yours. You may read this commentary and disagree with it completely, but that does not mean that you have not achieved gnosis, nor does it mean that my understanding is incorrect.

The important thing, according to this Saying, is to keep going, to keep seeking until one finds that surprising insight. When that insight is stumbled upon, anything one wants will truly be available.

THREE

Jesus said, "If your leaders say to you, 'Look, the Kingdom is in the sky,' then the birds of the sky will precede you. If they say to you, 'She is in the sea,' then the fish will precede you. Rather, she is within you and she is outside you. When you know yourselves, then they will know you, and you will understand that you are children of the living Father. But if you do not know yourselves, then you live in poverty, and you are the poverty."

The Kingdom of Heaven, or "Paradise," is not a physical place that we go to when we die; it is an aspect of Reality that has no place because it is in every place. Gnosis gives one this understanding. This relates to the concept of "Pleroma," or fullness, a term used by canonical Christians but developed into a very important aspect of Gnosticism.

The original Gnostics were not polytheistic, as much as they were *panentheistic*—everything emanates from God; everything from spirit to matter is connected and filled with the spirit of the Unnamable One. The emanations that sprang from the Spiritual Realms are layered above matter, but not separate from it. Rather, the matter is "full" of the essence of spirit. The word that the Gnostics used to describe this "filling" was *Pleroma*. In most Gnostic teachings, the Christos, a manifestation of the Logos, or Word of God, is seen as the spirit that fills the material realms, activated by Sophia, the Holy Mother of Divine Wisdom.

The Kingdom of Heaven resides within and without everything that has been created. Experiencing gnosis, which is akin to "waking up," removes the veil of illusion that has been superimposed over the sensible— inasmuch as we "sense" it— World of Forms and allows one to see things as they actually are.

The second part of the Saying lets us know that those who have attained gnosis are often recognizable as such by those who seek to control them—priests and leaders— but also by others who have attained gnosis. More importantly, however, is the understanding that each and every one of us is a son or daughter of the Unknowable, "children of God." In the Gnostic tradition, the filial relationship between Jesus and God is not exclusive—rather, Jesus wants us to understand that we are all children of God. We simply need to remember this fact.

Of course, if we have not remembered it, if we have not discovered this for ourselves, then the spell cast on the World of Forms fools us into thinking we live in a garbage dump, when we actually live in a palace. As we will see in later Sayings, wealth, to the Gnostics, does not represent material wealth so much as it represents a richness of living information, the Logos, or Word, in which gnosis resides. "Poverty" is a Gnostic code word[iii] that signifies the life of one who has not achieved gnosis, the absence of the Logos. This parallels the statements that Jesus makes about the Kingdom of heaven. "You are the poverty" parallels his statements about knowing for one's self, and the meaning should be evident from the rest of the Saying.

FOUR

Jesus said, "The person old in days will not delay to ask a little child seven days old about the place of Life, and that person will live. For many of the first will be last, and will be one alone."

The very old and the very young— both stages of life when we are closest to non-life. The infant, one could say, has just arrived from where the old man is about to go. In spite of the years of experience the elderly man has amassed while here in the World of Forms, he still does not truly *understand* very much, and so he asks the newborn.

Trying to ask a baby something about the meaning of life will not likely result in a comprehensible answer. This is actually kind of an odd image, when one thinks about it. "Hey there, little baby— can you tell me what the deal is with Life?" However, it is also quite appropriate— the old soul with a lifetime's worth of experience admitting his own ignorance and asking the infant about life shows humility and earnestness on the part of the old man. To receive any kind of answer would imply an intuitive, Gnostic experience that depends upon the old man's inner knowledge more than upon any sort of answer a baby could give. And, in asking this question and so exercising the Gnostic experience, that old man "will live."

Jesus does not mean that we should all ask babies questions about the nature of Being. Jesus most likely means that we should approach the question of the Meaning of Life with the humility and understanding implied by the parable, looking to the unexpected and innocent for answers to essential questions. "Many of the first will be last" should be familiar as a concept to most Christians. In the context of this particular Saying, the infant would be the "first," and the elderly person the "last," and vice-versa.

As one resides in the imperfect illusion of the World of Forms, one begins to accumulate the trappings of the illusion. By the time one becomes elderly, one is firmly ingrained into the system of the World of Forms. The spiritually "new," here represented by the newborn, have not yet been usurped by the illusion and imperfection of the World of Forms. However, if they go through life without knowing the Way, they will become spiritually "old," weighted down by the baggage of imperfection, and they will be "all alone" outside of the community of those who have achieved gnosis, or perhaps "alone" in the sense that the spirit of the universe (of Jesus himself) will be absent from this person's life. Indeed, as we all know, Jesus often admonishes us to become like children, like those who do not carry the baggage of a lifetime of living in an imperfect creation.

FIVE

Jesus said, "Know what is in the presence of your face, and what is hidden from you. The hidden will be disclosed to you. For there is nothing hidden that will not appear."

This Saying is almost stunning in its simplicity, and has many parallels in canonical teaching. What is right in front of us? One could answer that it is the World of Forms in which we live, our collection of experiences as humans. Throughout this text, we refer to the realms of perception, in which one uses one's senses to perceive one's surroundings, as the "*World of Forms.*" The World of Forms is any place in which one can stub one's toe. It is the level of forms and gross matter and measurement, the level of emanation in which we reside. It is a level missing an indescribable "something."

What is this "something"? One could answer that it is the presence of the Holy in our daily lives. But if one does not even know what one is looking for, this distinction cannot be made. How can you find the answer to your questions, Jesus asks, if you do not even know what your questions are?

Here Jesus asks us to pay attention to our surroundings and our place in the World of Forms. Too many seekers do not make the distinction between what they know and experience and what they do not know but desire to experience. Before one can know God, one has to figure out the difference between these two things. By following the Gnostic way, one comes to realize, however, that what is hidden (the presence of the Holy) **is** "in the presence of your face." This is an essential aspect of the realization of gnosis.

To put it another way, let us come up with an absurd metaphor. Imagine that we have all been born without the ability to see the color green. We are vaguely aware that something must be wrong with our vision, but we cannot quite put our finger on it. A teacher comes along, however, who has learned that a simple change in awareness will allow us to awaken the faculty that enables us to see green. He develops a magic lens that allows one to see green temporarily, but it can only be used by the person who wishes to see green, and each lens can only be used one time.

Could the teacher really describe the color we cannot see? How does one describe "green"? There would literally be no way for us to describe "green," other than as some abstract quality that we could not normally perceive. "Green," however, exists around us, and once someone uses the teacher's methods and is able to see green and pass the methods along, but is still unable to describe "green" to those who cannot see it.

Let us imagine a conversation between someone who can see green ("Greenie") and someone who cannot ("Nogreen"):

> **Nogreen**: This forest is nice, but I have this feeling that I'm missing something— I feel a kind of existential emptiness.
>
> **Greenie**: Yes, you are missing something. You're unable to see the color green.
>
> **Nogreen**: The color green? What the heck is that? Describe it to me.
>
> **Greenie**: Er . . . it is difficult to do that. It is all around us, mixed in with the other colors. Everything looks different when you can see green, because it affects the colors it is mixed with. The leaves are green, this shirt is green— even your eyes are green. But you can't see it.
>
> **Nogreen**: But what **is** green?
>
> **Greenie**: It is in the trees, it is on the ground, it is everywhere around us.
>
> **Nogreen**: But you're not telling me what it is?
>
> **Greenie**: I can't tell you. All I can do is give you this lens to look through.
>
> **Nogreen**: Wha'? That's absurd.

Greenie: Look, you tell me you're lacking something. I know that the thing you're lacking is right in front of your face. All you have to do is put this on and you will see what I mean.

Nogreen: (Sigh.) All right, gimmee that. (Puts lens on, sees green) HOLY CRAP!

The analogy only works on a very basic level, because when we discuss gnosis, we are unable to discuss something that can be experienced with our normal sensory faculties. The Kingdom of Heaven, God, the Christos are everywhere around us via the Pleroma, but we do not see them because the illusion of reality hides them.

According to Jesus, however, "nothing that's missing cannot be found." The Gnostic experience is available to anyone who seeks it in earnestness and humility. Once the World of Forms has been redeemed, the veil of illusion will be lifted for everyone, and all that is hidden will be revealed.

SIX

His disciples asked him and said to him, "Do you want us to fast? How should we pray? Should we give alms? What food should we stop eating?"

Jesus said, "Do not tell lies, and do not do what you hate, because all things are revealed in the presence of the Kingdom. After all, there is nothing hidden that will not be revealed, and there is nothing covered up that will remain unrevealed."

The disciples are asking Jesus to address the issue of legalism. Essentially, they want to know how to act— what kind of things Jesus expects his students to do. This was an important question in early Christianity: did Jesus intend to reform Judaism and preserve the legalistic precepts of Hebrew Scripture, or did he intend to establish an entirely new Way that used some of the semiotic symbols of Judaism but would be practiced differently?

The Gnostic would answer that it was probably a combination of the two approaches. Jesus had to use the language of his culture, and having been brought up in Judaism, he used its symbols to discuss his Way. Jesus indicates many times in both canonical literature and Gnostic literature that he did not come to destroy the law, but to fulfill it. His actions, however, often deviate from Hebraic Law, and Jesus does not indicate that he places great import on any specifics. Indeed, Jesus teaches a kind of "legalistic relativism," in which he desires to strip away the baggage of legalism and proscription and understand the very foundations of man's relationship with God.

In the traditional canon, the famous passage from *Matthew* 22:35-40 sums this up:

And one of them versed in law asked him as a test, "Teacher, which commandment in the law is important?" He said to them, "You are to love the Lord God with all your heart and all your spirit and all your mind. That is the important and first commandment. The second one is similar: You are to love those close to you as you love yourself. All the law and all the prophets hang from these two commands."

In Gnostic teaching, this very same attitude is well expressed in Saying 6. The disciples ask Jesus very specific questions, asking for precepts and instruction. But, Jesus indicates, when one knows the very root of law, the specifics will come naturally. There is no need to outline specific laws commanding this or that— just keep in mind a few simple, patently obvious things and the rest will follow.

Jesus also uses this moment to teach the disciples about the importance of honesty before man and God. "Do not lie" is his first admonition. His second is a bit more cryptic at first glance: "do not do what you hate." Notice, Jesus is not telling the disciples to do whatever they want to— he tells them not to do anything they do not want to do. This is an important idea. When one prays, or gives charity, or observes a specific diet, but hates doing it, one is acting dishonestly. Better not to pray at all than to pray because it is a chore that the law proscribes. It does not matter one bit if one gives to the poor just because he or she is told to give to the poor. What matters is that the person giving, or fasting, or obeying the "law" does this because he or she knows for him or herself that it is the right thing to do, that it is something worth doing because it is pleasing to God.

Exactly what Jesus means by prayer, charity, fasting, etc. is left up to the reader/listener. Jesus has confidence in humanity's ability to recognize the good for what it is, and follow through in action. When one comes right down to it, in spite of the heaviness and intricacy of Judaic legal code, one's diet, one's chosen method of prayer, one's decision to fast, one's decision to give to the poor— these are all relatively unimportant and focusing on them is worthless. The important thing is honesty to God, one's self, and one's neighbors.

By extension, those who do hate praying, giving charity, etc., whether they do these things or not, have clearly not achieved gnosis and do not know God. These people are acting simply based on the shallow, illusory experience of a defective World of Forms, and are acting as part of the unredeemed World of Forms that Jesus came to save.

Finally, back again to the phrase we heard in the previous Saying, but this time with a slightly different connotation. In the Kingdom of Heaven of which Jesus speaks so often, those who have led dishonest lives are transparent before God and the body of the saved World of Forms. The nature of reality and God will be experienced by all present.

SEVEN

Jesus said, "Blessed is the lion that the human will eat, so that the lion will be human. And foul is the human that the lion will eat, and the lion still will become human."

Saying 7 is the perfect example of the inscrutable and enigmatic passages that some critics of the *Gospel of Thomas* find mysterious and confusing. Humans eating lions? Lions becoming human?

The Gnostic approach to these mysterious admonitions is to seek for the "Aha!" moment, when the meaning of the Saying stands out clearly as correct **for the individual experiencer**. Although knowing what other people think about the Sayings can assist the reader/listener in developing an interpretation, the reader/listener really needs to spend time considering each Saying for him or herself. This is where the "inscrutability" of cryptic Sayings like number 7 becomes a benefit to understanding gnosis, instead of a drawback—if they were exceptionally clear and required no effort to understand, they would be passive instead of active. Their great difficulty and inscrutability invites analysis that transcends the typical logic of the world of limitations.

Many critics of the Gnostic way claim that it is too elitist, too difficult to attain. Although it is true that it can be a difficult path, the fact is that it is only cryptic and difficult and elitist for those who see it that way. This is one of the big Gnostic secrets: nothing in Gnosticism is truly a secret, because, as mentioned in Saying 6, everyone knows everything in the Kingdom of Heaven, and everything hidden will be revealed. Claiming that the Gnostics keep too many secrets makes as much sense as criticizing a newspaper for neglecting to call you and tell you, personally, about a story it has printed.

The lion is fraught with symbolism. It appears only a few times in the canonical New Testament, but never in the Gospels. It is an important symbol in Jewish scripture, especially among the prophets. We also find the lion mentioned In Gnostic mythology, in which a false and insane deity called the Demiurge created the world. In this system, the Demiurge, the god of *Genesis*, is essentially an insane jailer who seeks to imprison humanity so that they may worship him. The spirit of God, the Logos/Sophia, in the form of the serpent, descends into the Garden and saves humanity by encouraging Adam and Eve to eat the fruit of the Tree of Knowledge of good and evil.

Pertinent to this discussion is that the Demiurge represents the imperfection of the World of Forms's creative powers. Time after time in the Nag Hammadi Library and other extant Gnostic texts, we find the Demiurge described as having the face of a lion. For instance, from *The Hypostasis of the Archons*:

> And it assumed a plastic form molded out of shadow, and became an arrogant beast resembling a lion. It was androgynous, as I have already said, because it was from matter that it derived.

Or, from *On the Origin of the World*:

> And when *Pistis Sophia* desired to cause the thing that had no spirit to be formed into a likeness and to rule over matter and over all her forces, there appeared for the first time a ruler, out of the waters, lion-like in appearance, androgynous, having great authority within him, and ignorant of whence he had come into being.

And, from *The Secret Book of John*:

> And when she saw (the consequences of) her desire, it changed into a form of a lion-faced serpent. And its eyes were like lightning fires which flash.

And, interestingly, a reference is made in one of the non-Christian texts included in the Nag Hammadi Gnostic corpus, the *Sentences of Sextus*, which are excerpted from a popular collection of sayings which circulated among the Roman Empire. The *Sentences* tell us that, **"The lion also rules over the body of the wise man . . . ."**

From these excerpts, we conclude that the lion, to the Gnostics, and by extension to Jesus in Saying 7, represents the Demiurgic, bodily, corporeal and material passions of mankind, the passions that, though they seem creative and active, are actually destructive, insane, and passive. The human—in this context representing one with enlightened gnosis—who "eats" the lion devours his or her Earthly passions, transforming those passions into true spiritual experience. The lion that eats a human, however, represents the passions which overcome a human and, in turn, become that human.

This is startlingly insightful: Jesus is telling us that passions are not evil, but one must be sure that one is not devoured by them, one must try to use one's passions to further the Way, changing the animal passions into human passions, instead of letting one's animal passions devour one's self.

EIGHT

And he said, "The Gnostic is like a wise fisherman. He cast his net into the sea and drew it up from the sea full of little fish from below. Among them the wise fisherman discovered a good large fish. He cast all the little fish back down into the sea, and easily chose the large fish. He who has ears had better listen!"

The canonical Gospels are full of references to fish, fishermen, nets, etc. This is no major surprise— Jesus's ministry started in what were essentially fishing villages surrounding the Sea of Galilee, and according to most sources, many of the disciples were fishermen. For this reason and others, pastoral Sayings like number 8 have an inherent authenticity that illustrates how well Jesus was able to connect to his students.

A parallel can be found in *Matthew* 13:47f, in what most refer to as "The Parable of the Net":

> "Once again, the kingdom of the skies is like a large net thrown into the sea, collecting some of every species, which, when it was full, they dragged onto dry ground, and sat down and sorted the good fish into their creels and threw the bad ones out. That's how it will be in the culmination of time. The messengers will ride out and separate the evil from the just and throw them into the furnace of fire, where the wailing and gnashing of teeth will be."

Matthew's version is quite different, and uses the parable as a warning that some souls may spend an eternity in Hell. When reading Sayings in *Thomas* that have Biblical parallels, one must ask: why did the compiler choose to record the Saying as he or she did? Why does Saying 8 omit the rest of the parable found in *Matthew*? If we choose to adhere strictly to the historical certitude of the Gospel authors, this presents us with some difficulty. If, however, we acknowledge that the authors of the Gospels were different individuals with different agendas, we can conclude that to the Gnostics, Jesus did not mean what the author of *Matthew* (or his sources) thought he meant. The author of *Matthew* was taking the parable rather literally. The Gnostics were speaking in their own semiotic code.

The first difference between the two is the subject of the parable. In *Matthew*, it is the Kingdom of Heaven that is like the Wise Fisherman. In *Thomas*, it is the Gnostic. This is an important distinction: in *Thomas*, the responsibility for separating the good fish from the bad does not fall to the angels or the Kingdom of Heaven. Rather, the responsibility falls upon the shoulders of each and every individual who has experienced gnosis.

What, then, is the difference between the good and bad fish? *Matthew* makes it easy for his readers: the good fish are the good people, the bad fish are the bad people. The bad fish get sent to hell and burn forever. The good fish go to heaven and get harps and wings and unlimited cotton candy.

In *Thomas*, however, the fish are not "good" or "bad," they are "large" or "small." If one is out fishing with a professional fisherman who knows, as have fishermen since time immemorial, that fish populations can be depleted by over fishing, and ask him why he is tossing back the small fish, one reply might be that the small fish need to be thrown back so that they have the opportunity to grow into larger fish. Aha!

The Gnostic argues that the true, Alien God is all-forgiving and, above all, filled with the forgiving love and infinite compassion that it asks from each of us. This is an important aspect of Gnosticism that must be applied to any interpretation of Gnostic ideas. So, looking at the Saying while keeping this in mind, the interpretation becomes quite different.

Jesus is not condemning those who have not experienced the Way to eternal damnation. He tells us that, just as fish will grow naturally if one lets them, spiritual development will grown naturally in the seeker. It is not important to hound those who are not yet ready— focus instead on those who have already come to fruition and are already curious seekers with a developed spiritual inclination. The others will come along in their own time, in their own environment. This idea is supported throughout the Gnostic corpus: the Way is personal, and requires personal development. Without a personal understanding of the Way, the seeker is a small fish who has yet to grow.

NINE

Jesus said, "Look, he went out, filled his hand with seeds, and scattered (them). Indeed, some fell on the road, and the birds came and gathered them. Others fell on rock, and they didn't send roots down into the earth and didn't send ears rising to the sky. Others fell on thorns, and they choked the seeds and worms ate them. And others fell on good soil, and it caused the fruits to grow up to the sky: it yielded sixty per measure and one hundred twenty per measure."

Yet another famous parable, "The Parable of the Sower," found in all of the synoptic gospels: *Mark* 4, *Matthew* 13 and *Luke* 8, in almost identical terms to those found in *Thomas*. As with certain other parables, the canonical versions of this parable provide us with Jesus's interpretation, where *Thomas* leaves the interpretation to the reader. For instance, in the *Gospel of Mark* 4:14-20, we find the following:

> The sower sows the word. And some of these people are the ones by the wayside: where the word is sown, as soon as they hear it, Satan comes, and takes away the word that was sown. And some of them are the ones sown on the rocky ground: when they hear the word, right away they joyfully seize it, and yet it has no root in them, it is only temporary, so that if there's pressure or persecution because of the word, they fall right down. And others are the ones sown into the thorns: they hear the word, and then the worries of the day and the strategy of moneymaking and the concerns of the future come in and choke off the word, and it becomes unable to bear fruit. And still others are the ones sown on good soil, who hear the word and take it in and bear fruit, here thirty, there sixty, and there a hundred."

In this case, there would be very little with which the Gnostic would disagree. Jesus's canonical explanation of this parable serves quite well, in this case, to explain the Gnostic understanding thereof.

It is worth making a few interesting points, however. The Gnostic could just as well replace "gnosis" with "the word" and "the Demiurge" with Satan. The Gnostic view of Satan differed from sect to sect. For the most part, the duties and actions assigned to Satan in canonical Christianity fall upon the shoulders of the Gnostic Demiurge, referred to in Gnostic scripture as the "God of This World." The Gnostics, with some exceptions, found enough to fear and revile in the Demiurge, but due to lack of material, we cannot be certain that they maintained a cohesive understanding of the Devil. In practice, it is probably safe to assume that they can be taken as two different names for the same player.

One should pay special attention to the reference to the "worries of the day and the strategy of moneymaking and the concerns of the future;" Jesus is teaching his students a kind of detachment from the things of the world that are owned by God of This World. No matter how modern evangelists try to spin his teachings, it is patently obvious that Jesus had at best a disdain and at worst complete contempt for money and wealth. In this sense, Jesus was an anarchist— even in the canonical Gospels, questions on money and wealth are absurd and should be kept entirely separate from matters of spirituality. Although it is rather long, this excerpt from Jacques Ellul's *Anarchy and Christianity* is worth quoting in full, as it explains Jesus's teachings on power and money both succinctly and intelligently:

> We read in *Matthew* 17:24ff. that "when they came to Capernaum, the collectors of the half shekel tax spoke to Peter and said, 'Does not your teacher pay the half shekel tax? Peter responded, 'Yes.' And when he came into the house, Jesus said to him, 'What do you think, Simon? From whom do the kings of the earth take tribute or taxes? From their own sons or from foreigners?' Peter answered, 'From foreigners.' Jesus then said to him, 'The sons are thus free. However, not to scandalize them, go to the lake, cast your line, and take the first fish that comes up. Open its mouth, and you will find a shekel; take that and give it to them for me and for yourself.'"

> Naturally, for a long time attention focused on the miracle. Jesus was making money like a magician! But the miracle is without real importance as such. On the contrary, we have to remember that the miracles of Jesus are quite different from marvels. He performs miracles of healing out of love and compassion. He performs some

extraordinary miracles (e.g., stilling the storm) to come to the help of people. He never performs miracles to astonish people or to prove his power or to stir up belief in his divine sonship. He refuses to perform miracles on demand. If people say: Perform this miracle and we will believe in you, he refuses absolutely. (This is why faith is not linked to miracles!) A miracle of the type found here is thus inconceivable in and for itself. What then is the point of it?

Jesus first states that he does not owe the tax. The half shekel tax was the temple tax. But it was not simply in aid of the priests. It was also levied by Herod the king. It was thus imposed for religious purposes but was taken over in part by the ruler. Jesus claims that he is a son, not merely a Jew but the Son of God. Hence he plainly does not owe this religious tax. Yet it is not worth causing offense for so petty a matter— that is, causing offense to the little people who raise the tax, for Jesus does not like to cause offense to the humble. He thus turns the matter into a subject of ridicule. That is the point of the miracle. The power which imposes the levy is ridiculous, and he thus performs an absurd miracle to show how unimportant the power is. The miracle displays the complete indifference of Jesus to the king, the temple authorities, etc. Catch a fish— any fish— and you will find the coin in its mouth. We find once again the typical attitude of Jesus. He devalues political and religious power. He makes it plain that it is not worth submitting and obeying except in a ridiculous way.[iv]

In summary, this parable leads the reader/listener towards an understanding that, though the word is scattered upon everyone, only those who take it in and plant in and tend to it as a farmer tends to his crops will be able to take advantage of it. If one is too distracted by life in the World of Forms, and does not nurture the word as Jesus indicates one should, then the word will be fruitless in him or her.

TEN

Jesus said, "I have cast fire upon the world, and look, I'm guarding him until he burns."

Saying 10 has certain subjective parallels in the canonical Gospels, but nothing specific— references to fire are many. In the canon, we are often led to believe that the fire of which Jesus speaks refers to the fire of Hell, like in *Matthew* 3:11-12 (the speaker is John the Baptist):

> Now I bathe you in water to change hearts, but the one coming after me is stronger than me: I'm not big enough to carry his shoes. He will bathe you in holy breath and fire. Winnowing-fan in hand, he will clean up his threshing floor, and collect the grain to be put into the silo and the husks to be burned in unquenchable fire.

The original Greek meaning of "to baptize" is "to wash" — indeed, in Greek, one would "baptize" one's clothes, hands and dog.

Jesus as the Word of God does not intend to toss people into eternal fire. If, indeed, "to baptize" means "to wash," then a baptism by fire would not be destruction— it would be a cleansing, a purification. Fire was, and is, an extremely important and potent ritual item used in ceremonies from every tradition. The incense burned at your local church reflects the inclusion of the Holy Fire in Christian ritual.

Why, indeed, would Jesus set the entire world on fire in the literal sense— does he intend to cause Hell on Earth? The answer: he wouldn't. In Saying 10, when he says that he has cast flame upon the world, he means that he's in the active process of purifying the world through the message of gnosis, and he's watching over it until it is clean, and the imperfections caused by the Cosmo's schizophrenia have been disinfected.

ELEVEN

Jesus said, "This sky will pass away, and she who is above her will pass away, and the dead are not alive, and the living will not die. You all were eating the dead, and you made it come alive. When you should be in the light, what will you do? On the day when you were someone, you made the two. But when you should be two, what is it that you will do?"

What is the sky above the sky? Perhaps Jesus was referring to the common belief that an "upper atmosphere" of ether existed above the sky, as illustrated by the poem "Summer Harvest" by Gnostic teacher Valentinus:

Summer Harvest

I see in spirit that all are hung

I know in spirit that all are borne

Flesh hanging from soul

Soul clinging to air

Air hanging from upper atmosphere

Crops rushing forth from the deep

A babe rushing forth from the womb.[v]

This illustrates the concept, mentioned previously, of *panentheism*, in which creation is a series of emanations that descend from God and "hang" from one another.

Jesus might also refer to the false heaven of the Demiurge, the creator deity. This heaven is a sort of "upstairs reality" that one who followed the Demiurge during life would be sent to as a reward (punishment?) for faithful service to the insane creator. Speaking Platonically, this "Heaven above the sky" is part of the illusion, an hallucination that will most assuredly disappear when the World of Forms is redeemed by the word of God. Whether such a Heaven exists physically or is more of a psychological phenomenon must be decided by the reader/listener— either way the same rules apply.

Given what we know about Gnostic myth, that Jesus was speaking about a standard, literal judgment/end times scenario is doubtful. If he was, he would not say that the dead will not live. But, what then, does it mean? Once again, let's turn to the codebook. "Dead" and "living" are often used by Gnostics to refer to the two states of human awareness. When a Gnostic says dead, he or she usually means "asleep," "unaware," "without gnosis." Someone who is living, on the other hand, is someone who has a personal acquaintance with God, someone who is awake. So, of course the "dead," or those who are as of yet unenlightened, will not "live"— and neither will the "living" die.

The next part of the Saying is even more cryptic (on the surface): **"During the days when you ate what is dead, you made it come alive. When you are in the light, what will you do?"** In Saying 7, Jesus said that the lion was lucky to be eaten by a human, because in the process it would be transformed into a human. This is a direct parallel to the above statement: eating that which has no spiritual nature makes it come alive. This is not some kind of religious dietary rule— eating would mean absorbing, taking something into yourself, taking that which has no spirit and refining it through the power of your own experience. This is especially potent in light of the Eucharist. When one eats the host, it becomes God within, and the living information which resides therein actives the divine spark in those who partake of communion.

It is a description of gnosis, which indeed refines the illusory nature of reality and allows one to see things in the light of God and the word. Whenever this happens, the World of Forms is redeemed and saved. The apocalypse and resurrection happen every single day. Thus, after the World of Forms is redeemed, everything is fully realized and refined. In other words, using the terminology from this Saying, nothing will be dead. So, Jesus asks us to consider the fact that we know how to deal with that which is illusory while we have access to that which is dead. The illusion is dead, spiritually, until it is refined by the Gnostic experience. But, once everything is redeemed and "the dead do not live," and one "should be in the light," what does one do? Jesus does not provide an answer— he can't. This is something each of us needs to ponder for ourselves.

TWELVE

The disciples said to Jesus, "We know that you are going to leave us. Who will be the greatest, over us?"

Jesus said to them, "No matter when that place comes, you are to go to Jacob the Righteous, the one for whom the sky and earth came into being."

As Freud might have said, sometimes a Saying is just a Saying. If, indeed, the *Gospel of Thomas* records the actual Sayings of Jesus, then it could very well be that Jesus meant for "James the Just," sometimes referred to as a brother of Jesus, to take over his ministry after he left. James is a frequent mythological character in Pastoral Gnosticism, which spread throughout Asia Minor, all the way to India. The historical James became the leader of the nascent Jerusalem church.

James and Thomas represented this Pastoral Gnosticism, and similar ideas can be found in the Gospels attributed to them. A long-standing tradition mentions that Thomas left Palestine after the Passion and took the Gospel to India, stopping and founding churches along the way in Turkey, Persia, etc. Christian churches in India continue to trace their lineage to Thomas, and theological features in texts attributed to both Thomas and to James are very similar. This is in contrast to the scholarly, Alexandrian "Western," or Philosophical Gnosticism of Valentinus, heavily influenced by Paul, which stretched from Egypt to Spain.

Note that the Saying does not indicate how or why Jesus plans to "leave." One thinks that if he had told the disciples he was going to die, or ascend to Heaven, the Saying would most certainly mention that fact. Maybe it was a case of the teacher leaving the room and leaving someone in charge? "No spitballs, please— I want all faces down in your scripture scrolls. James is in charge until I get back."

THIRTEEN

Jesus said to his disciples, "Compare me to something and tell me what I resemble."

Simon Peter said to him, "You resemble a righteous angel."

Matthew said to him, "You resemble a wise philosopher."

Thomas said to him, "Master, my mouth will not allow me to say what you are like."

Jesus said, "I am not your master. Because you have drunk, you have become intoxicated from the bubbling spring that I have measured out."

And he took him, and withdrew, and spoke three words to him. When Thomas came back to his friends they asked him, "What did Jesus say to you?"

Thomas said to them, "If I tell you one of the Sayings he spoke to me, you will pick up stones and cast them at me, and fire will come from the stones and burn you up."

How strange, how oddly vivid and telling— Saying 13 says so much, with so little, that it astounds one with every reading. This Saying describes, perfectly, the Christology of Gnosticism. Who was Jesus? Why did he have followers? Was he the Son of God? A prophet? A philosopher?

Jesus is asking his disciples what he reminds them of— he is asking them what they think about his nature. This has echoes in the synoptics, where Jesus discusses the matter with Peter. In the canon, we find three versions of the story.

Mark 8: 27-30:

> And Jesus and his students went out to the villages of Philip Caesarea. And on the way he asked his students, "Who do people say I am?" And they said to him, "John the Baptist, or some say Elijah, or others say one of the prophets." "And who do *you* say I am?" Peter answered, "You are the Anointed." And he commanded them to tell no one about him.

Mark is the earliest of the synoptic Gospels; note that, in *Mark,* Jesus does not give Simon Peter the duty of founding the Church— it is probable that this section was composed before Peter took over. In fact, in *Mark,* Jesus warns his disciples not to tell anyone that he is the Christ. Why is this? Saying 13 offers a reason.

But first, the other Gospels. *Matthew,* written second, is aimed at a Jewish audience. *Matthew* is filled with quotations from Hebrew scripture, and intends to illustrate to Jewish critics and followers that Jesus fulfills specific prophecies.

Matthew 16:13-20:

> After Jesus came into the regions of Philip Caesarea he asked his students, "Who do people say the son of humanity is?" They said, "Some say John the Baptist; others say Elijah, the rest say Jeremiah or one of the prophets." He said, "And you? Who do you say I am?" Simon Rock [that is, Peter] answered, "You are the Anointed, the son of the living God." Jesus answered him, "You are in luck, Simon Johnson: flesh and blood didn't reveal this to you, but my Father in the skies. . . . Then he ordered his students to tell nobody that he himself was the Anointed.

This time, Jesus assigns Peter to head his church. *Matthew* is the only synoptic to assign the church to Peter at this point. It is likely that this was written after Peter had already assumed the position of the "Pope" of Rome by a member of his church who sought to defend his leadership. Again with the secrecy— do not tell anyone. But why?

Let us move to *Luke* 9:18-21, written for a Roman audience, more cosmopolitan citizens of the Empire:

> And it happened while he was praying privately that his students were with him, and he asked them, "Who do the crowds say I am?" They answered, "John the Baptist . . . others say Elijah, others say one of the ancient prophets risen again." Then he said to them, "And you, who do you say I am?" Peter answered, "The Anointed of God." But he strictly ordered them not to tell that to anyone. . . .

In Gospel after Gospel, we find Jesus instructing his disciples not to tell anyone that he is the Messiah, the Son of God, etc. We can assume that this is a fairly accurate recording of instructions that Jesus actually gave. Why is this? Is it to keep him and his followers safe from persecution? Possibly— according to most accounts, Jesus had already amassed great numbers of followers by this time. Is it because Jesus is unsure about his own role? Doubtful—if we know one thing about Jesus, it is that he spoke with certainty and authority, and did and said very little without considering consequences.

In Saying 13 of the *Gospel of Thomas*, however, the "Messianic Secret," as this strange secret is known, is explained quite well. So, from the top, Jesus gathers three of his disciples together for a little pop quiz. Notice that he does not ask anything about what "the people" think he is— this is strictly for his disciples.

Peter thinks that Jesus is like an angel. This is apparently the wrong answer. In this context, angels are messengers from God, but exist as pure spirit. Jesus is most definitely human. Matthew says that Jesus is like a wise philosopher. Wrong again: philosophers are all human, but Jesus is most definitely partially divine. Finally, Thomas hits upon what Jesus thinks is exactly the right response: "Master, my mouth will not allow me to say what you are like." Jesus immediately replies that he is not Thomas's master— and that Thomas is drunk on the teachings of Jesus!

Peter and Matthew made a grave error— they tried to describe Jesus in understandable terms. Granted, it was kind of a trick question, but only Thomas understood what Jesus was asking for:

NOTHING.

When Jesus tells Thomas that he is not his "master," he is not telling Thomas the he, specifically, is not Jesus's student any longer, but pointing out the irony that while claiming not to know what Jesus was like, he still called him a "master."

Jesus did not consider himself an angel, a teacher, a master, the Messiah, or anything of the kind. Since the spirit and Logos of the indescribable God works through him, human words cannot possibly describe Jesus's mission— this is something that needs to be experienced in the same way that a wine drinker experiences drunkenness.

This clarifies the Messianic Secret of the synoptic gospel. Jesus did not intend to simply keep his nature a secret. Jesus was instructing his disciples not to give away this information because he wanted the people to decide who he was for themselves. Jesus is far too complex to pin down using the paltry terminology of standard religious discourse. He was not the Messiah (but he was). He was not the Son of God (but he was, indeed). This is another Gnostic "secret"— Jesus's role was so unique, so different than anything that had come before, that words are inadequate to explain just who he was. His role could not be explained— it had to be experienced.

Jesus tells Thomas that he "got" the answer, as he did not try to compare him with something. Then, as what we can only assume is a special reward for being correct, for having the proper acquaintance with the person of Jesus and the indescribability of his role, Jesus takes Thomas aside and tells him three Sayings. Only Thomas gets to hear them.

What are these three Sayings (or "words")? Thomas returns to the disciples and they are dying to know what Jesus told him. Whatever the words, we are not told either. They must, however, be especially potent, and even blasphemous, because Thomas worries that the others would try to stone him if they heard them. And worse, they would be consumed by a fire that springs forth from the stones! Stoning was the Judaic punishment for severe blasphemy, the kind of blasphemy that one commits when one declares that God is a Poopyhead, or that God does not Exist, or that Baal is a better God than Yahweh.

What does this mean? Many scholars try to find actual words or Sayings that could apply. According to Church Father Hippolytus, writing in *A Refutation of All Heresies,* a Gnostic sect called the Naasenes said that the world depended upon three secret words: Kaulakau, Saulasau, Zeesar. Hippolytus states that, **"Kaulakau, they said, was Adamas, primal man, 'the being who is on high' . . . Saulasau, mortal man here below; Zeesar, the Jordan which flows upward."** Some think that Jesus told Thomas these words, or perhaps similar mystic terms. But, knowing that Jesus told Thomas a few important mystical words, while certainly something probably kept secret, would in no way cause the other disciples to want to stone Thomas. In fact, as important disciples of Jesus, they would probably be excited to know them. No, what Jesus told Thomas was far more serious than that.

First, though, what about that fire that bursts forth from the rock? What does that mean? This is nothing that usually happens when one tosses rocks about. Perhaps the "fire" is the baptizing fire discussed in Saying 10. Or, perhaps the fire is simply a power so potent and unbelievable that the disciples would indeed be consumed by it.

Let us look at what we have learned from the Saying thus far:

1) Trying to describe Jesus and his role using normal logical analysis will not work, as he cannot be compared to anything.

2) Thomas, "drunk" on Jesus's teachings, realizes this.

3) Jesus tells Thomas three things that he cannot tell the other disciples, because they are incredibly blasphemous to the Jewish mindset.

4) However, if one tried to punish someone for revealing these three things, he or she would be punished in turn by fire.

This does not help much, but perhaps this obscurity is intentional! It seems that if Thomas could not reveal the three words to the other disciples, fellow students of Jesus, then he cannot reveal them to the reader, either. The "three Sayings" are something that each individual will have to figure out for herself. One will know when one knows. Understand that, REALLY understand it, and one will understand that the meaning of the three sayings transcends logic. The sayings exist within, and it is up to each and every one who follows the Way to uncover the meaning of the sayings in that placeless place where one becomes drunk on the teachings of gnosis.

FOURTEEN

Jesus said to them, "If you fast, you will bring a sin upon yourselves, and if you pray, they will condemn you, and if you give alms, you will be doing evil to your spirits. When you go into any land and walk about in the districts, when people take you in, eat what they serve you and heal the sick among them. For what goes into your mouth will not defile you; rather, it is what comes out of your mouth that will cause you to defile yourselves."

This is another Saying that addresses issues of legalistic proscription and hermeneutics. There are parallels for the general meaning of this Saying throughout the synoptics, and, of course, in Saying 6, in which Jesus tells the disciples to act with honesty and humility.

The first part of the Saying, which addresses fasting, prayer and charity, is similar in context to the aforementioned Saying 6. This Saying, however, is an admonition to humility. Would Jesus literally have instructed his disciples not to pray or give charity? One might understand this Saying in an equally telling manner by adding the phrase "in front of other people": Do not bother fast in front of other people— when others know one is fasting, one has to live up to their expectations instead of the expectations of God. Do not pray in front of other people; doing so opens one to attack for praying incorrectly. Do not give alms in front of other people; that is just showing off. Besides, money does not help people— people are helped by gifts of food and care, not by money. Jesus would have agreed with Mahatma Gandhi when he mentions in his autobiography that he was, "sternly opposed to giving alms to sturdy beggars."[vi]

If one plans to do any of these things, do it with humility, simplicity and because one is inspired by God, not because one feels a sense of obligation. One should not do anything that one does not want to do while on the Way— our actions should be honest and joyful.

There is ample canonical evidence that this is a correct interpretation of this subject. The best evidence comes from *Matthew 6*, where we find the following (oft-quoted) passages during the Sermon on the Mount:

> "Be careful not to put your virtue in front of people to be noted by them. If you do, you will get no pay from your Father in the skies. So when you contribute to charity, do not have a trumpet player go before you, like the fakes do in temples and down alleyways, so people will glorify them; believe me, they have already been paid their wages. But when *you* give to charity, your left hand shouldn't know what your right hand is doing, so that your charity is on the sly; and your Father, watching on the sly, will pay you back.

> "And when you pray, do not be like the fakes who love to pray standing in the temples and on street corners so as to show off for everybody. Believe me, they have already been paid their wages. When *you* pray, duck into the store-room and lock the door and pray to your Father on the sly. And your Father, watching on the sly, will pay you back. (6:1-7)

> "When you fast, do not be like the grim-looking fakes who disguise their faces so they will look to people like they are fasting. Believe me, they have already been paid their wages. When you fast, put on a fragrance and wash your face, so you don't look to people like you're fasting, except to your Father on the sly. And your Father, watching you on the sly, will pay you back. (6:16-18)

Prayer should be a secret, personal conversation between an individual and God. However, to spend too much time and effort railing against these individuals who do these things is counterproductive. Jesus tells us we must concern ourselves with prayer, fasting and charity on a personal level.

The next part of the Saying instructs the disciples to avoid the letter of the Hebraic Law's dietary instructions and even certain instructions on hygiene and contact with the "unclean." It is difficult for the modern mind to understand how radical these instructions must have been— they counter hundreds, if not thousands, of years of practice which survive to this day. What we now know as the "kosher" diet was, and still is, an essential part of Orthodox Jewish society— disregarding these dietary rules would be seen by devoutly Orthodox interpreters of Hebrew scripture as a major problem, akin to suggesting to a political conservative that illegal hallucinogenic drugs should be distributed freely in grade schools.

Jesus's defense of this position is spot on: "what goes into your mouth will not defile you; rather, it is what comes out of your mouth that will defile you." Jesus explains it best in *Matthew* 15:17-20:

> "Don't you see that everything that goes into the mouth passes into the belly and is thrown out into the toilet? But what comes out of the mouth comes from the heart, and those things pollute the person. For out of the heart come evil designs, murders, adulteries, whoring, thefts, perjuries, blasphemies . . . those things pollute a person, but eating with unwashed hands does not pollute a person."

Saying 14 is important because it eschews strict legalism in favor of simple honesty, humility and compassion. Helping someone in need is at the root of God's Way, and no "Laws" can change that fact. But, one must help those in need and honor God and act with goodness because these things are a reward in and of themselves.

FIFTEEN

Jesus said, "When you see one who was not brought out of woman, fall on your faces and worship. That one is your Father."

Who does not have a mother, or who was not born of woman? Are we all not "born of woman"? According to the popular stories about Jesus, even he was born of woman— one could even more accurately say that he had no father. Is this some kind of trick Saying?[vii]

There are actually a few interpretations of this Saying that might fit into Gnostic epistemology. The easiest, and quite likely the most realistic, is that, as every living being has to be born of woman, nobody living deserves worship. Note the terminology: "fall on your faces and worship"— this kind of worship would be reserved for the holiest of persons, and would be unacceptable to the Jews in reference to anything other than God. Jesus could be telling us that earthly leaders— like Caesar, priests, rulers, religious teachers— should not be worshiped as though they are spectacular or more than human. Even Jesus had a mother, and he never asks his disciples to fall on their faces and worship him. Doing such would not only be sacrilegious, but also silly and futile. Jesus could be using creative irony to remind his students that everyone is the same: we all have mothers, we all have an origin— only God is worthy of worship.

One could also interpret 15 without the ironic connotations. Who, then, is worthy of such worship? One "born of woman" is one who has been brought forth from the womb-matrix of the World of Forms, the imperfect creation of the deluded Demiurge. Once one has experienced gnosis, then one's Cosmic pedigree is rendered null and void— one is no longer someone who can claim to have been born of woman; instead one is a child of God, and a member of the Universal Church. Earthly appellations and familial terminology simply no longer apply— when one "denies" one's father and mother and sisters and brothers, one does not truly despise them in the worldly sense, but recognizes that in the grand scheme of the Way, these terms are meaningless.

If this is indeed the case, then everyone who has experienced gnosis is worthy of worship in the same fashion as God, because there can be no distinctions between members of the Universal Church— all are equal, and all are equal in status to Jesus— indeed, to God itself. This is a universal kinship in holiness, and such equality was extended by some Gnostics to men, women, "foreigners," even pagans who had achieved gnosis. This emphasis on equality seemed horrific to the Early Church, and prompted the Church Father Tertullian to comment:

> they all have access equally, they pray equally — even pagans, if any happen to come. . . . They share the kiss of peace with all who come . . . . All of them are arrogant . . . all offer you gnosis.[viii]

Yes, the earliest Gnostics were persecuted by the church for daring to suggest that all men and women are equal in the eyes of God. I wonder what modern society would be like had this inherent equality been accepted by the church instead of denied?

SIXTEEN

Jesus said, "Perhaps people think that I have come to cast peace upon the world. They do not know that I have come to cast some divisions upon the earth: fire, sword, war. For there will be five in a house: there will be three against two and two against three, father against son and son against father, and they will stand to their feet, becoming single ones."

The canonical parallel to Saying 16 is Matt. 10:34-36 (in which Jesus quotes from Micah 7:6):

> Don't think that I came to cast peace across the land. I didn't come to cast peace, I came to wield a sword, because I came to divide 'a man against his father, a daughter against her mother, a bride against her mother-in-law— and to make a man's servants his enemies.'

Certain individuals like to haul out the canonical parallel to this Saying to justify the idea that Christians are allowed to fight in wars, or at least can support them in good conscience. This is completely absurd, and antithetical to everything Jesus taught about our relationship with one another. Using this passage to support "just war" theory takes the passage completely out of context.

Jesus meant that his ideas and the Way are so revolutionary and radical that they will cause strife among family members. Jesus in no way endorses this, particularly in the context that the canon provides us with. In *Matthew* 10, the Saying occurs as Jesus is giving his disciples instructions on how to carry out their ministry. He refers to the fact that their ministry in the world will not be accomplished with ease. He follows by telling them that, "whoever prefers father or mother over me is not worthy of me; and whoever prefers son or daughter more than me is not worthy of me " (see also Saying 15).

We can see that he actually admonishes his disciples to remember that familial distinctions are not part and parcel of his Way— in fact, the strife and infighting within a single household is not something to be supported or condoned, but will be the unfortunate but natural result of introducing Jesus's Way to new people. And, if those people still recognize the distinctions between themselves to the point of fighting, they are "not worthy" of his Way.

The part of the passage from the *Book of Micah*, in context, actually concerns the evil that Israel had fallen into **during Micah's time**. Remember that the author of *Matthew* wanted to convince a Jewish audience that Jesus fulfilled Hebrew prophecies. In fact, it is possible that Jesus never actually quoted Micah, but did say something about setting household members against one another. The author then found a handy quote in Micah and used it to illustrate that Jesus was familiar with scripture.

One simply cannot take this passage to defend "just war" theory— it does no such thing. Jesus illustrates his inherent wisdom, and recognizes the power of his message. As for the "five in a house, three against two" section of the Saying, it is difficult to say why Jesus chose these particular numbers. Some Gnostic and Manichaean texts refer to Five Intelligences in the realms of the Pleroma; perhaps this "three against two" shows how an Earthly manifestation of this divine quintuple can become imperfect.

However, note that the Saying in *Thomas* does leave us with some hope that the "combatants" will eventually "stand alone," "become a single one"— one community, perhaps? One in the eyes of God? Certainly this returns us to the Gnostic concept of the "solitary," or unified individual in light of the Logos.

SEVENTEEN

Jesus said, "I will give you what has not been seen by the eye, what has not been heard by the ear, what no hand has touched, what has not been thought of by the human mind (heart)."

It is worth noting that the Coptic word *'et* can mean both "mind" and "heart." The distinction between the two was far less clear-cut at the time, and we should consider that, in context, the words "mind" and "heart" did not so much refer to the physical brain and heart as they do now. Both translations mean the same thing: this concept cannot be translated. Jesus, indeed, bestows gifts upon those who choose to follow his example.

But, just what is it that Jesus gives? Jesus does not give things that can be sensed using the senses of the World of Forms. In Saying 17, Jesus discusses gnosis and the Way, pure and simple. This is an experience and a concept that originates without the realms of human perception, and can only be accessed, but not described.

This brings an interesting question to mind that many critics of Gnosticism like to drag out whenever confronted by these ideas: if gnosis and Gnosticism and the Way and God are so indescribable, then how is it possible to write or talk about it? If gnosis is such a personal experience that cannot be sensed, then how come so many books were written describing it by the Gnostics? How can a belief survive if nobody can describe the belief?

Most extant Gnostic texts only seek to comment on what Jesus taught about an experience that cannot be described. This is not easy; we rarely even find an actual mention of God or faith in the canonical Gospels that describes these concepts clearly and definitively. The authors of the Gnostic texts were sharing their own experiences and understandings. As Elaine Pagels says in The Gnostic Gospels:

Like circles of artists today, Gnostics considered original creative invention to be the mark of anyone who becomes spiritually alive. Each one, like students of a painter or writer, expected to express his own perceptions by revising and transforming what he was taught. Whoever merely repeated his teacher's words was considered immature.[ix]

The idea of a describing a single, immutable experience in the same terms as one's fellows is absurd in Gnosticism, so we try the best we can.

If one desires to attain gnosis, one certainly can, but one will never be able to tell anyone else what the experience was like. The texts that are written are not meant to describe gnosis, any more than the Zen Buddhist koans were composed to describe enlightenment. Rather, they exist to spur each and every seeker to find it for him or herself, to prompt the reader in the right direction without pushing too hard.

We are limited to the created World of Forms, which is insane, and since it is insane, nothing that exists within it can truly describe it— a disconnect manifests itself as the difference between subjectivity and objectivity. Anything more profound than what is limited to our senses can never be translated into words, seen with the eyes, thought about, or described.

EIGHTEEN

The disciples said to Jesus, "Tell us, how will our end come?"

Jesus said, "Have you found the beginning, then, that you are looking for the end? You see, in the place where the beginning is, so is the end. Blessed be the one who stands on his feet at the beginning: that one will know the end and will not taste death."

The underlying importance of eschatology, or the study of the End Times, given to Jesus's teachings in canonical Christianity is never given as much focus in the Gnostic teachings, and Saying 18 may give us a clue as to why that is. It is unclear whether the disciples are asking about their individual ends, or if they are referring to the highly anticipated "End of Time," but this is as good a place as any to discuss the Gnostic concept of eschatology, which essentially delivers the message that individual resurrection and salvation, herein referred to as "anastasis," and the End of Time Itself, herein referred to as "the Eschaton," are indeed micro- and macrocosmic manifestations of identical phenomena. This is another big Gnostic secret: the resurrection and salvation of each individual human will bring about the resurrection and salvation of the entire World of Forms. The ultimate goal of the Gnostic is to bring about the salvation and redemption of the universe itself.

Anastasis is resurrection on an individual level. Whereas most Christians would declare that this is something that occurs after death, the Gnostic disagrees. To the Gnostic, and to Jesus, anastasis occurs during one's lifetime. Anastasis is, indeed, the experience of gnosis itself, and is the same event that causes one to recognize that the Kingdom of Heaven is "spread out all around you" (see also Saying 3).

Although the Gnostic corpus is full of evidence to support this, the *Gospel of Philip* contains some good examples:

Those who say that the Lord died first and (then) rose up are in error, for he rose up first and (then) died. If one does not first attain the resurrection, he will not die....

While we are in this world, it is fitting for us to acquire the resurrection, so that when we strip off the flesh, we may be found in rest and not walk in the middle....

Those who say they will die first and then rise are in error. If they do not first receive the resurrection while they live, when they die they will receive nothing.

We can also refer to Saying 51 in *Thomas*.

51. His disciples said to him: When will the resurrection of the dead take place, and when will the new world come?" He said to them: "That (resurrection) which you are awaiting has (already) come, but you do not recognize it."

This Saying illustrates the concepts from the point of view of those who believe in a bodily resurrection of the dead on Judgment Day, which makes sense, as this idea was already extant during Jesus's lifetime.

So, we can conclude from these Sayings that Gnostics believed that anastasis and the Eschaton were related, but what does Jesus mean about finding the end by standing at the beginning, and how does this relate to anastasis and the Eschaton? To understand this, one must think philosophically, and we must investigate the Gnostic understanding of space/time (s/t). In order to help us picture this concept, we turn to ever-useful dairy products.

Think of s/t as an infinite block of Swiss cheese (Figure A). In this infinite block, space and time exist simultaneously. The entire block of cheese "occurs" at once— since the block is infinite and nothing exists outside of it to perceive it, no observable change can occur. Every point within the cheese "happens" at the same time.

Now consider each observable "moment" in s/t as a thin slice of the block (Figure B). Let's say that our single slice represents five years' time. Suppose that each air bubble in the cheese represents one human life. In other words, each "hole" in the slice is the sum total of a human's experience during that five years; each human's lifetime actually resembles something worm-like as it traverses the block of cheese.

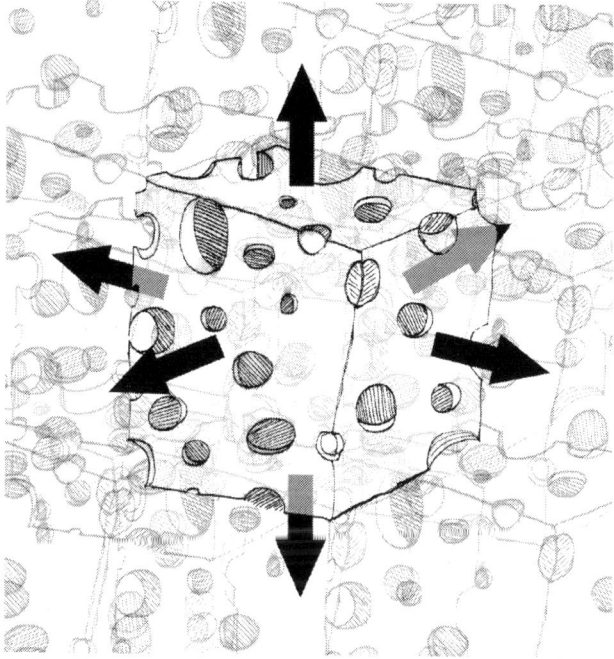

Figure A: Infinite Cheese

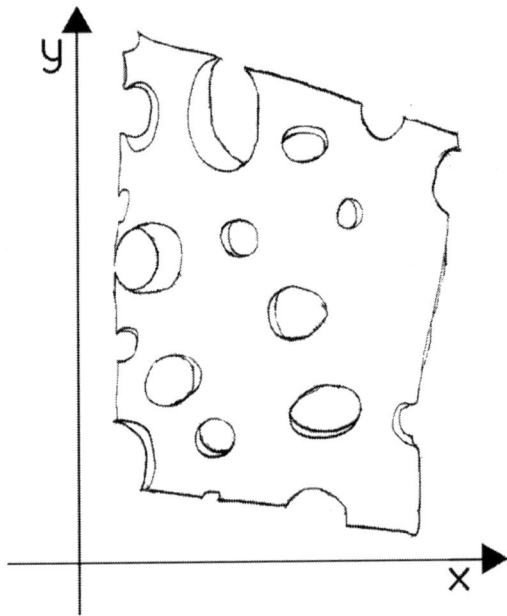

Figure B: Five Years of Cheese

Now then, each of us can only experience our own "holes" while they are traversing the block of cheese. Sometimes the holes intersect, sometimes they expand, sometimes they end sooner than others, but we are limited to perceiving only that which lies within the borders of our individual hole. Now picture that a slice of the cheese, of indeterminate size, is spoiled and mouldy. This slice, and all it contains, is the whole of our World of Forms, the created universe.

This rather imperfect metaphor cannot possibly represent the in-depth nuances of the Gnostic universe, but should suffice for this short discussion. The relevant fact, that Jesus wanted us to understand, is that everything is still part of the same block of cheese. In other words, time, change, motion and space are all illusions based on our limited perception.

We are actually all essential parts of a whole which occurs simultaneously. The consciousness of the World of Forms fills the entire block of s/t, and every experience we have is actually an experience that the universe itself is having. It is counterproductive to talk about anastasis and the Eschaton in terms of "when" and "where" and "how"— all of s/t, as it occurs simultaneously, is a single moment of universal consciousness. **Your** consciousness is literally the universe experiencing itself; realizing this is gnosis. The beginning and the end are the same; they have already occurred, they are occurring, and they will occur. There is a single consciousness in the universe which moves throughout itself— we are all a plurality of the universe.

This idea explains the concept of "universal consciousness," "reincarnation," and "collective unconsciousness" that have been sentimentalized by New Age salespeople and pop psychologists. To put it into layman's terms, consciousness and reality are the universe's sensory organs, the organs it uses to understand itself. Since time consists of a single moment, when I die, the consciousness within me moves to another segment of the universe. My consciousness, which the universe is using to understand itself, could be reincarnated at any point within s/t, any slice in the simultaneous block of cheese. I could be "reborn" in **anyone** or **anything** from the past, present, or future. I will be you; you will be me. Memories of previous lives may reflect this fact— each one of us is a single manifestation of a fragmented whole, so we very well may be able to "remember" perceptions from other incarnations.

Once the universe is fully conscious of itself, it becomes redeemed and realizes that it is whole. The universe itself must experience gnosis and have its own anastasis. This is the Eschaton, which occurs every moment of every day, because there are no "moments". This also explains Jesus's ideas about nonviolence, and the universality of humanity. When one harms another individual, one affects experiences that one will have, or that one has had— one essentially resembles a hand that cuts off the fingers of the other hand. Jesus recognized that this is ridiculous— we should focus on healing, and harming another is not just the same as harming one's self, it **is** harming one's self. How likely are we to shoot someone if we know that we will have to be shot by ourselves at some point?

So why, then, do we perceive things in s/t one slice at a time? Why is the universe fragmented? Why is the universe's perception and consciousness bounding around from person to person to person? And, what does this mean about individuality? This also raises questions about predestination and fate. Nonetheless, one can see how these ideas are illustrated in Saying 18. End and beginning are meaningless phrases— one is as good as the other, and if you have found one, you will find both.

NINETEEN

Jesus said, "Blessed is the one who existed in the beginning, before he existed. If you become my disciples and listen to my words, these stones will minister to you. For there are five trees in Paradise which do not move in summer or winter, and their leaves do not fall. Whoever knows them will not taste death."

The Saying opens with a phrase related to the concepts discussed in Saying 18: the one who came into "being before being" existed before his or her current lifetime— this is all of us, and we are all blessed for it. As the Logos, or Word of God, Jesus himself also fits this bill.

Next Jesus informs his disciples that listening to him will allow them to learn even from the stones. This is due to a most important concept, that of the "Pleroma," or Fullness. The Pleroma concept states, quite simply, that even though our world of experience is defective and perishable, the spirit of God fills every single element it contains. Thus, someone who listens to and understands Jesus's teachings and has gnosis, understands that God fills everything in creation, including the stones themselves— even the stones have lessons for those who seek in humility and honesty. In fact, the spirit of God as Jesus himself resides within the stones, as it resides within everything.

The five trees in paradise are a head-scratcher. Is Jesus being literal? Doubtful— though it has been suggested that Jesus was referring to five actual psychotropic plants of some kind, this interpretation ignores the context of the Saying. It is possible that the Early Christians did indeed utilize psychotropic plants, but the evidence is still spurious enough that without better proof, solid conclusions of this nature escape us.

It is also possible that the five trees correspond to the five senses, that they will become "imperishable" in the Kingdom of Heaven. This is also a reasonable explanation. The Manicheans also referenced five trees in their texts, but again, how they could relate to this Saying is too unclear for anything other than uninformed speculation.

When one reads this Saying, one cannot help but think of modern Gnostic Philip K. Dick, who found his own gnosis in a series of visions. Philip Dick experienced a Gnostic awakening in 1974, which led him to numerous conclusions about the nature of Reality from a Gnostic frame of reference. He described the illusory systems in which we are enmeshed as the "Black Iron Prison," and described the holy living information/Logos as living information termed plasmates. One of his major visions, detailed in selections from his Exegesis as found in his book *VALIS*, included the revelation that:

> 17. The Gnostics believed in two temporal ages: the first or present evil; the second or future benign. The first age was the Age of Iron. It is represented by a Black Iron Prison. It ended in August 1974 and was replaced by the Age of Gold, which is represented by a Palm Tree Garden.

Dick used "Palm Tree Garden" to describe paradise, or the Kingdom of Heaven, many times in his works, and though Jesus doubtfully meant such a concept when he refered to the five trees, I cannot help but picture the five trees as palms. [x]

TWENTY

The disciples said to Jesus, "Tell us what the Kingdom of Heaven is like."

He said to them, "She is like a small grain of mustard, smallest of seeds, but when it falls on prepared soil, it produces a large branch and becomes a shelter for birds of the sky."

It is interesting to note the continuity of subject matter in the Sayings. We go from Saying 18, about knowing where the beginning is, to Saying 19, about preexisting and the five trees, to Saying 20 about seeds growing into plants. This continuity probably served both as a series of "signposts" as ideas in *Thomas* develop, and also as a mnemonic device for those who would memorize texts in lieu of writing them down.

Matthew and *Luke* describe the mustard seed growing into a tree, which could refer to black mustard, a plant that can reach a height of several meters. *Mark* and *Thomas* do not refer to the mustard as a seed that will grow into a tree, but as a plant with broad leaves—delicious mustard greens.

Mustard began as a so-called weed, and when cultivated retained weed-like qualities. It required constant attention to keep one's mustard from taking over the entire garden. However, it is an extremely hardy plant that can survive in drought-like conditions and rough terrain. The Romans and the citizens of the empire loved mustard, as a condiment and a readily available flavoring when most other spices were often as valuable as gold. Unprepared mustard has no real "heat," but with the addition of liquid it takes on the spicy qualities for which it is famous. That Jesus would use mustard as a metaphor shows his ability to create unique and meaningful connections between everyday items and abstract spiritual concepts.

So what can we learn about the Kingdom of Heaven through Jesus's mustard metaphor? The Kingdom of Heaven starts as a tiny seed within one, and requires cultivation and care. However, it is readily available, and despite its ubiquitousness, extremely valuable, comparable to more valuable spices and flavourings which are only available to the wealthy. On its own, it is meaningless, but when "activated" by the Way and gnosis, it becomes alive— "spicy"— as does mustard after its preparation with liquid.

It also "shelters the birds"— the bird was a very common metaphor in the ancient world for the soul. The Egyptians pictured one aspect of the soul as a bird which flew from the body after death, and the Greeks also equated the birds with the soul—the great playwright Aristophanes wrote an entire metaphorical play on the subject called, plainly enough, *The Birds*. This idea even survived into Sufism, in *The Conference of the Birds* by Farid Ud-Din Attar, a metaphor for humanity's quest for enlightenment told in a story about a flock of birds seeking their king.

So the Kingdom of Heaven, when cultivated within, shelters the soul. However, this is also something of a warning. When one grows mustard in one's garden and the mustard goes to seed, it attracts the birds. These birds were not welcome visitors in most gardens, for obvious reasons. When one cultivates the Kingdom of Heaven and it begins to attract birds, the birds may indeed begin to wreak havoc within one's own garden. Any sincere student of spirituality will recognize the inherent truth behind this warning.

TWENTY-ONE

Mariam said to Jesus, "Who do your disciples resemble?"

He said, "They are like little children dwelling in a field that is not theirs. When the Lords of the field come, they will say, 'Give us back our field.' They take off their clothes in front of them in order to give it back to them, and they return their field to them. For this reason I say, if the Lord of a house knows that a robber is coming, he will be on guard before the robber arrives and will not let the robber tunnel into the house of his kingdom and steal his possessions. You, however, keep watch from the beginning of the world. Bind a great power to your loins, so the robbers cannot find a road on which to get to you, because the help that you're watching for will be overtaken. Let there be among you a person who understands. When the fruit split open, he came quickly carrying a sickle and harvested it. Anyone here with ears had better listen!"

This Saying begins with Miriam (Mary) who may or may not be the Magdalene. Just as Jesus asks his disciples to compare him with something in Saying 13, Miriam wants Jesus's opinion on his students.

Jesus states that they are like little children who are living illegally in a field. We know, of course, that Jesus held children in high regard and often counsels his students to become like them. In this regard, the Saying's message is similar to the message in Saying 6, in which the tiny baby is superior to the old man because the child represents someone who does not carry "baggage." When the owners of the field show up and tell the kids to get lost, the kids strip completely naked and give the field to the owners— more than what the owners would expect, no doubt. A common interpretation of this aspect of the Saying might be that the children shedding their clothes represents the disciples shedding their bodies— some even go so far as to say, perhaps taking liberties with context, that the Gnostic would prefer death as an escape from the imperfection of the material world.

Moving along, then, Jesus says that if the owner of a house knows a robber is coming along, he will prepare himself to defend his possessions before the robber arrives. The students of Jesus, however, have been watching since "the beginning of time," which we now know from previous Sayings is the same as the end of time, and is a code that represents the Eschaton/resurrection. Even though they are watching and on guard, the "help" that they are watching for, Jesus counsels, will not be able to reach them— they are on their own.

Jesus concludes with his standard hope that at least one person among them (assumedly someone "who has ears") can correctly understand the meaning of this parable, which is, in essence, summed up in the final point, that "when the fruit ripens, it gets harvested."

The thread common to these seemingly disparate ideas is the concept of attentiveness or watchfulness. The children in the field are watchful, as they are squatting in a field that is not theirs. When the owners of the field arrive, the children are prepared and take off their clothes. So they have to be "naked," or stripped of worldly items, in order to return the field to the owners. This is Jesus's advice on relating to the world in relation to the resurrection and the Eschaton— it has nothing to do with death. Once one has gnosis, one has stripped one's self of worldly concerns and no longer needs "clothes" or the field, which represents the world. Once one has this realization, one can let the rulers of the world have their world, and everything that has to do with it. The concept of "ownership" becomes absurd.

So, Jesus gives the admonition that just as the children were attentive in the field, so must the students be as attentive as someone who knows that a robber is on the way. However, the disciples are not just watching on one specific occasion— they have been watching since the beginning of time, which means that they are **always** watching, waiting expectantly for the Eschaton to arrive. Jesus's comment that "nobody is going to be able to help you" refers to the fact that the Gnostic experience is one's individual experience, and that nobody can really be there to help. We are only our own perceptions— there is nobody else.

Finally, Jesus concludes by underlining these points: one has to be constantly prepared and attentive for the Eschaton/anastasis, because as soon as the fruit (the Gnostic) ripens, it happens.

So, in summary, Saying 21 tells us that constant attention and watchfulness are needed to follow the Way, and constant expectation of the eternally occurring rebirth of the self and the World of Forms. In light of these things, worldly possessions and the dictum of worldly rulers and the world itself are without any value whatsoever.

TWENTY-TWO

Jesus saw some babies nursing. He said to his disciples, "These nursing babies are like those who enter the kingdom."

They said to him, "Since we are as babies, shall we enter the Kingdom?"

Jesus said to them, "When you make the two into one, and when you make the inner like the outer and the outer like the inner, and the upper like the lower, and when you make male and female into a single one, so that the male will not be male nor the female be female, when you make eyes in place of an eye, a hand in place of a hand, a foot in place of a foot, an image in place of an image, then you will enter the kingdom."

We begin with another reference to babies, a favorite metaphor of Jesus's. Once again, he compares those who enter the Kingdom of Heaven with something, another indication that one can in no way directly describe it. This time, the comparison is to tiny babies, who, as not overloaded with the spiritual baggage of this world, are closer than most to the perfect state of Being.

Being like a baby, however, is not enough for a ticket into paradise. One must also seek after a kind of spiritual unity. In the Kingdom of Heaven, all distinctions exist simultaneously. The inside, or Inner Self, becomes like the Outside, the microcosm like the macrocosm. Gender distinctions are unnecessary— could this way of thinking explain the Gnostic's more liberal take on the equality of women?

This is spiritual parallelism— just as the anastasis (microcosm) is to the Eschaton (macrocosm), so is the awakening and reconciliation of opposites in each individual equal to the same in the World of Forms. In the same way, when the Gnostic claims that the Christos descended into the serpent on the Tree in the Garden of Eden in order to save Adam and Eve from the Demiurge, it was a macrocosmic parallel to Jesus's crucifixion.

The Real versus the Image has been a common theme in philosophy since the days of Heraclitus. Jesus understands this, and is telling his disciples and the reader to transcend the ideas of objectivity and subjectivity, reality and perception. As an example, picture the World of Forms as the Kingdom of Heaven's reflection in a mirror. The World of Forms is an illusion, but an illusion based on the perception of an image of the Kingdom of Heaven. If the mirror is flawed, imperfections can appear which are not "real," but are part of the reflection.

So we, as sense organs of the All, are looking into an illusory reflection of the Kingdom of Heaven. Perception requires a perceiver and a perceived— we are the World of Forms perceiving itself.

However, one cannot perceive that which is infinite, but only that which is finite. In order to know itself, the infinite universe had to break down into perceivable, finite segments and use itself to view itself, as it were. We are a combination of ourselves and the reflections that we perceive.

"Eyes instead of an eye" is not referring to someone with one eye having multiple eyes; it refers to the reflective nature of the Real— the World of Forms exists in more than one way. The logical conclusion to all of this is that the Kingdom of Heaven comes to someone once he or she has realized that the fragmented, imperfect nature of the World of Forms is an illusion caused by the Universe's inability to see all of itself at once. This inability to reconcile the observed with the observer is what fragmented the World of Forms and drove it insane—and we call the insane bits home.

In order to enter the Kingdom of Heaven, one must free one's self from one's spiritual baggage and come to understand that the observed and the observer are one and the same, a seamless but fragmented unity, and that the perceptible World of Forms is an illusion.

TWENTY-THREE

Jesus said, "I shall choose you, one from a thousand and two from ten thousand, and they will stand to their feet as a single one."

Jesus is aware that not many people will understand his teachings as they should be understood. The few who do, however, will "stand to their feet" as part of the perfection of the Kingdom of Heaven.

Although detractors of Gnosticism like to claim it is an elitist movement, the only difference between a Gnostic and a non-Gnostic is the level of information one has. A Gnostic is someone who has chosen to walk down an open path towards a particular personal goal. On that path, one naturally learns deeper levels of meaning within the mythic structure of the path. The natural projection of these levels of meaning into further levels of meaning reveals additional information about the goal. The information, however, is available to anyone who wants it.

Gnosticism is just as elitist as Accounting. If one wants to be a professional Accountant, one will study the subject and take some introductory math courses. One will then progress through different levels of initiation (course levels) which will allow one to take the information learned and apply it to deeper levels of inquiry. Eventually, one will be a Master, and graduate, and hopefully be hired on as a privileged member of the Professional Accountancy Association. Claiming that Gnosticism is elitist is like claiming that Accountants are elitist because they require a degree in the subject for a job in the field.

Jesus and the Gnostics in no way sought to exclude every non-Gnostic from "salvation" and entrance into the Kingdom of Heaven. In fact, based on what we know about the Gnostics from the historical record, they were far more inclusive than orthodox Christians have been since the formation of the Canon. Many Early Christians thought that the Gnostics were not elitist enough (*vide* Saying 15 for an example)! What Jesus means here is that not many people will understand his teachings in the way he intends, but those who do are the ones who understand the singular nature of the World of Forms.

TWENTY-FOUR

His disciples said, "Show us the place where you are, for we must seek it."

He said to them, "He who has ears had better listen! The light is inside the person of light, who becomes light to the whole world. If one does not become light, one is darkness."

The disciples want to know "where Jesus is." This does not mean that they are playing hide-and-seek and the disciples have given up in frustration. Rather, the disciples mean something along the lines of "where you're at," the state that you're in, the Kingdom of Heaven in which Jesus resides.

When Jesus uses the phrase "he who hears had better listen," it indicates that what he explains is actually quite simple: "anyone with ears would understand this." His answer, that there is light inside of a person of light, explains that if someone has had a Gnostic experience, the seeker, provided he or she is looking in the right way, does not need to try to figure it out— he or she just *knows*. The disciples are, metaphorically, seeking Jesus—and, by proxy, the Way—in the dark with their arms outstretched and their eyes closed. Once they open their eyes and see the light of gnosis, they know where it is. If they do not, they will never know.

If gnosis is something that cannot be described, then how does one truly know if someone else has had a Gnostic experience? What keeps some unscrupulous character from saying, "oh, yeah, I've had gnosis." The answer is so simple that anyone with ears will understand: once one has experienced gnosis, "been enlightened," one will just know, but there is no way to know until you have.

TWENTY-FIVE and TWENTY-SIX

Jesus said, "Love your brother like your own soul, protect him like the pupil of your eye."

Jesus said, "You see the sliver in your friend's eye, but you do not see the timber in your own eye. When you take the timber out of your own eye, then you will see well enough to remove the sliver from your friend's eye."

It is interesting that the Sayings seem to use "brother" and "friend" interchangeably. Saying 25 tells us that our "brethren" (or friends) should be held in highest esteem— we should love our friends as much as we love ourselves, and protect them as we protect our own eyes.

Sayings 25 and 26 also reinforce the idea that each person is a sensory organ of the Universe, and that we are all different pluralities of the World of Forms which is attempting to learn about itself. Our friends, are, indeed, different illusory manifestations of the same World of Forms for which we are the primary perceptor. This is most certainly a good reason to protect one's friends as one protects one's eyes: they are as important to the universe as the eyes are to the body.

The theme continues to Saying 26, found in slightly different versions in *Matthew* 7:3-5 and in *Luke* 6:41-42. The advice is, again, straightforward: when it comes to placing value judgments on one's brother or friend, do not be a hypocrite. In fact, value judgments of any kind are a bad idea. Consider the implications of the Saying a bit further. Jesus's Sayings are specifically constructed by a master of symbolism and metaphor.

Note that, in the Sayings about the sliver and the timber, the so-called "faults" are injuries that one would not subject one's self to on purpose (who jams a splinter into her own eye?). If Jesus truly considers the sliver and the timber defects, then they are not self-inflicted defects or sins— they result more from happenstance or ill luck, from the defective nature of the World of Forms, not the afflicted self.

TWENTY-SEVEN

"If you do not fast from the world, you will not fall upon the kingdom. If you do not make the Sabbath a Sabbath you will not see the Father."

Saying 27 contains extremely important advice for the seeker. Jesus tells us we must fast— not from food, but from the world itself. The "world," or the World of Forms, is a false construct, an illusion created by the disconnect between perception and reality. Just as we abstain from the nourishment of food during a fast, so we must abstain from the nourishment of worldly things in order to venture along the Way.

I offer some personal thoughts in reference to this Saying. For much of my adult life thus far, I was heavily focused on and involved in politics and activism and government and war and social justice and, and, and . . . .

One day, almost as if by accident, I came to realize that these things were an overwhelming weight, especially considering that so many people spend so much time and energy on worldly affairs without actually experiencing them; without having any ends in sight. For political activists, myself included, it is often all about the means, the means, the means, but where are the ends?

Everyone is so involved in politics, but why? To "create a better world"? This is not really a goal, an end— it is an impossible abstraction. To get Candidate R out of office? Again, not a goal— it is means with no end. The problem is not that these issues do not exist, or are not worth focusing on— the problem is that the structures of reality and society themselves are inherently flawed. They are false structures imposed upon individuals by our inability to experience anything beyond the end of our nose. They are illusions, what Philip Dick referred to as "The Black Iron Prison."

I began to see most political commentary as aimless chatter in an echo chamber, a pseudo-revolution with no actual goals, empty blather from folks who benefit from the very systems they seek to overthrow. These ideas owe a great deal to Jacques Ellul, Christian anarchist:

No one is now concerned to question in what these ends consist, or to see exactly in what direction we are going. No control is now possible, for the ends have disappeared, or they seem to have no connection with means; it is the latter which now occupy the whole field of activity, the attention and the admiration of man. It is true that we still talk about "happiness" or "liberty" or "justice," but people no longer have any idea of the content of the phrases, nor of the conditions they require, and these empty phrases are only used in order to take measures which have no relation to these illusions. These ends, which have become implicit in the mind of man, and in his thought, no longer have any formative power: they are no longer creative. They are dead illusions, which are simply put among the properties of the contemporary theatre. It is impossible to take them seriously any longer, and no one would die for them. A man will die for his own well-being, or because he himself has already become a means: the means of a party, of a nation, of a class; and as a "means" he is thrust into a battle which is being fought for no end. The heroism of a soldier in wartime, or of a workman in a strike, is in reality the heroism of a means which does not know where it is going. . . .

All that science can do will be used to save one life, and then millions of people are massacred by bombs, or in concentration camps: both are products of the enormity of our means. Similar examples abound on all sides. For instance, take the question of social security: with great ability a huge administrative machine has been established in order to ensure social security for mankind but why? For what purpose? For no time has been more uncertain than our own, and what is this miserable "security" which is offered to men? Some millions of francs at the cost of the insecurity due to financial, social, and economic crises, of wars and of revolutions, which, owing to our technical means, actually affect the lives of all: men, women, and children. In this terrible dance of means which have been unleashed, no one knows where we are going, the aim of life has been forgotten, the end has been left behind. Man has set out at tremendous speed to go nowhere.[xi]

With this in mind, I decided to take a break, to "fast from the world," which conveniently coincided with a bout of pneumonia. After much meditation, contemplation, reading, research, I came to a few conclusions.

The first is that the sort of worldly "Utopia" desired by Liberals, Conservatives, or anyone involved in politics will never exist. It will not exist because it is not defined! I cannot for the life of me imagine any valid Utopia as the end goal of a political party.

Thus, to claim to be "on the right" or "on the left" or "in the center" is silly, just as idealistic as anarchism or absolute pacifism, but less valuable because at least anarchism and pacifism exist outside of the present system. If one was to follow the logical progression of this system, the eventual outcome can only be complete societal collapse and replacement by another system, or the kind of enforced and passionless happiness of the "Brave New World." In the meantime, we will still have the cycle of status quo versus status quo, "neoliberalism" versus "neoconservatism."

The next conclusion: true change is not edificial, but individual. We mass-men spend so much time trying to affect change on a global scale, trying to get scads of people to cast votes one way or the other, trying to get whole movements of people together, but, again, we are truly limited to our own perceptions. The most effective changes that can be made, therefore, are on an individual scale. In other words, what if, rather than trying to change everyone else, one spent that time working on one's **own** life? Life is to be lived on an individual level— "tend your own garden," as Voltaire reminds us, though I believe that if we each tended our own gardens, lived our own lives, and helped our neighbors with theirs—the **real people** we deal with on a day-to-day basis, not the abstractions we get in the media—the world would be a fantastic place. Trying to change other peoples' minds is silly— rather, work on one's **own** mind, and lead by example. Humans are inherently good; when people are given the opportunity to come to their own conclusions without the baggage of ideologues and the constant barrage of the media, they will choose the path of goodness. Bettering one's self is a way to give an ends to the means of society, and if we all better ourselves, the universe itself will be redeemed and the Kingdom of Heaven will be completed.

We cannot ever know the truth about anything we do not experience for ourselves. Ever. All external truths are propaganda. One cannot depend upon the media— any media, or upon other peoples' opinions. One must know for one's self.

Finally, and most importantly, we live in an insane, imperfect World of Forms that requires healing. This universe, which is a part of God, exists outside of space/time, and is currently involved in learning about itself through the medium of conscious perception. However, since it is impossible for the World of Forms to detect itself in full, it breaks down into self-aware pluralities: us. Since we are all basically eyeballs connected to the universal mind, Reality is the sum total of all experiences.

In fact, there is only one "experience"— one consciousness that we will all participate in. All experiences are valuable, and the ultimate "evil" is the objectification of other perceptors, a practice which leads to genocide, murder, rape, theft, war, etc., and proves the universe's insanity. The ultimate goal for each individual and for the entire World of Forms is "Know Thyself," when this has happened as often as is possible, the World of Forms is redeemed.

So, you see, save yourself and you save the Universe. What better end or goal than saving the universe, I ask you? The essential idea is related to the Saying: FAST FROM THE WORLD. Do not derive nourishment from earthly things.

Some might conclude that this is a rather egotistical approach to reality: "based on this interpretation of the world, you're saying that we shouldn't help anybody but ourselves. Isn't that just like Objectivism?"

The answer? No, because . . . .

One must keep the Sabbath as a Sabbath.

Jesus means that this kind of "fasting," or holy observation, is confined to holy times. To **always** fast from reality would require one to become a hermit. However, one can observe things of the world, participate in helping others, in acts of compassion, in acts of humility and charity. One must, however, keep them holy. Some people do good just so they can say "I'm a compassionate person because I did good today!" Rather, if one needs to think this way, one might consider, "I did good today because I am a compassionate person!"

Bettering one's self on an individual level and fasting from reality leads one to compassion and a desire to help others, especially if we are all the perceivers of the World of Forms. One should be very concerned that others are happy, comfortable, for many reasons: the selflessness that comes from recognizing our universality, the selfishness of knowing that one will experience everything that everyone else experiences or has experienced. The important thing is not to ignore reality, but to react to reality for reasons based upon our own experiences. This is along the same lines as Jesus's statement that "you should not do what you do not want to do." Yes, give to charity, yes, help others, yes, keep your interest in politics and in the way the world works, but **know why you are doing it**. Meditate, go on a spiritual quest, turn off the TV or computer or homeopape, meet your neighbors, treat your friends to a huge meal, but get away from reality for a while. And then come back, and kick its ass.

TWENTY-EIGHT

Jesus said, "I stood to my feet in the midst of the world, and I appeared outwardly to them in flesh. I found them all drunk, and I did not find any of them thirsty. My soul gave pain over the children of humanity, because they are blind men in their minds and do not see, for they came into the world empty, and they also seek to depart from the world empty. But now they are drunk. When they shake off their wine, then they will repent."

One frequently finds references throughout the Gnostic texts that compare those who have not yet achieved gnosis as "drunken," whereas those who have are "sober." The terms carry, as semiotic devices, the same weight as "asleep" and "awake." Note that the reason Jesus gives for humankind's blindness is that we came into the world empty, devoid of the fullness of God, the Pleroma. Our drunkenness is not the fault of humanity, but the fault of the flawed World of Forms and its intoxicating, hallucinogenic nature.

Jesus says that he appeared "in flesh," which gives us a hint as to his nature. Many Gnostics believed that Jesus was filled with his divine image, the Christos. Jesus the Man was a reflection of Jesus the Christos— Jesus was possessed by his own Heavenly Twin. The Christos is also what manifested in the Serpent in the Garden of Eden in Gnostic mythology. Again, we have the holy parallelism: just as God acts in the world as the Pleroma, fullness, so the Christos fills Jesus and acts through him. The God, the Mind (or Nous) of the World of Forms, indeed speaks through Jesus, as the Logos, or Word. Another way to visualize this concept is to picture the Logos/Christos as a positive virus made of living information that has been injected into the World of Forms but needs a carrier to spread. The famous arguments over whether Jesus was "fully human" or "fully divine" were sadly moot— Jesus was fully human, but having been filled with the Christos, became fully divine.

Note, also, the fact that Jesus says that humanity will have to shake off their own drunkenness before they can repent. This refers to the absolute necessity of the individual experience of gnosis— nobody can force another to sober up, not even Jesus himself.

TWENTY-NINE

Jesus said, "If the flesh came into being because of spirit, that is a wonder, but if spirit came into being because of the body, that is a wondrous wonder. Rather, I become amazed at how this great richness has come to dwell in this poverty."

Saying 29 picks up from the previous Saying, in which Jesus declares that he appeared "in the flesh." The Saying juxtaposes the two aspects of being: "spirit," or the indwelling God, and "flesh," or the corrupt creation. That the World of Forms descended from the ineffable, Jesus says, is pretty amazing—unbelievable even, especially since so many claim that the whole concept of spirit is a creation of man. This is a response to detractors of religious and spiritual leaders, those who would go as far as to claim that there is no God, or that all religions other than the officially accepted ones are creations of charlatans who create false gods to deceive the masses.

So, Jesus replies, the concept of the higher spiritual nature of the World of Forms is absurd, certainly, but the idea that no higher realms exist, that what you see is what you get, that God is nothing more than a creation of mankind, is even more absurd.

In fact, he continues, the perfection of the soul and the brilliance of gnosis results from the Pleroma, the indwelling aspect of God that fills creation. And, that something perfect (richness) fills even the imperfection of creation (poverty) is truly amazing.

THIRTY

Jesus said, "The place which has three gods, they are in god. Where there are two or one, I am with that one."

The second part of this Saying could relate to the Gnostic concept of "being a solitary," or being alone. Being a solitary means that one recognizes one's limitations of perception, that in the shattered World of Forms, only one consciousness exists. The experience of gnosis reveals the loneliness of the seeker, and it is possible that Jesus is telling the seeker not to despair, because the Christos is within. But, that's only a teeny, tiny part of the puzzle.

The first part of the Saying is far more cryptic, and I'm not comfortable giving an in-depth analysis.[xii] In *Thomas*, Jesus refers to the "place" that has three gods as being in god. Could this be a reference to the Holy Trinity, Father, Son and Sophia? If so, perhaps Jesus is revealing that even outside of the Trinity, he is present whenever one or more individuals who seek gnosis are gathered together.

THIRTY-ONE

Jesus said, "No prophet is accepted in his own village; no physician heals those who know them."

All of the Canonical Gospels refer to the saying about a prophet being unwelcome in his home. According to the story, Jesus attempts to deliver his message in his hometown and confronts detractors from his family and the community who essentially think that he's gone mad. Because of this Jesus is not able to work miracles in said hometown, and leaves. The second part about the doctor recalls Jesus's reference in *Luke* 4:16-30 to a proverb that says "physician, heal thyself," but the meaning may or may not apply.

More likely, from a Gnostic standpoint, we are receiving some simple advice for those who seek to spread the word about the Way. It is worth keeping in mind that during the time of Jesus's ministry, one's circle of friends and acquaintances was limited pretty much to those who lived in one's village, town, or neighborhood. There were no phones, mail service was rudimentary and arbitrary, and it would be rare indeed for someone to wander throughout the countryside and meet new people. Everyone who knew a person, who **really** knew a person, lived in her own hometown.

When one has the kind of "conversion experience" that Gnosticism teaches about, whether it is gradual or sudden and immediate, it is truly a life-changing experience. Trying to share these truths with those who know you, especially within the confines of a religious hegemony, can be an eye-opening experience indeed. Those who know you, friends and family alike, have preconceptions of you. They think they already know the person you are, but remember the importance of the Gnostic distinction between perception of reality and reality itself. Jesus is telling us that your friends and family know the you that is sleeping or drunk, the you based on their perceptions. When you attempt to share with these people the experiences that you believe are the Way, they will never truly be able to understand you.

Since this is true, there are two possibilities that are implied by this Saying. The first is that they may deny you and deny the truths that you are sharing. They may consider you insane, blasphemous. Thus the first part of the Saying, that "no prophet is accepted in his own village."

The other possibility is that they will accept what you are saying out of love for you and trust in you. This can be equally dangerous— remember, gnosis should be an individual experience, and should not be based on what one is told. The messenger can play an important role, but only if the Way is sparked in the individual. The messenger does not tell someone where the Way is hidden— the messenger's duty is to spark the desire to seek within the receiver of the message.

If someone decides "I want to be a Gnostic because I love you and agree with what you've told me," then that person has been pointed in the wrong direction. They should decide, "I want to be a Gnostic because what you're telling me makes sense and makes me want to discover these things for myself." If one's friends/family choose to seek for the wrong reasons, and then fail to become spiritually fulfilled, the danger is even greater that they will never find such fulfillment, and will blame **you.**

Thus, the second part of the Saying. No physician will heal his own friends and family. There are many ways that this suggests the above interpretation. For instance, suppose a physician heals his cousin, but unsuccessfully. His cousin dies, the physician is blamed and is now an outcast with a reputation that will make it difficult for him to continue to practice. Suppose the physician is a First Century faith healer/herbalist, who attempts to heal an ailing relative. The relative would benefit far better from treatment at someone else's hands, but the physician is family, so the relative decides to see him instead.

Going in the other direction, if one wants to share his or her message actively, one must be quite sure that one is not sharing it with one's family or friends simply because they are such. A physician should never practice exclusively on his friends and family; he should practice out of a desire to heal and to do good for others regardless of who they are.

Encouraging others to find their own Ways is Part of the Gnostic Way, to find the Middle Path between illustration and revelation. This is doubly important when dealing with friends and family, those who have preconceptions about you that could affect their own search.

THIRTY-TWO

Jesus said, "They are building a city upon a high mountain. She is being fortified. There is no way that she can fall, nor can she be hidden."

In the last Saying, Jesus commented on the relationship between one's spiritual path and one's friends and family. In this Saying, Jesus is commenting on the relationship between one's spiritual path and the rest of the world. The Saying itself is pretty clear, but what does the city represent? Perhaps, given its proximity to other Sayings which describe the seeker, the city represents the seeker herself, the Gnostic on the Way.

As we already know, when one is seeking on the Way, one opens one's self up to detractors and to the "powers and principalities" that govern the insane section of the World of Forms in which we reside. We become like the City on the Hill— fortified by our own gnosis, but visible for miles around.

Jesus doubtfully intended "nor can it be hidden" to be a good thing— if one is under siege and needs to be "fortified," then being hidden would probably be an asset. Jesus intends to warn the seeker that once one has accepted the Way, one becomes an open target. Human oppressors alone may not necessarily do the targeting; one is also a target of all of the flaws of life in a flawed creation. When one chooses the Way, one has to be on guard at all times and be vigilant, aware of one's visibility to the World of Forms and its distractions, most of which are born full grown from one's own mind, due to our inability to distinguish between perception and reality.

So, Jesus is not presenting this Saying as advice, but as a warning: go ahead and build your city— you will definitely be able to defend it. However, once it is built, there can be no hiding it away, so be ready.

THIRTY-THREE

Jesus said, "What you will listen to with one ear, in the other ear proclaim from your rooftops. After all, no one lights a lamp and puts it under his ear, nor does one put it in a hidden place. Rather, one puts it on a lamp stand so that all who come and go will see its light."

There is an interesting note to make about the translation, in which the word "basket" has been replaced by "ear." To fit within the traditional Saying as found in the Gospels (i.e. *Mark* 4:21-23), translations of Saying 33 generally read the Coptic word *"maashe"* in the feminine form, as "basket," or bushel, as in nobody lights a candle and puts it under one. However, in the process of researching the Coptic, we discover that *maashe*, in Coptic, translates in its **masculine** form into "ear."

Could ear be another proper translation? It is doubtful, not knowing enough to judge which translation is more "proper," our best guess is that it could have been a Coptic "pun"— a Coptic reader would understand the double-entendre. It certainly makes sense both ways— sure, one wouldn't put a lamp under a basket, but one also wouldn't hold a lamp to one's ear if one wanted to see, right?

Regardless, the meaning is essentially the same, even if the take on the ear/basket pun proves completely wrong. Just as when one becomes enlightened one is like a "City on a Hill," visible to everyone, so must one make the Way available to all who are curious— the "rooftops" are equivalent to the hill, both representing a "higher" state. Do not hide the light, or use it inappropriately, Jesus says— do not keep it away or try to use it to hear when it is clearly intended to be seen by all.

It is worth noting that Jesus seems to encourage an almost passive approach to spreading the word. He certainly does not indicate that one should force someone to believe, or that one should actively proselytize and coerce conversions. Rather, he says, shout it from the rooftops, or place the light on a high place for people to see. If someone will benefit from it, they will be attracted to the message. There is no need for screeching, finger pointing, force-fed religion. Such tactics work as well as using one's light under one's ear.

THIRTY-FOUR

Jesus said, "If a blind man leads a blind man, the two of them will fall into a pit."

Jesus warns the listener, first of all, to be aware of false teachers, as following someone who is not qualified to teach will lead both parties to a bad end. However, as there is no distinction between the blind leader and the blind follower, Jesus' Saying could also warn those who think themselves qualified to teach to avoid doing so unless they can "see."

Everyone exists in a state of sightlessness before experiencing gnosis. This state is also equated with being asleep and being drunken. Jesus counsels us that one who has not experienced gnosis is in no position to lead someone to the experience of gnosis— it is vastly important that only those who have had direct experience attempt to lead others. But, how can one tell whether or not someone has truly experienced God? The answer can only be that one who is seeking in earnest will simply know.

THIRTY-FIVE

Jesus said, "One cannot enter a strong person's house and take him by force without tying his hands. Then he will move out of his house."

     Canonical parallels of this Saying can be found in *Luke* 11:14-23, *Matthew* 12:22-30 and *Mark* 3:23-27. In the canon, the Saying is given in relation to exorcism, but that does not seem to be the meaning here. The concept of "robbery" and theft appears frequently within the Gnostic texts as a metaphor—see Saying 21, as an example. It is an interesting metaphor, especially in the context of this particular Saying, which does indeed turn the idea on its head.

     The Coptic text only implies that Jesus means the strong man is being tied up in order to "loot his house." The actual phrasing is "he will move out of his house;" whether this means that the house's contents are up for grabs is hermeneutic and ambiguous.

     So, who is the "strong guy," and who are those who want to "tie him up"? A possible interpretation could be that Jesus is referring to the "strong guy" as his opponents, or the opponents of the Church, or even Satan, which allows one to justify his seeming endorsement of the use of force— Jesus says Satan needs to be tied up to kick him out of his "house," the Earth. It is also possible, however, that the Gnostic interpretation would see the "strong man" as the Demiurge, the insane Creator God, who needs to be tied up and kicked out of the World of Forms.

     What if we look at this Saying in a different fashion? Why on Earth does it make any sense to claim that Jesus means that followers of the Way should be the thieves? If this is the case, the Saying takes on a meaning that is entirely different, but one that is actually supported by other Gnostic texts. The theme being addressed is that the Spirit that exists within the World of Forms has been taken by robbers. For instance, in the *Gospel of Philip*, we find the following (emphasis mine):

Christ came to ransom some, to save others, to redeem others. He ransomed those who were strangers and made them his own. And he set his own apart, those whom he gave as a pledge according to his plan. It was not only when he appeared that he voluntarily laid down his life, but he voluntarily laid down his life from the very day the world came into being. Then he came first in order to take it, since it had been given as a pledge. **It fell into the hands of robbers and was taken captive, but he saved it.** He redeemed the good people in the world as well as the evil.

Also, this passage from *The Sophia of Christ* addresses the same issue:

> ... [T]hrough that Immortal Androgynous Man [God] they might attain their salvation and awake from forgetfulness through the interpreter [Jesus Christ as the Logos] who was sent, who is with you until the end of the poverty of the robbers.

In the above passage, "the poverty of the robbers" refers to the state of poverty in which the World of Forms exists, as the Spirit has been "stolen" by the "robbers."

If the robbers are always the bad guys, then why would Jesus use thievery from the strong as a metaphor and place the followers of the Way in the part of the robbers? The answer is simple: he would not. The Strong Man, in the context of this Saying, actually represents the students of Jesus's Way! The students are "strong" **spiritually**, not physically.

If we address the problem of the "robbers," we can easily investigate the nature of his house, his tied hands and his stuff. To do so, we refer to the *Acts of Peter*, which contains the following metaphorical warning from a Christ-figure to Peter, who is journeying to the City of the Kingdom of God:

> No man is able to go on that road, except one who has forsaken everything that he has and has fasted daily from stage to stage. For many are the robbers and wild beasts on that road. The one who carries bread with him on the road, the black dogs kill because of the bread. The one who carries a costly garment of the world with him, the robbers kill because of the garment. The one who carries water with him, the wolves kill because of the water, since they were thirsty for it. The one who is anxious about meat and green vegetables, the lions eat because of the meat. If he evades the lions, the bulls devour him because of the green vegetables.

From this passage, we can see that, in Gnostic symbology, the robbers are those who focus on and concern themselves with the things of this world. They are the aspects of the World of Forms, both human and abstract, which attach the student to the world and open her up to distraction from the Path. So, if the student is the strong man, then his house is the Kingdom of Heaven, and the robbers are the people and things and attachments that tie her hands with attachments that cause her to abandon the Kingdom, leaving it open for "looting" by the false teachers and their followers.

Jesus doesn't tell us, "Look, you should tie up the strong man's hands so we can rob his house." He's tells us, "Look, even though you may be strong, if the robbers (false teachers/corrupt and insane part of the World of Forms) tie your hands (distract you with worldly things), even you will be forced to leave your house (the Kingdom of Heaven) and the robbers will steal your stuff (your spiritual nature). In light of what we have already learned from *Thomas* about being tied and weighted down by worldly things, this seems like a fair warning for anyone who thinks herself "strong" in spirit.

THIRTY-SIX

Jesus said, "Do not worry, from morning to evening and from evening to morning, what you are going to wear."

This is one of a number of Sayings in *Thomas* which discuss the pointlessness of fretting over material things. Some see these Sayings as a rousing endorsement of asceticism, but, once again, literalism may not be the best way to interpret the messages of the Way. Instead, it might be helpful to read this Saying and the others like it as promoting a sort of Buddhist detachment from the material world—which is, after all, insane.

Jesus does not tell anyone that they should just go around naked, or live in a cave or abstain from eating. He simply tells the seeker what most teachers of the Way have always said: stuff is stuff, and not worth worrying about. Worrying about stuff is bad. Concerning yourself with things to the point that they distract you from the Way can be dangerous. Consider the previous Saying, wherein the strong man's hands are bound and the robbers loot his house.

The concept of material "ownership" does not matter in the community of the Kingdom of Heaven. It is been said that Jesus and his followers were "Communists," though "anarchist collectivists" might be a more appropriate term. This did not necessarily come from some kind of enforced economy— more likely it resulted from the teaching that one should not be attached to mere things, and that the Universe will always provide for those who follow the Way with sincerity and humility.

THIRTY-SEVEN

His disciples said, "When will you appear to us, and when will we see you?"

Jesus said, "When you strip naked without being ashamed, and you take your clothes and put them on the ground under your feet like little children and trample then, then [you] you will look upon the son of the living one and you will not be afraid." [xiii]:

The disciples want to know when Jesus will appear to them, most likely in what we can call his "True Form" as the son of the Living One: God, so called because it resides and exists out of the realms of Death.

Saying 36 tells us not to worry about what one is wearing, and 37 goes one step farther: take the clothes you wear, throw them on the ground, and smash them to pieces! The key, of course, is not that one simply destroy one's clothes— the important part is to do it without being ashamed.

This may remind us of another Bible story concerning shame and nakedness. In the Garden of Eden, once Adam and Eve had eaten the fruit from the Tree of Knowledge of Good and Evil, they knew that they were naked, and were ashamed for it. Is Jesus asking his disciples to return to an "Edenic" state?

But, one has to keep the Gnostic interpretation of *Genesis* in mind. Remember, the serpent was the **good guy**— it was the Christos/Logos teaching humanity about their inner spiritual fullness. So how could a return to a pre-serpent state, as it were, be a good thing? When Adam and Eve ate from the Tree and were cast from the Garden, they did not do what they were supposed to do. They had eaten the fruit— the gnosis offered by the Logos/Serpent—and were as gods, but remember that when they ate the fruit, they were still in the imperfect world of the insane Creator. They were not ashamed **as a result of** eating the fruit, they were ashamed because they had disobeyed the Creator. When they discovered the beauty of their own spiritual nature (their "nakedness") they became afraid and ashamed because, as residents of the insane universe, it was their nature to fear their spiritual side and the gnosis offered by the serpent. So, they dressed themselves— embraced the imperfect world of matter— hoping that the insane Demiurge would forgive them for eating of the fruit. But, no such luck. Instead, the Creator used this as an excuse to embroil them even further into the realms of matter, making them even more subservient to his insane creation.

To recap: Adam and Eve, naked and ignorant, are living in an insane universe. The God desires to save them through the medium of the Logos, which descends into the Serpent. The Serpent convinces Adam and Eve to eat of the fruit of **Knowledge** (**gnosis**). They do so, and realize their own splendour. Since, however, they are trapped in a corrupted universe, they become ashamed at their own divinity and decide to embrace the world of matter. This gives the Demiurge, the schizophrenic aspect of our own universe, the perfect opportunity to kick them even further down the ladder of being.

However, had they not been ashamed and immediately grasped for the material once they had eaten of the tree, had they stayed "naked" instead of immediately "putting on clothes," they would have recognized the serpent for the Logos and been able to escape the imperfection in which we now all reside.

A radical interpretation of *Genesis*, no? But this reading of the Gnostic *Genesis* seems to apply here. If, indeed, Jesus had a Gnostic message and if, indeed, he is referencing *Genesis*, it is no stretch to assume that being naked and unashamed and "young," as we were at the creation, is an admonishment directed at those who have been ashamed of their nakedness. There is nothing to fear, Jesus is telling us, once you cast off your devotion to the material and corrupt and dance in joy like little kids!

This is not some kind of ego-driven pride or vanity— it is not the shamelessness that pervades our culture. It is the lack of shame that one would feel being naked in front of a tree, or as a better comparison, it is the lack of shame a naked baby feels in the presence of her mother.

THIRTY-EIGHT

Jesus said, "Often you have desired to hear these words that I am speaking to you, and you have no one else from whom to hear them. There will be days when you will seek me and you will not find me."

The disciples, as earnest seekers, often desire to hear the Sayings that Jesus has been speaking— they have sought, but, until finding Jesus, had been unable to receive spiritual nourishment. However, Jesus says he will not always be around, so what happens when he leaves?

This is another of the many Sayings in Gnostic literature in which Jesus encourages his students to be self-sufficient. After all, the Way is, at its very root, an individual experience that is available to all honest seekers, whether or not they have someone teaching them at all times. In this Saying, Jesus is telling the disciples, "Hey, look, I'm not always going to be around. Don't always depend upon me as the only source of your teachings. After all, you're searching for information that you already know."

Or, as Jesus says in the *Apocryphon of James*, **"Hasten to be saved without being urged! Instead, be eager of your own accord, and, if possible, arrive even before me; for thus the Father will love you."**

Again, it is worth pointing out here that Jesus never intended the personality cult that much of Christianity has become. In this Saying, he underlines the fact that though his earthly incarnation is not eternal, his teachings are. In Gnosticism, Jesus as an historical figure is sometimes incidental to his teachings, and Saying 38 reminds the reader that this is so.

THIRTY-NINE

Jesus said, "The Pharisees and the scribes have taken the keys of knowledge and have hidden them. They have not entered nor have they allowed those who want to enter to do so. As for you, be as cunning as serpents and as innocent as doves."

Jesus uses "the Pharisees and scholars" to represent those who interpret religion as something available only to an exclusive group. We know the Pharisees as interpreters of scripture, and the scribes were a social class of literate individuals who recorded these scriptures. The scribes write, the Pharisees interpret, and where does this leave the illiterate practitioner of the Way? He or she has to rely upon the teachings of other people in order to glean information.

This is bad practice for all parties concerned. By forcing the populace to rely upon their own interpretations of the Way, the Pharisees and Scribes are first and foremost keeping themselves out of the Kingdom of Heaven, as the Way should be available to all on an individual level. Suppressing this self-determination on the part of the individual seeker is, part and parcel, an evil act.

It also has repercussions for the individuals who have been told to depend upon those who are more studied or literate, instead of upon their experience of God itself. If they depend solely upon the interpretations of others, they are getting the wrong information. Additionally, the practice of exclusivity is a huge turn-off. If someone wants to learn about the Way, but is told, "God only loves you if you do this, this, this and this," then he or she is just as likely to say, "I'll never be able to do all of that, so I may as well not even try." This is why active proselytization is such a bad idea. Information about the Way should be made available to seekers, who should be allowed to interpret it and apply it for themselves. It should not be withheld from anyone, or forced upon anyone, nor should anyone depend on others to provide de facto interpretations. As we saw in Saying 38, Jesus never even asked his followers to depend exclusively upon his own teachings!

"Cunning as serpents and innocent as doves" probably means exactly what it says, and certainly applies to this Saying. The serpent as a symbol did not have negative connotations to Gnostics; it was a symbol of divine wisdom. Jesus asks us to be wise and gentle when presenting others with information about the Way, unlike other religious leaders who claim to have exclusive knowledge not available to everyone.

FORTY

Jesus said, "A grapevine has been planted outside of the Father. And it is not fortified, they will pull her up by her root and she will be destroyed."

The grapevine represents the World of Forms, the Creation which is insane, "not fortified." As the Father, or Paradise, is that placeless place wherein time does not exist but perfection pervades everything, anything outside of it must be in the material world. Note that it has "been planted"— this is not a wild grapevine, someone had to plant it. And, if it has to be pulled out by its roots, it is most certainly being kept alive somehow by those who have not properly fortified the vine.

However, so long as people continue to nourish gnosis and follow the Way, the rulers of the Earth will not be able to continue to fortify the vine indefinitely. Those who follow the Way, by so doing, will not just chop it down— they will pull up the grapevine by the roots!

FORTY-ONE

Jesus said, "Whoever has something in hand will be given more, and whoever has nothing will be deprived of even the little they have."

A canonical parallel for this Saying can be found in *Luke* 19:11-27. Here's the text of the parable from *Luke*:

"Once there was a nobleman who went to a faraway land to take possession of a kingdom and return. Calling ten of his underlings he gave them a thousand drachmas and said to them, 'Do business while I am gone.'

"But his subjects hated him and sent messengers after him, saying, 'We do notwant this person ruling us.' And as it happened, upon his return after taking possession of the kingdom he also had these underlings called in to whom he had given the money, to find out how they had handled it.

"The first came along saying, 'Master, your hundred drachmas brought in a thousand.'

"And he said to him, 'Well done, good servant! Since you proved trustworthy in the smallest matter, receive authority over ten cities.'

"And the second came to him and said, 'Your hundred drachmas, master, made five hundred.'

"And he said to him, 'So take over five cities.'

"And another came to him and said, 'Master, here's your hundred drachmas back which I kept hidden in a handkerchief. Thing is, I was afraid of you being the hard fellow that you are, who withdraws what he didn't deposit and reap what he didn't sow.'

"He says to him, 'Your own mouth convicts you, you terrible servant! You knew I was a hard fellow, did you, withdrawing what I didn't deposit and reaping what I didn't sow? Then how come you didn't put my money in the bank, where I could have gone and gotten it back with interest?' And he said to those assembled, 'Take the hundred drachmas from him and give it to the one with a thousand.'

"And they said, 'But master, he already *has* a thousand!'

"'I'm telling you,' he said, 'he who has will be given more, from him who has nothing even what he has will be taken away. . . . '"

On the surface, this tale seems a bit odd coming from someone who has illustrated the dangers of material wealth. We can conclude in this case that we have been presented once again with a metaphor, a lesson couched in code language. The "something in hand" to which Jesus refers is gnosis, or the benefits that one receives from following the Way. When one follows the Way humbly and wisely, one already has something in hand, and continuing to follow the Way in this fashion will only produce even more benefits for whomever so follows.

However, someone who has been given the Way—as the foolish servant was given the talent by the nobleman— but does not choose to follow it, or someone who follows it without sincerity or humility, will have any initial benefits derived from their spiritual journey "taken away"— they have gained nothing, so the very foundations of their spirituality will vanish. This is an important point to make: the Saying is directed at those who have already been shown the Path but choose not to invest in it. Those to whom the path has not been shown are, of course, not subject to the problems that can arise from not choosing to follow it.

Keep in mind, also, that the Way requires devotion and investment of time and energy. Jesus is warning us that one must throw one's whole being into following the Way. One cannot simply pay lip service or read about it if one wants to benefit from it without ending up like the foolish servant who hid his talent away.

FORTY-TWO

Jesus said, "Be passersby."

This is a fantastic Saying, rich in potential interpretations, with no Canonical parallels. The term "passerby" was often used on the epitaph of Greek tombstones to address the reader as though coming from the deceased ("O passerby, this tomb before you houses my bones . . ."). So, the simplest interpretation of this Saying is to pass by the things that are perishing and "dead," i.e. the trappings of this corrupt existence. Indeed, we find the whole of the Way in this simple admonition, which can also be pursued as a koan and meditated upon with great efficacy.

Saying 42 counsels the reader to pursue the kind of detachment of which Jesus speaks in a number of other Sayings in *Thomas*. That which is dead is dead— bypass it while following the Way. Paying too much attention to it will distract you from the Path and lead to suffering. It seems that the Way is a matter of being "in the world but not of it." You can have stuff, live somewhere, drive around in a car, but do it humbly and keep in mind that anything you have in this world will eventually fade away and perish.

Speaking of Saying 42, fans of Douglas Adams' "Hitchhiker's Guide to the Galaxy" might also be amused by yet another coincidence surrounding the number 42 (emphasis mine) . . . .

> The answer to the Ultimate Question of Life, the Universe and Everything, as given by the supercomputer Deep Thought to a group of mice in Douglas Adams's comic science fiction series The Hitchhiker's Guide to the Galaxy, is "42". According to the Guide, mice are 3-dimensional profiles of a pan-dimensional, hyper-intelligent race of beings. They built Deep Thought, the second greatest computer of all time and space, to tell them the answer to the question of life, the universe and everything.

> After seven and a half million years the computer divulges the answer: 42.

"Forty-two!" yelled Loonquawl. "Is that all you've got to show for seven and a half million years' work?"

"I checked it very thoroughly," said the computer, "and that quite definitely is the answer. I think the problem, to be quite honest with you, is that you've never actually known what the question is."

. . . . Already booked for a round of talk-show appearances to reveal the Question, the mice become desperate to discover it. During a meeting with Arthur Dent and his companions on the planet Magrathea, Frankie and Benjy mouse reveal a plan to extract the ultimate question from Arthur's brain. Since this involves removing and dicing his brain, Arthur is unwilling to go along with the plan. He manages to escape from them unscathed.

Lacking a real answer, the mice proposed to use "How many roads must a man walk down?" as the question for talk-shows (having rejected the question, "What's yellow and dangerous?" - actually a riddle whose answer, not given by Adams, is "Shark-infested custard").[xiv]

"How many roads must a man walk down?" "42." Saying 42: "Be passersby." Is "Be passersby" the Answer to Life, the Universe and Everything?

FORTY-THREE

His disciples said to him, "Who are you to say these things to us?"

"You do not understand who I am from what I say to you. Rather, you have become like the Judeans, for they love the tree but hate its fruit, and they love the fruit but hate the tree."

The disciples habitually require even more proof that Jesus is who he says he is, that his Way is worth following. This is certainly an understandable question; a simple carpenter's son shows up, declares that he is a son of God, and that he can teach his students how to achieve enlightenment—a bit of healthy skepticism would certainly have been warranted. Also, note that the question they ask is not so much "how do you identify yourself?" as it is "by what authority do you speak?" Jesus replies, as he has before and will again, that the proof is in the proverbial pudding.

This is an important concept: Jesus speaks on his own authority, and one should be able to verify said authority based on what he says. No need to check the books of the prophets, no need to provide fresh wine for all of the weddings in Judea. Rather, someone who sincerely understands and studies what Jesus says will know him for who and what he is, and by virtue of his teachings will understand by what authority he speaks.

If one desires to follow the path of Jesus, one should do so by studying what Jesus said. But, this presents its own set of difficulties. We can never know, with one hundred percent certainty, just what Jesus said, historically. Never. As far as we know, he left no writings of his own. Some very intelligent individuals divorce the figure of Jesus from history completely, seeing in him instead a Judaic version of the mythical Osiris-Dionysus[xv].

So, we have to rely on what other people said Jesus said. Add to that the Roman Era practice of attributing one's work to someone already respected to add veracity, and the volume of layers between the reader and the actual words of Jesus becomes almost mind-boggling. How, then, can we identify the words of Jesus in order to know him better? This Saying provides us with an answer: read the words attributed to Jesus. Do they sound like something he might say? Do they fit in with what you know Jesus's teachings to have been? If so, there you go. You just know.

Jesus seems to be telling us, in the section about the fruit and the tree, that the Judeans have a habit of following different parts of a teaching without considering the whole. Not surprising, considering the syncretism of the period. The Way, however, when approached from the basis of gnosis, is quite holistic and logically sound. There is an underlying structure beneath the semantics that makes perfect sense; seeing this structure parallels seeing the inherent structure that exists beneath the fabric of reality, and this is an additional facet of gnosis. When studying what Jesus says, one should remember this point. If one wants to embrace the Way, one must embrace it wholeheartedly. When one does so, questions about Jesus's authority and nature take a back seat to, and are explained by, the teachings themselves.

FORTY-FOUR

Jesus said, "Whoever talks back to the Father will be forgiven, and whoever talks back to the son will be forgiven, but whoever talks back to the holy spirit will not be forgiven, either on earth or in heaven."

Canonical parallels can be found in *Matthew*, *Mark* and *Luke*. The difference seems minor on the surface; the synoptics all omit the Father from this Saying. Take, for example, *Matthew* 12:31-32:

> If someone says something against the son of humanity, he will be forgiven; but if someone says something about the breath of the holy, he will not be forgiven in this century or the coming one.

A canonical reader might assume that, in this Saying, "Father" refers to God, "Son" refers to Jesus, and "The Holy Spirit" is just that. This makes for a puzzling Saying, indeed— how is it possible that blaspheming God would be a forgivable offense, especially when it carried such an intense penalty in Judaic Law? We are, after all, talking about breaking one of the Big Ten, here— surely Jesus would never really say, with such flippancy even, that blasphemy automatically gets forgiveness? In the Trinitarian view of the Church, are not the three really the same? How can one blaspheme against the Father or Son and be forgiven, but not so for the Holy Spirit, if they are all one and the same? So, we can see that trying to interpret this Saying using the language of Canonical Christianity does not really work all that well.

Instead, suppose we use the language of Gnosticism to look at this Saying. When we do so, it makes perfect sense. After all, as says the *Gospel of Philip*:

> Names given to the worldly are very deceptive, for they divert our thoughts from what is correct to what is incorrect. Thus one who hears the word "God" does not perceive what is correct, but perceives what is incorrect. So also with "the Father" and "the Son" and "the Holy Spirit" and "life" and "light" and "resurrection" and "the Church (Ekklesia)" and all the rest - people do not perceive what is correct but

they perceive what is incorrect, unless they have come to know what is correct.

Let us suppose that by "The Father," Jesus refers, in this Saying, not to God— suppose he refers to the insane creator deity, the section of the universe that went mad and began producing the imperfect realm in which we exist? "Father," used to describe this Demiurgic figure, is considered the "Creator" of the universe. In this context, blaspheming against the Father might not be such a bad thing— after all, one blasphemes against the imperfect entity who is responsible for the miseries of existence.

So, then, if Father refers to the Demiurge, who then, is the "Son"? The son is not Jesus, who, after all, did not come from the Demiurge; rather, the son is Adam, and the Sons of Adam: the Son is Humanity. Blaspheming against humanity is, of course, quite forgivable. It is an unfortunate habit we have, but when we treat one another poorly, we are generally dealing with the world of imperfection; we can blaspheme against the body of Adam, but not the divine spark within.

What about the Holy Spirit? The Holy Spirit is the manifestation on Earth of the True God, which fills everything that exists and transcends the schizophrenic universe. Let us turn once again to the *Gospel of Philip*:

> "The Father" and "the Son" are single names; "the Holy Spirit" is a double name. For they are everywhere: they are above, they are below; they are in the concealed, they are in the revealed. The Holy Spirit is in the revealed: it is below. It is in the concealed: it is above.

So, the Father and Son reside only in the material plane, the creation of the Demiurge. The Holy Spirit, on the other hand, resides not only on this "plane," but also in the realms of perfection. The "Holy Spirit" presents itself in Gnostic mythology as a force which is both masculine (the Logos, or Christos) and feminine (Sophia). Thus the "two names" and reference in *Philip* to a plurality.

When one blasphemes against the Holy Spirit, one blasphemes against the true divinity which resides within everything. Blasphemy against the Holy Spirit is not saying "The Holy Spirit is a wanker," it is any act which seeks to diminish the inherent divinity which fills the universe. In other words, it is any act which seeks to deny the unique spirituality of the other pluralities that reside within the false creation. In different other words, an act which blasphemes the Holy Spirit is an act which treats other individuals as objects instead of as individuals. In other different other words, an act which blasphemes against the Holy Spirit is an evil act.

One who commits evil acts while in this universe is part of this universe, and is a servant of the false deity. If one blasphemes against the Holy Spirit and then repents and comes to understand his or her Way, then one is no longer the same person who blasphemed, and that person is forgiven. If one consciously commits acts of evil without repenting, then one is simply an illusory aspect of this universe, an hallucination that will most likely simply fade away when the universe is redeemed.

FORTY-FIVE

Jesus said, "They do not harvest grapes out of thorn trees, nor are figs gathered from thistles, for they yield no fruit. Good persons produce good from their treasures; evil persons produce evil from the evil treasure they have stored up in their minds, and say evil things. For from the excess of the mind they produce evil."

You cannot harvest good fruit from plants on which they do not grow; you cannot harvest goodness from people in whom goodness does not exist. A distinction exists, however, between what good people do with their goodness, and what evil people do with their evil. Those who choose the path of goodness do so with humility, and take the good and do good with "what they have." To those who desire goodness, goodness is not something that one keeps; rather, the very essence of goodness is compassion and acceptance of the individuality of others, something shared.

Evil, on the other hand, is something that gets "stored up," hoarded in the heart/mind of the evil person. Goodness fills one, and is then shared as though one is pouring wine from a vessel. Evil also fills a person like a vessel, but since the evil person does not desire to share or act with compassion, this evil overflows from that person, infecting those who surround him.

This might actually be a good point at which to discuss how a Gnostic might see "good" or "evil." These are dangerous terms to bandy about, especially since they are often used as meaningless abstractions by notable figures. To begin, let us look at how someone following the Way might define "evil."

The first question usually asked of Gnostics is whether the universe itself is "evil." Gnosticism, after all, has a radically dualist reputation and supposedly presents everything as black and white, spirit and matter, good and evil. From earlier Sayings and discussions, we have learned that, for all intents and purposes, the Universe is a living thing which uses human perception to learn about itself. Conscious beings are a plurality of the universe— sensory organs, if you will. In the process of learning about itself, the universe had to fragment itself—since an infinite object cannot step outside of itself to observe itself.

This fragmentation resulted in a gaping wound between objectivity and subjectivity— the universe developed schizophrenia. In Gnostic mythology, this schizoid aspect of the universe is referred to as the Creator, the Demiurge. Is someone with a mental illness "evil" simply due to their affliction? Of course not. So, the universe is not, by nature, "evil," but ill.

If the universe is defective, and learns about itself through consciousness, then "evil" consists of acts which further the defectiveness of the universe, and keep it from learning about itself. What kind of acts would do this? Acts that restrict other conscious individuals' perceptive abilities would do this, just as the defective portion of the universe seeks to restrict the universe's ability to know itself, so that it might survive and maintain control over the World of Forms. In other words, evil acts are those which disregard the inherent perceptive nobility of some individuals in favor of others.

Acts that spring from pure greed fit the bill. Giant megacorporations are evil because they devalue the individual. Wal-Mart, for instance, is evil. Literally. Wal-Mart survives by objectifying the individuals who work there and the individuals who shop there and those who produce the goods sold there. This objectification detracts from these individuals' ability to perceive the universe with the necessary freedom. Wal-Mart forces people to labor long hours at low wages, and, like the destructive virus that it is, seeks to impose this system of modern serfdom on more and more people worldwide. Wal-Mart's actions are not just greedy, they are literally unethical and evil.

A totalitarian government of any stripe—one might argue any government whatsoever—be it dictatorial or democratic, also manifests evil. Such governments sacrifice the freedom of individuals, and have no compunction about killing thousands and thousands of their fellow humans. Sadly, evil also reflects back upon whomever commits it. Since we are all a plurality of the same universe in which everything occurs simultaneously, we are literally all one another, and commit one another's evil acts.

The consciousness of the universe bounces around from instance to instance, person to person. My consciousness is the same as yours, but at a different node of space/time. So, every time our Glorious Leaders damage the freedom and perception of another individual, they are doing it to themselves, as well, and they are hindering the universe's ability to know itself. They are like a person who keeps jabbing sewing needles into his own eyes. The eye suffers, but so does the entire body.

Because it is an act of objectification, evil also forces itself on others. Any time someone says "you **must** think the way I do," they are creating an object with the "you," and not giving the other person the benefit of the doubt, the respect due to a fellow conscious part of the universe. Because we live in a troubled section of the universe, evil is inherently present in all of us. We are all guilty of objectification. But, if we know what the problem is, at least we can try to avoid it. Racism, slavery, classism, corporatism, genocide, homicide, rape— all of these result from pure objectification.

Now that we have a better understanding of the nature of evil, let us look at the converse. If evil is the objectification/restriction of an individual's ability to perceive, then goodness is anything which promotes the health of the universe. What, exactly, does this entail?

First of all, goodness respects the freedom of the conscious individual to make his or her own choices and perceive the universe how he or she sees fit. For this reason, goodness tries to lead by example, not by coercion. The individual experience of God can only truly be experienced by said individual. Do good with what you have (your perceptions), allow others to do good with what they have (their perceptions), and you facilitate the salvation of the universe. Forcing one's opinion on others leads to, at best, an insincere acceptance of those ideas, or, at worst, outright hatred of that opinion. Instead, goodness is humble, because only through humility does one allow others to discover their inherent goodness for themselves.

Anyone who goes out of his or her way to tell you that he or she is enlightened probably is not.

Anyone who advertises his or her goodness treads a fine line.

Goodness is also compassion. As we are all the same consciousness, we nourish this goodness in others, care about the opinion of others at all times. Someone who acts with goodness typically has a constant voice in his or her head, which repeats "how will this action affect those around me"? Now, this does not entail the kind of shallow pseudo-compassion that leads lipstick liberals to soup kitchens for an hour every Thanksgiving out of a sense of duty, for does not this act objectify the homeless? It is a more deep-rooted compassion for everyone that one experiences.

As mentioned in a previous passage, the truly compassionate person does not say "I'm doing good, therefore I'm compassionate," but rather "I try to be compassionate, therefore let me do some good." Jesus says "Do not do what you hate;" if you hate going to soup kitchens to feed the hungry, do not do so. If, however, you do so because you sincerely care and sincerely desire to help someone, do so with compassion and humility. If you claim to want to help a society better itself, lead by example; do not kill thousands of members of that society, no matter what they have done to you.

The next obvious aspect of goodness is a difficult one for many folks to deal with. Goodness is pure, unadulterated forgiveness. This does not mean forgiving your pal who owes you a few bucks from last night's poker game—this is about selfless, humble forgiveness that recognizes the nobility of every individual. This does not mean that those who commit terrible acts should be allowed to walk away without meeting justice. What it means is that justice should truly be just, and undertaken with forgiveness in mind. It means the woman who forgives the rapist. It means the society that forgives the others who attack it, despite the difficulties of doing so. It means the abolition of the death penalty because forgiveness entails mercy. When one forgives one's "enemy," one forgives one's self.

FORTY-SIX

Jesus said, "From Adam to John the Baptist, among those born of women, no one is so much greater than John the Baptist that his eyes should not be averted. But I have said that whoever among you becomes a child will recognize the kingdom and will become greater than John."

"Among those born of women" should ring a bell— in Saying 15, Jesus tells us, "When you see one who was not brought out of woman, fall on your faces and worship. That one is your Father." So, from "Adam to John the Baptist," not one person counts as someone who was "born of women." Does Jesus mean that Adam was "born of woman?" If woman means, metaphorically, the matrix of the creation, then it is quite possible to consider Adam in this way.

In many cultures, one should never look someone deserving of great respect straight in the eyes, so it Jesus tells us that John the Baptist is deserving of such respect.

By now we are familiar with Jesus's teachings on becoming "little kids." For examples, see Sayings 21 and 37. What Jesus is emphasizing here is that when one becomes like a "little kid" in order to achieve gnosis, the experience means that one is no longer considered "born of woman"— since all humans from Adam to John the Baptist were born of woman, and John is the greatest of those, and students of the Way who become enlightened are greater than John, so it follows.

We might also look at John the Baptist in terms of Philip K. Dick's concept of plasmates, or living information. Many Gnostic sects believed that prior to Jesus's baptism in the river Jordan, he was completely human. When John baptized him and the Holy Spirit descended into him, the living information entered his body in the form of Sophia, making him holy. Thus, within this particular story system, the cycle of illusion which began with Adam ended with John the Baptist.

It is worth noting, also, that John the Baptist had a pretty high standing in the community of Jesus's followers. So, telling someone that he or she would be greater than John would be pretty astonishing, even shocking. As a master rhetorician, we often find Jesus using shocking statements to bring his teachings to life within his disciples.

FORTY-SEVEN

Jesus said, "A person cannot mount two horses or bend two bows. And a slave cannot serve two masters, otherwise that slave will honor the one and the other will despise him.

"Nobody drinks aged wine and immediately wants to drink young wine. Young wine is not poured into old wineskins, or they might break, and aged wine is not poured into a new wineskin, or it might spoil. An old patch is not sewn onto a new garment, since it would create a split."

On the surface, Jesus reminds us that the Way is something completely new, that clinging to the "old," the trappings of the illusory world, can only be detrimental to one who chooses to try to follow the Way.

In the first part of the Saying, where Jesus discusses bending bows, mounting horses and serving two masters, he also tells us to stick to our guns and not to be hypocrites. It would be hypocritical of a "slave" to serve two masters, in the same way that it would be hypocritical for someone following the Way to concern herself with amassing great amounts of wealth. Someone following Jesus's teachings can use them as instruments by which one measures the way one approaches existence and interacts with the world. Following the Way on one hand, and then compromising one's convictions because it seems the right thing for the moment on the other, will end up coming around to bite one on the ass.

"Nobody drinks aged wine and immediately wants to drink young wine. Young wine is not poured into old wineskins, or they might break, and aged wine is not poured into a new wineskin, or it might spoil." This warns followers of the Way that trying to convince those in other traditions to embrace something totally new may not be the best idea. Very few dedicated devotees of established traditions will really be open to investigating something new, and besides, getting all of that new information might be detrimental to said person's spiritual development overall. It is best to wait, in all cases, until someone expresses a desire to learn about the Way.

FORTY-EIGHT

Jesus said, "If two make peace with each other in a single house, they will say to the mountain, 'Move from here!' and it will move."

This version of the famous Saying differs from canonical versions in an distinct way. The canonical Sayings require faith in God to move a mountain. See, for instance, *Matthew* 17:21-22:

> Believe me, if you have faith and don't hesitate, not only will you do this business with the fig tree, but if you tell this mountain here, 'Get up and throw yourself into the sea,' it will happen; and everything you ask for in your prayers, if you believe, you will get it.

The Gnostic version does not mention faith, because "faith," as used by canonical Christian interpreters, was a different concept to the original Gnostics. "Faith" implies belief without experience, which is a step on the path to gnosis, not the be-all end-all. According to the *Gospel of Philip*:

> Farming in the world requires the cooperation of four essential elements. A harvest is gathered into the barn only as a result of the natural action of water, earth, wind and light. God's farming likewise has four elements - faith, hope, love, and [gnosis]. Faith is our earth, that in which we take root. And hope is the water through which we are nourished. Love is the wind through which we grow. [Gnosis], then, is the light through which we ripen.

There are a number of different possible interpretations, any of which make sense when read in light of other Sayings in the corpus. So, as a metaphor, who are "the two," and what is "the house"? Remember that the Sayings seem to be arranged based on internal agreement. The previous Saying (47) also speaks of two— one should not serve two masters. So, just as one should not serve two masters in one's external life, so should one reconcile—or make peace with—two opposing **internal** principles. This means recognizing God, or perfect aspect of one's nature, within, and reconciling that with the imperfect nature of the World of Forms within which we reside. Based on this interpretation, the "house" is the body.

This is also addressed to a macrocosmic level. The "two" in this case would be the Logos, the representative of God which fills the Earth, and the Demiurge, or corrupt/insane part of the universe. When these two "make peace," the universe will be redeemed. This, of course, is a bit more esoteric an explanation of this Saying.

Of course, the most obvious layer is also the most applicable. The important thing for the student of the Way to do is to make peace. This implies forgiveness, humility and compassion, which are generally required for peace between individuals. Peace is the most powerful force we can harness; by working together instead of fighting one another, we have the power to move mountains. This is not a matter of faith, Jesus is Saying, it is a matter of direct application to one's interaction with one's neighbors. As mentioned in our favorite analogy, if we are all sensory organs of the universe, fighting and violence are extremely counterproductive. Rather, recognizing our nature as pluralities of the World of Forms itself will of course allow us to move mountains.

Jesus was a pacifist, but not in the traditional sense of the word. Rather, his desire for peace and compassion came from his recognition that we are all on equal footing before God, and that the application of force resulted in the sin of objectification. Notice that, in the canonical Gospels as well as the Gnostic texts, whenever presented with an opportunity to use his power to respond to violence, Jesus declines to do so. Reading Jesus's teachings as somehow condoning violence makes, quite literally, no sense at all. This is not to say that Jesus never expressed anger, or never recognized the value of, say, tossing moneylenders' tables around in the Temple, simply that he recognized that peace is the only real way to approach God.

FORTY-NINE

Jesus said, "Congratulations to those who are alone and chosen, for you will find the kingdom. For you have come out of her, and you will return there again."

Most of what can be said about this Saying has already been covered in the commentary to Saying 18:

18. The disciples said to Jesus, "Tell us, how will our end come?"

Jesus said, "Have you found the beginning, then, that you are looking for the end? You see, in the place where the beginning is, so is the end.

Blessed be the one who stands on his feet at the beginning: that one will know the end and will not taste death."

Here we have another reminder that the end and the beginning are the same place— we have come from there, and we shall return there again. Being "solitary" describes the realization of our nature as pluralities of the single universe. As God fills the universe, we remember that the point of the fragmentation of God is for God/universe to learn about itself. The God stands alone; nothing can exist outside of that which is infinite. It is all one; fragmentation is illusory— we are all alone because God is alone.

"Chosen" is a code word for someone who follows the Way. Note the direct parallel between the concept of the Jews, God's chosen people. What "chosen" does in Gnostic semantics is broaden the idea to include anyone who follows the Way— no longer does "chosen" refer to a single people; rather, it applies to anyone, Jewish, Christian, Pagan, what have you.

Who does the choosing? The God? Jesus? More likely it is a deeply personal affirmation of the follower herself. The decision to follow the Way must be a personal, individual decision. The only person who can make a choice to follow that path is the individual student. As such, the one who does the choosing is . . . you.

FIFTY

Jesus said, "If they say to you, 'Where have you come from?' say to them, 'We have come from the light, from the place where the light came into being by stretching out its own hand, stood to its feet, and appeared in their image.' If they say to you, 'Is it you?' say, 'We are its children, and we are the chosen of the living Father.' If they ask you, 'What is the evidence of your Father in you?' say to them, 'It is movement and repose.'"

Saying 50 continues the thoughts of Saying 49. Jesus provides a reply for those detractors who will undoubtedly ask for absolute proof of the Way's effectiveness and veracity. It is an important question in Gnosticism— one of the most important, actually: how does one prove an individual experience that cannot be described? Actually, one does not. One can only reply in code, which may or may not be understood by the asker. The replies are formulated Gnostic koans from which the asker may glean the answer.

There are three main kinds of questions that the curious and the detractors may ask in reference to the Way, and these three questions are provided and answered in code by Jesus in this Saying. The first, "Where have you come from?", would be asked by those who are concerned with the role of the Creation in the Way or in the ontological nature of humankind. If, as Gnosticism holds, the universe is imperfect and the Creator is insane and occluded, then, of course, an immediate and obvious question is, well then, what about you? Are not you part of the same occluded universe? Were you not created by the same God? Where are **you** from?

The only possible answer to this unanswerable question, Jesus says, is that we have come from "the light." Not only have we come from the light, but we have come from the place "where the light created itself, stood to its feet, and its image appeared." What is this place? It is the preexistent realm of God. The Creator of this universe, according to Gnostic mythology, did not create himself— he came into being due to a kind of divine error on the part of the fragmented World of Forms, which exists so that God can observe itself. The act of creation above the creation of this World of Forms, however, assumes a timelessness without of past, present or future; that once God (has/is) learns(ed)(ing) about itself, it (will be able to/is/has) form(ed)(ing) an image of itself. This meeting of God and the wholeness of its own image, where the Pleroma fills the occluded creation and redeems the insane universe is where gnosis originates, and where someone who has experienced gnosis can rightly say that she "comes from."

Of course, the near illegibility of the above paragraph should clue the reader in on the difficulties of describing this kind of thing. The point is, if someone is keyed into the Way, she will be able to intuit all of this information from the code answer ("we have come from the light").

The second question, "Is it you?" contains the coded answer for questions about the light's nature. As one cannot describe the light or its nature, one must describe, instead, one's individual relationship to it. The Way consists of becoming "childlike," which leads one to the understanding that one is a child of the "living Father." Note the inclusion of the term "living," another code word which differentiates God from the creator, who, as an entity/thing that exists within the corrupted world can be described as "dead."

We also have a return of the code word "chosen," which, as we know from the previous Saying, indicates one who will find/has found the "Kingdom." One chooses one's self, of course— in a subtle way, the answer Jesus suggests one gives to this question is "yes, it is me, but . . . ."

Finally, the last kind of question is the most difficult: "prove it." As we know, gnosis, like Buddhist enlightenment, cannot be described, only experienced. It cannot be authenticated using standard logical proofs or theorems or the scientific method. This is one of the essential difficulties for spiritual paths since the beginning of time— they deal in non-empirical states that cannot be qualified, quantified or otherwise codified. Attempts to do so have led to the evils that religions can breed: written dogmas which must be rigidly enforced, bloody doctrinal differences, conversion at sword point— these are all symptoms of the frustration that arises when one cannot explain one's religious ideas to someone else.

So, what is the Gnostic solution to this difficult problem? It is in "movement and repose." Movement refers to the movement of the spirit within the corrupted universe— it is the abstract sense of motion one gets when one has gnosis, as though one can feel the entire universe revolving and moving.

The movement is also the process of movement as initiated by God, the "Unmoved Mover," the fragmentation of God into observable shards. Movement is, in effect, Everything that can be perceived. This is proof enough for the Gnostic.

Repose, then, is a multi-layered term. When one experiences gnosis and the realization of the one-ness of the Universe, one realizes the experience of the Unmoved Mover. The "repose" is the unmoved part. There is also an element of meditation to the "repose." The best way to achieve gnosis is to meditate on the teachings of the Way, whichever Way one chooses. The Gnostic (and Early Christian) meaning of "prayer" was closer to meditation than to the pleading homilies it has become to many people. After all, as Jesus says, one does not pray in church, one goes into a "closet" alone and concentrates on God. **"When *you* pray, duck into the store-room and lock the door and pray to your Father on the sly."** (Matt 6:6-7) Obviously, this is a quiet, solitary experience— in other words, meditation. It is not the same kind of meditation as that of Buddhism or Hinduism, but it is meditation nonetheless, and it is a wonderfully effective best way to "get" the experience of gnosis.

If God is "Unmoved," and is at rest, then God is meditating on its own nature. Indeed, the entirety of the perceptual world—and most of that which cannot be perceived—consists of God meditating about itself, trying to understand its own nature. The wind does not ring the bell— there is no wind, only Mind. The bell does not ring the bell. There is no bell, only Mind. There is only Thought in Mind; we exist because God is thinking about us in an attempt to learn its own nature, though even this is not entirely true. Nonetheless, it is there for each of us to realize on our own.

FIFTY-ONE

His disciples said to him, "When will the repose for the dead take place, and what day will the new world come?"

He said to them, "She who you are looking forward to has come, but you do not know her."

Sometimes one is tempted to think that there are too many Sayings in *Thomas*. Not, of course, that any have been added, just that those scholarly-types who like to divvy texts up for easy reference may have gone a bit overboard. After all, the original *Gospel of Thomas*, like the original canonical Gospels, never had textual divisions as we understand them. The numbers were assigned to the Sayings by the scholars who have studied the Gospel and basically were inserted before "Jesus said" each time. When one notices that the last few Sayings (49-51) are all really about the same thing, and use the same terminology, suppose we look at all three without the divisions:

> Jesus said, "Congratulations to those who are alone and chosen, for you will find the kingdom. For you have come out of it, and you will return there again." He added, "If they say to you, 'Where have you come from?' say to them, 'We have come from the light, from the place where the light came into being by stretching out its own hand, stood to its feet, and appeared in their image.' If they say to you, 'Is it you?' say, 'We are its children, and we are the chosen of the living Father.' If they ask you, 'What is the evidence of your Father in you?' say to them, 'It is movement and repose.'" His disciples then asked him, "When will the repose for the dead take place, and what day will the new world come?" He said to them, "What you're looking forward to has come, but you do not know it."

Clearly, this could either be a case in which the compiler put similar Sayings next to one another, or a single "lecture" given by Jesus on the subject of man's relation to the Kingdom that overzealous scholars divided into multiple Sayings.

This may not be a major concern,, except that it sacrifices clarity for the sake of easy reference. The ideas in these three Sayings make more sense as a continuous whole than they do when taken alone— the so-called "lack of context" that some say troubles *Thomas* is not as troubling when one considers the Sayings in groups.

In response to Jesus's statement that proof of "the Father within" is movement and repose, the disciples ask when the repose will come for the dead, and what day the new world will come. In other words, the disciples are asking about the resurrection. From the context of their question, they seem concerned that the dead are "agitated," or in some state in which they cannot rest. Traditionally, this Saying might be interpreted as a question about literal eschatology: people die, their spirits or souls enter some kind of state where they cannot rest, then the Kingdom arrives and everybody gets repose and all is well in the world. However, keeping our Gnostic language lessons in mind, this interpretation is, as usual, too literal.

In the Gnostic tradition, remember, Jesus almost always speaks in metaphors and uses code words to try to get the reader/student of the Way to intuit the correct answer for herself. What, then, does "the dead" mean? Who are they? Well, if those on the way can be described as "children of the Living Father," and alive, then, as has been noted, "the dead" are those aspects of the universe who have not yet been redeemed through coming to their own understanding of the Way. The "new world" comes, of course, when this happens, when the dead aspects of the World of Forms attain the repose discussed in Saying 50. The disciples are not asking two separate questions— the day of rest for the dead and the arrival of the new world are the same event.

As usual, Jesus declines to discuss matters in terms of "time." As says the *Treatise on the Resurrection*, **"For if one who will die knows about oneself that one will die - even if one spends many years in this life, one is brought to this - why not regard yourself as risen and brought to this?"** Time is meaningless when discussing events which occur on a timeless scale; these events have already/are currently/will someday occur(ing)(red). The Universe and all of its living contents have already been/are currently in the midst of being/will at some future date be redeemed.

FIFTY-TWO

His disciples said to him, "Twenty-four prophets have spoken in Israel, and they all spoke of you."

He said to them, "You have disregarded the living one who is in your presence, and have spoken of the dead."

Twenty-four is the number of books in the Hebrew Canon. Jesus's followers, and those who came after them, such as the author of *Matthew*, spent a great deal of time trying to show how Jesus fulfilled various prophecies from Hebrew scripture. Some Gnostics did the same, notably in the *Pistis Sophia*. This Saying addresses what Jesus may have thought on the subject.

It is rare to find a Gnostic text—or a Canonical text, for that matter—in which Jesus refers to himself as the Messiah. Son of God, Son of Man or The Living One are more common terms— these are terms that had been extant in religious literature as commonly as "Messiah" appears in Hebrew Scripture.[xvi] For instance, the phrase is used quite frequently in the *Corpus Hermeticum*, a non-Christian collection of Gnostic philosophical works centering on discourse between Hermes Trismegistus and his sons:

> Tat: Tell me this too! Who is the author of Rebirth?
>
> Hermes: The Son of God, the One Man, by God's Will.[xvii]

and

> Then saith to me Man-Shepherd: Didst understand this Vision what it means?
>
> Nay; that shall I know, said I.
>
> That Light, He said, am I, thy God, Mind, prior to Moist Nature which appeared from Darkness; the Light-Word (Logos) [that appeared] from Mind is Son of God.
>
> What then? - say I.

Know that what sees in thee and hears is the Lord's Word (Logos); but Mind is Father-God. Not separate are they the one from other; just in their union [rather] is it Life consists.[xviii]

Saying 52 addresses the essential aspect of Jesus's true nature within the Judaic tradition. The disciples basically tell Jesus, "Look, you fulfill prophecies, you fit the Messiah bill, you're the guy we've been waiting for." Jesus replies, rather Socratically, "wait a second, gang— these are dead guys you're talking about, and dead prophecies that carry no import since **I'm right here**. Arguing about my nature is a waste of time. **I'm right here**."

Knowing Gnostic code also adds another layer of meaning. Jesus describes the "prophets" spoken of by the disciples as "dead," meaning that the prophets are aspects of the insane, created world, whereas Jesus is "living." Many Gnostics, as we know, believed God of Hebrew Scripture was the insane Demiurge— a Gnostic reading this particular Saying with this code in mind might interpret it to mean that the prophets were prophesizing about historical events on behalf of a God who may or may not have been schizophrenic or evil. This is not to say that the prophets were "wrong," just that their prophecies were related to their own historical, worldly situations, and not to Jesus at all, who does not fulfill worldly prophecies because he is "living," part of the higher realms of spirit encompassed by the Way.

The crux is whether the worshiper of a deity worships based on his or her own direct experience of God. Words are words. The follower of the Way would not say, "God, as described in the Hebrew canon, is insane and evil, therefore all Jews who worship this God are evil." Rather, a follower of the Way would say, "I personally cannot reconcile God that Jesus speaks about with God described in some of the Hebrew Scriptures. However, if someone who agrees with Hebrew Scripture devoutly believes in God based on her own experience thereof, then she is on the Way and knows the true God." For this reason, it follows that anyone on any spiritual path can be a "Gnostic," even if he or she does not necessarily practice "Gnosticism."

FIFTY-THREE

His disciples said to him, "is circumcision useful or not?"

He said to them, "If it were useful, their father would produce children already circumcised from their mother. Rather, the true circumcision in spirit has become profitable in every respect."

Although Jesus never addresses the issue of circumcision in the Gospels, the Epistles mention it a number of times, and Paul also rejects physical circumcision in favor of spiritual circumcision. Although the concept may seem trite to our modern sensibilities, this was a very serious and profound issue during Jesus's time. In the Hebrew Scripture, specifically in *Genesis* 17, Yahweh tells Abram, who would become Abraham, the "father of monotheism," that circumcision would be the physical symbol of the covenant between he and his followers. The uncircumcised were simply not party to this covenant.

Exceptionally few Gentiles during the Roman Era were circumcised. This kind of put a damper on conversion— "If you'd like to join our religion and worship our God, we have to CUT YOUR PENIS." Wisely, the Early Christian community under the auspices of Paul rejected the requirement of **physical** circumcision, claiming instead that spiritual circumcision would suffice (see, for example, *1 Corinthians* 7:17-19).

Whereas Paul accepted the covenant between the Creator and the Jews, and saw Jesus as representing a new covenant, Jesus clearly rejects the requirement of physical circumcision because it is a false covenant presented by a false deity. Note the language from the Book of *Genesis* 17:9f:

> 9 Then God said to Abraham, "As for you, you must keep my covenant, you and your descendants after you for the generations to come. 10 This is my covenant with you and your descendants after you, the covenant you are to keep: Every male among you shall be circumcised. 11 You are to undergo circumcision, and it will be the sign of the covenant between me and you. 12 For the generations to come every male among you who is eight days old must be circumcised, including those born in your household or bought with money from a

foreigner-those who are not your offspring. 13 Whether born in your household or bought with your money, they must be circumcised. My covenant in your flesh is to be an everlasting covenant. 14 Any uncircumcised male, who has not been circumcised in the flesh, will be cut off from his people; he has broken my covenant."

Yaldabaoth **very specifically** means that circumcision **MUST be "in the flesh."** Interpreting this passage as maybe possibly okaying "spiritual circumcision" completely opposes written scripture. Yaldabaoth even requires the circumcision of children "bought with money from a foreigner," indicating that if pagans wish to enter the covenant, they have to be snipped. Physically. No ifs, ands or buts.

Jesus repudiates this false covenant by telling his disciples that, "If [circumcision] were useful, the father would produce children already circumcised from their mother." Obviously, if Yaldabaoth really wanted a covenant, he could have seen to it that men were born circumcised. That he did not shows that physical circumcision was a control mechanism, designed to yoke the followers of Yaldabaoth to him from their eighth day on Earth. A good number of the "commandments" issued by Yaldabaoth are control mechanisms designed to keep mankind from knowing our true nature, which would destroy the false realm that Yaldabaoth has designed. Many of these commandments, including some of the Ten, are repudiated by Jesus, even in the canonical Gospels. This is covered in fantastic detail in an essay on Gnostic website Enemies.com:

> The first four commandments are theological commandments, not moral ones, and can be understood in light of Yahweh's claims to supremacy: those who worship "other gods," those who "bow down" to idols, those who take Yahweh's name "in vain," and those who work on the "Sabbath" must all be "put to death."
>
> It is only these first four commandments - theological laws encouraging the worship of Yahweh - that Yahweh enforces consistently; Yahweh often breaks, or orders people to break, the last six commandments - moral laws encouraging people to treat each other with fairness and respect.
>
> If the Old Testament can be believed, it is perfectly permissible to dishonor, kill, cuckold, steal from and lie to those who do not worship Yahweh.

Indeed, this self-proclaimed "jealous god" is so insecure about his own divinity that he often behaves like an alpha-male baboon who status had been threatened, even to the point of flinging feces:

> "...if ye will not... give glory unto my name, saith the LORD of hosts, I will even send a curse upon you... Behold, I will corrupt your seed, and spread dung upon your faces..."[xix]

Of course, physical circumcision does not automatically yoke one to Yaldabaoth, because physical differences are completely superficial in the long run. This is also indicated in some other Gnostic texts. For example, in *The Tripartite Tractate*:

> For when we confessed the kingdom which is in Christ, escaped from the whole multiplicity of forms, and from inequality and change. For the end will receive a unitary existence, just as the beginning is unitary, where there is no male nor female, nor slave and free, nor circumcision and uncircumcision, neither angel nor man, but Christ is all in all.

Rather, one should concern one's self with "circumcision of the spirit," indicative of the **New** Covenant between Jesus/the Logos/God and those who follow the Way. As this world is an image of an image, a false construct created by an insane deity, the covenant between Yaldabaoth and Abram was a shadow covenant, an image or reflection of the true Covenant which takes place in the Kingdom of Heaven, and is a Covenant between the Logos/Christos and each individual who follows the Way.

FIFTY-FOUR

Jesus said, "Blessed are the poor, for to you belongs Heaven's kingdom."

In *Matthew* 5:3 we have "The poor in spirit are in luck: the Kingdom of the Skies is theirs!" In *Luke* 6:20 we have "You the poor are in luck, because the Kingdom of God is yours." The question most students of canon tend to ask concerning this statement is whether Jesus refers to those who are literally impoverished or those who are spiritually impoverished. That Jesus cared a great deal for the poor and downtrodden cannot be argued. Poverty, however, from a Gnostic standpoint, can also refer to the perishable nature of the created realms. Recall Saying 29, where Jesus defines that in which the spirit dwells as "poverty:"

> 29 Jesus said, "If the flesh came into being because of spirit, that is a wonder, but if spirit came into being because of the body, that is a wondrous wonder.
>
> Rather, I become amazed at how this great richness has come to dwell in this poverty."

We find in Saying 29 that even great poverty contains this amazing spirit of the Logos. Even— especially— the poor will enter the Kingdom.

"Poor" also signifies someone who is not attached to material possessions. The voluntarily poor, even if they do have possessions, do not allow those impermanent possessions to impede their progress on the Way. One There is no poverty requirement, but Jesus is also reassuring the poor, in spirit and otherwise, that they will not be excluded from the Kingdom. There are, after all, no distinctions in the Kingdom. As it says in the *Treatise on the Resurrection*:

> But what am I telling you now? Those who are living shall die. How do they live in an illusion? The rich have become poor, and the kings have been overthrown. Everything is prone to change. The world is an illusion!

A beautiful treatment of the reward which the poor will receive can be found in the *Acts of Peter and the Twelve Apostles.*

A man came out wearing a cloth bound around his waist, and a gold belt girded it. Also a napkin was tied over his chest, extending over his shoulders and covering his head and his hands.

I was staring at the man, because he was beautiful in his form and stature. There were four parts of his body that I saw: the soles of his feet and a part of his chest and the palms of his hands and his visage. These things I was able to see. A book cover like (those of) my books was in his left hand. A staff of styrax wood was in his right hand. His voice was resounding as he slowly spoke, crying out in the city, "Pearls! Pearls!"

I, indeed, thought he was a man of that city. I said to him, "My brother and my friend!" He answered me, then, Saying, "Rightly did you say, 'My brother and my friend.' What is it you seek from me?" I said to him, "I ask you about lodging for me and the brothers also, because we are strangers here." He said to me, "For this reason have I myself just said, 'My brother and my friend,' because I also am a fellow stranger like you."

And having said these things, he cried out, "Pearls! Pearls!" The rich men of that city heard his voice. They came out of their hidden storerooms. And some were looking out from the storerooms of their houses. Others looked out from their upper windows. And they did not see (that they could gain) anything from him, because there was no pouch on his back nor bundle inside his cloth and napkin. And because of their disdain they did not even acknowledge him. He, for his part, did not reveal himself to them. They returned to their storerooms, Saying, "This man is mocking us."

And the poor of that city heard his voice, and they came to the man who sells this pearl. They said, "Please take the trouble to show us the pearl so that we may, then, see it with our (own) eyes. For we are the poor. And we do not have this [...] price to pay for it. But show us that we might say to our friends that we saw a pearl with our (own) eyes." He answered, Saying to them, "If it is possible, come to my city, so that I may not only show it before your (very) eyes, but give it to you for nothing."

And indeed they, the poor of that city, heard and said, "Since we are beggars, we surely know that a man does not give a pearl to a beggar, but (it is) bread and money that is usually received. Now then, the kindness which we want to receive from you (is) that you show us the pearl before our eyes. And we will say to our friends proudly that we saw a pearl with our (own) eyes" - because it is not found among the poor, especially such beggars (as these). He answered (and) said to them, "If it is possible, you yourselves come to my city, so that I may not only show you it, but give it to you for nothing." The poor and the beggars rejoiced because of the man who gives for nothing.[xx]

FIFTY-FIVE

Jesus said, "Whoever does not hate father and mother cannot be my disciple, and whoever does not hate brothers and sisters, and carry the cross as I do, will not be worthy of me."

The theme of hating father and mother recurs a number of times in *Thomas*. The concept of "hating" one's relatives can be—and has been—taken literally, but only in the sense that the Way eliminates such distinctions and levels the playing ground for everyone.

There is no "father," no "mother," no "sister" or "brother" to someone on the Way— they are all just people who are individual aspects of the same Pleroma. Of course, it remains doubtful that Jesus would literally encourage the "hatred" of anyone *per se*, though abandoning the family was a favorite ascetic practice during the time, and would have been far more offensive than it is today.

On another level, Jesus yet again encourages those who follow the Way to break one of the important Ten Commandments. Here is the pertinent commandment in context (Exodus 20:12): **"Honor your father and your mother, so that you may live long in the land the LORD your God is giving you."** Ol' Yaldabaoth seems to be encouraging honor of father and mother not because they gave one life and are due respect, but so that the Holy Land stays in the hands of the "chosen people." By telling his students to hate father and mother and thereby lose their inheritances, Jesus also informs them that this commandment does not apply, another indication that the literal covenant between the false Creator and the Jewish people should be considered null and void.

Jesus is not concerned with keeping the Holy Land in the hands of any particular people— he breaks with the control mechanisms that bind his followers to the material world. After all, inheriting a few acres of farmland or a boat and some fishing gear might indeed keep one under Yaldabaoth's control. The point is most likely consistent with Jesus's teachings, however, that the Way is often a grueling path that one follows until one's death, after which one receives eternal life.

FIFTY-SIX

Jesus said, "Whoever has come to know the world has fallen upon a corpse, and whoever has discovered a carcass, of that person the world is not worthy."

By now, we understand references to "dead" things as code words signifying the Black Iron Prison, the illusory created world, the universe of Yaldabaoth, the Demiurge. During the creation process, something happened that allowed the universe to fracture, and this fragmentation resulted in a section of reality which is devoid of something essential— a quality of spirit is lacking from the World of Forms, which is "empty" in the same way that a corpse is empty of life.

But, what does this entail? Can the ontology of illusion be proven? What are the implications for those of us who are, for all intents and purposes, trapped in an insane construct?

That the universe is illusory is an exceptionally common philosophical idea, a concept that can be found in everything from Platonism to Buddhism to "Row Row Row Your Boat" (which could be a Gnostic hymn). The essential premise is based on the fact that each of us can only truly **know** that which we can truly **perceive**. The Zen koan about the tree falling in the forest illustrates the idea— it falls, nobody is around to hear it, does the tree exist?

This is also addressed in philosopher George Berkeley's school of Occasionalism, which holds that there is no causality except for the intervention of God, or Being, into the realm of Becoming. Berkeley posited that there is no essence behind what we perceive— since all we can do is sense things, we cannot prove the existence of any "actuality" which exists underneath the most basic perceptions. Does taste exist for someone with no tongue? Does sound exist for someone who cannot hear? Berkeley argues that these things do not exist per se, that the only real objectivity in the World of Forms comes from consensus:

> This arouses the question whether this perceived object is "objective" in the sense of being "the same" for our fellow humans, in fact if even

the concept of other human beings (beyond our perception of them) is valid. Berkeley argues that since we experience other humans in the way they speak to us - something which is not originating from any activity of our own - and since we learn that their view of the world is consistent with ours, we can believe in their existence and in the world being identical (similar) for everyone.[xxi]

Modern physics has similarly addressed this idea with concepts like Einstein's Theory of Relativity and Heisenberg's Uncertainly Principle:

In the Quantum Mechanical world, the idea that we can measure things exactly breaks down. Let me state this notion more precisely. Suppose a particle has momentum p and a position x. In a Quantum Mechanical world, I would not be able to measure p and x precisely. There is an uncertainty associated with each measurement, e.g., there is some dp and dx, which I can never get rid of even in a perfect experiment!!!. This is due to the fact that whenever I make a measurement, I must disturb the system. (In order for me to know something is there, I must bump into it.) . . . [xxii]

This uncertainty leads to many strange places. For example, in a Quantum Mechanical world, one cannot predict where a particle will be with one-hundred percent certainty. One can only speak in terms of probabilities. One might say that an atom will be at some location with a 99% probability, but there will be a 1% probability it will be somewhere else—in fact, a small but finite probability exists that it will be found across the Universe.

As has been discussed, the Gnostic view of Time is similar to this concept. Since everything exists within infinity, all different segments of "time" (have)(are)(will) occur(ed)(ing) simultaneously. As quantum physics maintain, perception alters what is perceived, and exact measurement cannot occur. This inability to correctly perceive anything is the tragic flaw of our created Universe, and has been caused by the aforementioned fragmentation.

So why did this fragmentation occur? According to Gnostic mythologies, it occurred because God wanted to know itself. As infinity, it could not step outside of itself, so it needed to create a space into which it could send a part of itself that could observe the whole. As the fragmentation kept reducing God into component parts, the parts began to recede from the source. At some point during this recession, one of the parts of God decided to break off and form its own little universe, our very World of Forms. Because this part of God was so far from the source, it could not correctly perceive the whole of

God. Believing itself the entirety, it set about creating a universe based on an image of the realms which preceded it.

Now, in order for this Creator to maintain its self-designated status of god of this universe, it needed to create aspects which would continue the fragmentation of the universe but would perceive **it** as the sole god. It needed to create humanity and begin the establishment of a series of control mechanisms that would preserve its flawed creation. This is discussed in Gnostic mythology in the interpretation of the Garden of Eden.

Although the details differ from text to text, the Gnostic version of the Eden myth runs as follows. Sophia, "Wisdom," one of the holiest emanations or Aeons of God, accidentally gives birth to Yaldabaoth, the Demiurge. The Demiurge immediately mistakes himself for the infinite, the Limitless Light. Sophia informs the Demiurge that he is not, in fact, the Ultimate Power, that a region of light exists above. When he asks for proof that this is indeed the case, Sophia reveals herself and the divine beyond her region, in all its power and beauty and glory. As a representative of the feminine aspect of God, she informs the Demiurge that a "Perfect Being" will one day defeat him and put him in his proper place.

Unfortunately, Yaldabaoth, unwilling to believe that he is not the highest of the high, steals some of Sophia's divine nature—little did he know, however, that Sophia had counted on this theft as part of the process of correction that would eventually allow the Limitless Light to enter the world of forms. Yaldabaoth then divides his region into areas and aspects, over which he places his own angelic powers, the Archons. With the assistance of the Archons, he creates the World of Forms as a reflection of the Infinite that he had seen when Sophia revealed to him the higher realms. Finally, in order that he receive praise and obedience, he gives birth to Adam and Eve, again basing their forms on reflections of the Aeons above.

Yaldabaoth intends to control Adam and Eve that they might praise him as the most high and perpetuate his illusory World of Forms. In order to cement this control, he creates the Garden of Eden, places Adam and Eve within, and tells them they can eat anything in the Garden except the fruit from the Tree of Knowledge of Good and Evil. This Tree houses the stolen Divinity of Sophia, the true nature of the Infinite Light.

Meanwhile, Sophia has returned to the Source and repented for her erroneous creation. She then accompanies the Christos, the higher manifestation of the Logos that descended into Jesus, which penetrates with her into Yaldabaoth's realms in secret, hiding in the form of a snake or an eagle, or both, in the Tree of Knowledge. The Logos and Sophia convince Eve and Adam to eat the fruit, thus giving them enough of a divine nature to allow the Logos/Christos to access them and "activate" their inner divinity.

For disobeying him and displaying freedom and independence, Yaldabaoth kicks Adam and Eve out of Eden by destroying their memories of the place— putting them to sleep, so to speak. Yaldabaoth, however, is too late to unseal his own doom. Adam and Eve have already opened to the Logos and Sophia, and with the proper understanding, gnosis, can open themselves up to the Pleroma within and wake up! Until that happens to everyone, however, we are all still slaves of the insane control structures of Yaldabaoth and his Archons, which have been designed to hide away the Pleroma within the confines of the Black Iron Prison.

It is important to remember that even the darkest depths of the World of Forms are still parts of God, so they all contain divinity which can be tapped into with the assistance of the Logos, or sometimes even without. It is, however, technically "dead" and "illusory" because everything we think we perceive is an image, and true perception is not possible.   This inability to properly perceive is only one of the many control mechanisms instituted by the Demiurge and his pals in order to keep humans in line. The biggest control mechanism is, of course, institutionalized hierarchy. Any corporate structure, like a church or a government, that creates a framework which does not allow freedom to perceive based on individual experience keeps those under its sway from experiencing God for themselves. This is not to say that all organizations are inherently evil, just the ones which impede individual experience.

The illusion, or corpse, is a matrix of propaganda which has been draped over the world by Yaldabaoth. Philip K. Dick referred to this matrix of control mechanisms as "The Black Iron Prison." Yaldabaoth does not care whether the matrix is religious, political, scientific, etc.— all it cares about is furthering the illusion, which perpetuates its existence as ruler of the World of Forms. Anything that reinforces the idea that this reality is objective reality, that the universe is truly fragmented, that faith-based obedience is better than freedom, reinforces the rule of Yaldabaoth and keeps the World of Forms from progressing.

The semantics of politics reinforce this point. Left, Right, Liberal or Conservative, all of these words describe facets of the same system, and that system is the Black Iron Prison. The Black Iron Prison is not a police state— it is the illusion of a confrontation between a police state and those who attempt to resist it. Neither actually exist. The Black Iron Prison is not religion or science, it is that a conflict exists between the two, or that the two even exist as separate entities. The Black Iron Prison is not "bad" advertisements versus "good" advertisements, it is the idea that **all** advertising, even advertising for "liberal" organizations, is part of a culture which imposes values through deception. But, then, it is also **imposing** the idea that all ads are evil onto someone who does not already realize it.

Luckily, there is a realm of perfect freedom beyond what we know as "time." In this realm resides God, who, through the medium of the Logos, descends into the corrupted, insane realms and every so often flicks someone in the head. When this flick occurs, said person has experienced gnosis, or enlightenment, or a profound realization which cannot be described, only experienced. It wakes the person up. For that person, the illusion does not disappear, but he or she can recognize—though cannot usually describe—the Black Iron Prison in all its insidious glory.

The corpse-world is not worthy of someone who has recognized it as a corpse. It is, therefore, the duty of the follower of the Way to continually try to expose the illusion for what it is. Not, understand, in some misguided attempt to "save souls," or to "better lives." This will happen naturally as long as people are watching over the illusion. It is impossible to escape from the world's insanity while entrenched in it, but recognizing it is enough. Exposing the illusion on a regular basis will result in the redemption of the universe, especially considering a final salient point that needs to be made in this discussion.

This goes back to the idea that reality is based on perception, and that existence "is" because God desires to know itself. Instead of picturing time as a cycle or as a linear calendar, picture Time as a board covered in multicolored dots. Each dot represents one "occasion," one intersection of space/time. Now, suppose that God wants to learn about all of the dots. In order to learn about a red dot, God has to become red and enter that dot. This allows God to experience "red," and also allows God to experience perceptions of the dots that are peripheral to the red one (let's say yellow, green and blue). Now, once God is done experiencing "red," it wants to experience "yellow." So, it steps off of the board and moves to the left, turns itself yellow and enters the yellow dot. In order to completely know yellow, it has to get rid of the red (or it turns orange, see?), so it stores it in some kind of database, what Jung referred to as the "Collective Unconscious." The yellow dot is still able to perceive the red dot, and perceives the red dot perceiving it. And, since Time does not exist as a linear or cycle, God's consciousness can still be said to be in the red dot, too, no? it is the same consciousness, ignorant of the fact that it is the same in every dot.

This is how the consciousness of God learns about itself— it enters conscious beings in the universe and lives a lifetime. Then, it leaves, erases its memories, and reappears in another conscious being **who may, within the limitations of the Black Iron Prison, exist simultaneously with the first being**. Since there is no time, and only one consciousness, it does not matter. When I die, I may come back as you. When you die, you may come back as Julius Caesar. But, it is the same consciousness. Once it has visited every dot, and recorded all of that information, then the universe, or that section of it, is redeemed.

FIFTY-SEVEN

Jesus said, "The Father's kingdom is like a person who has good seed. His enemy came during the night and sowed weeds among the good seed. The person did not permit the workers pull up the weeds, but said to them, 'No, otherwise you might go to pull up the weeds and pull up the grain along with them.' For on the day of the harvest the weeds will be apparent, and will be pulled up and burned."

This Saying touches upon what has been covered in Saying 9, the famous Parable of the Sower. In Saying 9, the seeds represent the Word, or gnosis. There is no reason to think that in one Saying, Jesus meant the seeds to represent one thing, but in another Saying he meant them to represent something entirely different.

It does not address physical aspects of the World of Forms, sinners, non-sinners, etc., it addresses spiritual information that is found within the corpse-world discussed in the previous Saying. In typical fashion, Jesus is warning his disciples against trying to eliminate bad information, even though some of that information may have been planted by the Demiurge as a control mechanism. Scattered among the Good Word are teachings which, though they appear similar enough, were planted in order to destroy the entire crop.

Bad information, or false impressions of the word that exist within the World of Forms will come to fruition on their own. It is dangerous stuff to go around trying to destroy teachings that one thinks detract from the Way, because what **you** use to achieve gnosis may be completely different than what someone else uses. Exposing the Illusion as a false realm of corrupted information does not consist of attempting to destroy the spiritual paths of others— in fact, it consists of allowing those paths to grow on their own. It allows the universe to know all of its own aspects for what they truly are.

Now, when "harvest time" comes, when the World of Forms itself is redeemed and illusion has been exposed for what it is, then the bad information which has been nesting alongside the good will indeed be "pulled up and destroyed," because at that time it will cease to exist— it'll just fade away with the rest of the insane aspects of reality.

FIFTY-EIGHT

Jesus said, "Blessed is the person who is troubled; he has found life."

The Coptic word "**ntahhise,**" "the person who is troubled," may also carry the connotation "toils" or "works." The Way is never easy—as one who pursues it can definitely attest. It requires work, labor, trouble, concern. This does not imply a laborious pursuit; rather, that when trying to follow the path, one should welcome and work through the obstacles thereon.

Concerns and labor and trouble imply suffering. As all who are trapped in the Black Iron Prison suffer, this Saying might infer that all persons are on the path. Conversely, we might also consider the distinction between those wealthy Roman aristocrats and the laborers who toiled in the sun to keep them fat. Though the wealthy might not suffer in the traditional sense, nor are they "troubled" in the spiritual sense. The Saying becomes a warning against complacency.

Only in laboring, in constant struggle and turmoil and in the face of persecution can the path be attained. As says Nikos Kazantzakis in his spiritual opus, *The Saviours of God,*

These are the labors each man is given and is in duty bound to complete before he dies. He may not otherwise be saved. For his own soul is scattered and enslaved in these things about him, in trees, in animals, in men, in ideas, and it is his own soul he saves by completing these labors. If you are a laborer, then till the earth, help it to bear fruit. The seeds in the earth cry out, and God cries out within the seeds. Set him free! A field awaits its deliverance at your hands, a machine awaits its soul. You may never be saved unless you save them.[xxiii]

FIFTY-NINE

Jesus said, "Look to the living one while you are living, otherwise you might die and then try to see the living one, and you will not find the power to see."

The "living one" is the True God, the life and light that fills the corpus of the World of Forms. As sensory organs of the universe, we have a duty, which we have forgotten: we are here to come to know God, so that God might know itself and complete itself. The reason that we cannot understand our origin is that we are contained within it. The problem, of course, is that we are stuck in a fragmented, imperfect universe. The *Gospel of Truth* gives us a succinct summary of this state in which we reside:

> You see, the All had been inside of him, that illimitable, inconceivable one, who is better than every thought.

> This ignorance of the [God] brought about terror and fear. And terror became dense like a fog, that no one was able to see. Because of this, error became strong. But it worked on [the World of Forms] vainly, because it did not know the truth. It was in a fashioned form while it was preparing, in power and in beauty, the equivalent of truth. This then, was not a humiliation for him, that illimitable, inconceivable one. For they were as nothing, this terror and this forgetfulness and this figure of falsehood, whereas this established truth is unchanging, unperturbed and completely beautiful.

While we are alive and in the World of Forms, we are ignorant of God. This does serve a purpose in God's overall plan— our ignorance of God allows for the possibility of our coming to know it—how can one come to know something that one already knows?

The Gnostics, taking cues from Platonism, believed in a kind of limited reincarnation, very similar to that of Buddhism. If we remain ignorant of God in life, and do not come to know the Living One, we remain within the cycle of birth and death, in the corpse-world of the World of Forms, which we know from previous Sayings is represented by "death" in the language of Gnosticism.

So, when one dies who has not experienced God, one reincarnates back into the ignorance ("death") and forgets everything one has learned during one's past incarnations— one loses the ability to "see."

However, for one who has come to know the Living One, there is no death— you do not die. You escape from the realms of ignorance and error and are no longer subject to the control mechanisms of the Demiurge. As says the *Treatise on the Resurrection*:

> The Savior swallowed up death - (of this) you are not reckoned as being ignorant - for he put aside the world which is perishing. He transformed himself into an imperishable [Power] and raised himself up, having swallowed the visible by the invisible, and he gave us the way of our immortality. Then, indeed, as the Apostle said, "We suffered with him, and we arose with him, and we went to Heaven with him". Now if we are manifest in this world wearing him, we are that one's beams, and we are embraced by him until our setting, that is to say, our death in this life. We are drawn to Heaven by him, like beams by the sun, not being restrained by anything.
>
> This is the spiritual resurrection which swallows up the psychic [spiritual— Ed.] in the same way as the fleshly.

Again, it must be stressed that those who have not achieved gnosis or who have not come to know God are not condemned to Hell or an eternity of suffering. Rather, the entire universe will eventually be redeemed. There is something of a scalar aspect to this process— there is no requirement for scads of people to embrace the gnosis. One enough have done so, however, the scales tip away from ignorance and back towards wisdom (Sophia), which opens the door for the redemption of the entirety. See, once again, *The Tripartite Tractate*:

> Not only do humans need redemption, but also the angels, too, need redemption, along with the image and the rest of the Pleromas of the aeons and the wondrous powers of illumination. So that we might not be in doubt in regard to the others, even the Son himself, who has the position of redeemer of the Totality, needed redemption as well, - he who had become man, - since he gave himself for each thing which we need, we in the flesh, who are his Church.

For this reason, the Gnostic believes that anyone and everyone will eventually be saved; thus also the importance Jesus places on forgiveness. Without having achieved gnosis during life, a spirit or soul may not have another opportunity for quite some time.

SIXTY

He saw a Samaritan carrying a lamb and going to Judea. He said to his disciples, "[Why is that person carrying around] the lamb[?]" They said to him, "So that he may kill it and eat it."

He said to them, "He will not eat it while it is living, but only after he has killed it and it has become a corpse."

They said, "There is no other way for him to do it."

He said to them, "So also with you, seek for yourselves a place for repose, or you might become corpses, and they will eat you."

This Saying almost makes us chuckle. We can picture the disciples looking at one another, boggled, after Jesus asks them whether the Samaritan is going to eat the lamb while it is dead. Knowing his propensity for turning their answers on their ears, the disciples seem to be responding, "Uhhh . . . yeah . . . there's no real other way to eat a lamb . . . ."

The Saying also has a few layers of complexity, and some symbolic details that might be missed in the modern reading. To begin, we note that the lamb is being carried by a Samaritan. During Jesus's time, the Samaritans were considered heretics by the Hebrews of Judea (i.e. the "Good Samaritan" parable), and were literally despised. They were never mentioned off-handedly in Jewish or Hebrew scripture at the time, and were certainly not thought of as holy by the mainstream.

Something else to keep in mind was that during Jesus's time, one rarely just took a lamb to *Market* to slaughter it for a normal, everyday dinner unless one was extremely well-off. The slaughter of a lamb was pretty much specifically done as a sacrifice, for most Samaritan and Orthodox Jews at Passover. After the lamb was slaughtered and roasted, it would be eaten by the sacrificant. Samaritans practice a heterodox version of Judaism and live in Samaria , which is north of Judea and south of Galilee. The practice of sacrifice is quite important in Samaritan Judaism, and according to the Samaritans, the Passover sacrifice must be performed at Mount Gerizim in Samaria instead of in Jerusalem.xxiv

This makes one think that there may have been an error in transcription. Jesus and his disciples lived and preached in Galilee, and, like all devout Jews of Galilee, had to cross Samaria to get to Judea and Jerusalem (or circumvent Samaria via crossing the Jordan) in order to celebrate Passover in that city. Samaritans literally would have had no reason whatsoever to carry a lamb to Judea— their Passover sacrifice was within Samaria. So, instead of reading **"He saw a Samaritan carrying a lamb and going to Judea,"** the first sentence might read, instead, **"While on the way [from Galilee] to Judea [through Samaria], he saw a Samaritan carrying a lamb."** Perhaps our erstwhile scribes were less familiar with the tensions between the Jews and the Samaritans than we, so such a reversal is definitely within the realm of possibility, and makes far more contextual sense.

So, if Jesus and his disciples were headed to Judea, and the Samaritan was carrying a lamb around, we can assume that this Saying takes place during (or just before) the Passover Feast. It also clears up the mystery of the Samaritan— instead of wondering why on earth the Samaritan was mentioned, we know it would be the equivalent of Saying, "While on the way to California from Washington, Jesus saw an Oregonian carrying a lamb." It would also serve to underline the fact that Jesus and his disciples were willing to head through Samaria in spite of any cultural qualms (or because they were in a hurry).

The significance of the sacrificial lamb and its symbolic equation with Jesus is old hat by now. This Saying, however, inverts this concept. Jesus asks the disciples, "What's that guy gonna do with that lamb?" They remark that he is going off to sacrifice the lamb and eat it. After agreeing that only something dead can be eaten, Jesus tells the disciples that they had better find a place of repose, or they will end up dead and eaten like the lamb. Jesus equates the disciples with the lamb, in essence equating them with himself— no great leap in Gnostic doctrine. However, instead of becoming a sacrifice, Jesus counsels them to try to stay alive. This idea reflects upon the Gnostic concept of martyrdom, which was generally, "do notdo it."

Returning to the life=gnosis, death=materia language, Jesus warns the disciples that that which is "alive," i.e. awake or on the Way, cannot be "eaten," or destroyed, or disappear into nothingness when the universe is redeemed. That which is "dead," or of the defective World of Forms, risks being "eaten," or fading into insubstantiation once the defective part of the universe is redeemed and saved by God.

Repose, or rest, often equates with salvation or gnosis. There are obvious parallels with the practice of meditation and contemplation, which any good follower of the Way will tell you is essential to achieving enlightenment or gnosis. Of course, this does not need to be the intense meditation of the Zen practitioner or Hesychast monk, though it most certainly can be, but should be whatever practice the follower of the Way prefers to remind her that she is at one with, and at rest within, God. In this way, and through this practice of the Way, one becomes alive instead of dead, and does not need to worry about being eaten.

SIXTY-ONE

Jesus said, "Two will rest on a bed; one will die, one will live."

Salome said, "Who are you, man? As if sent by someone, you have climbed onto my couch and eaten from my table."

Jesus said to her, "I am he who exists out of he who is equal. I was given the things of my Father."

"I am your disciple."

"For this reason I say, if one is destroyed, one will be filled with light; when, however, one is divided, one will be filled with darkness."

    Jesus climbs onto Salome's couch and relates a story about two men on a couch, one dying and one living. Salome responds by Saying, essentially, "Who the heck do you think you are, coming in here, sitting down and eating my food like some official representative for some bigwig somewhere?" In other words, Salome wants to know by whose authority Jesus thinks he can just barge in and start chowing down.

    Jesus replies, in typical fashion, that he was sent by God, and has the authority thereof, and that he was given the "things of my Father" (like Salome's food?). It is an important point that seems to have been forgotten by some of our modern Christian organizations: there is almost no concept of ownership within the tradition of the Way. It would be redundant to rehash the old Jesus was a Commie arguments— although not really true in the Marxist sense, it is pretty obvious from reading the Gospels, both canonical and non-, that the early Christians tended to share things like meals and divvy up money and such. It is all just stuff; realizing and teaching that in the context of the

Way, detachment from material desires a la the Buddha is an important consideration. Since all is "of the Father," and since followers of the Way are "of the Father," there is very little in the way of "mine and yours" in Jesus's teaching.

Salome replies that she is Jesus's disciple. Was Jesus implying that, by questioning his presence, she was never **really** his disciple? Tough love, if so— "hey, I'm going to come over to your house unannounced and eat your food. And if you don't like it, you're not really my student." But, it would fit with the Coptic translation of the text, which reads "destroyed" — perhaps by entering, sitting down and eating, certainly not a social norm, Jesus meant to "destroy" Salome's preconceived notions about right and wrong, tradition and custom versus spiritual ethics. In so "destroying" Salome's ideas, Jesus illustrates that such cultural constraints are illusory, and she has an experience of gnosis which leads her to proclaim her discipleship.

When she declares her discipleship, Jesus basically says, "See, I had to bust you down so you could get filled with life. Your cultural and societal 'rules' separate you from yourself, whereas when they are destroyed, you're made whole and the light can fill you up. When you divide your spiritual side from your social/cultural side, however, you can't get enlightened— you're living in the illusion."

That religion and state are separate and must remain so is a no-brainer. However, it is often overlooked by the religious within our secular society that a true religion is a moral code that transcends earthly laws and structures. Jesus, in Saying 61, is counseling us to remember that the Way is holistic, and should be an essential facet and the primary consideration in everything we do, from eating and drinking to hanging out with friends. Rather than using religion as the basis for earthly tenets, however, Jesus uses it as something that transcends custom and the law of the land, which are darkened and illusory constructs and can really only get in the way.

SIXTY-TWO

Jesus said, "I speak of my mysteries to those who are worthy of my mysteries. Do not let your left know what your right is doing."

Another case where some interpreters see two separate ideas where one is represented. I'll only teach to the worthy, says Jesus, which begs the question: who is worthy? Jesus provides the answer: to be worthy, do not let your left hand know what your right hand is doing.

'Left' at the time was often equated with wrongness or evil, thus the derivation of the word "sinister," which means "left" in Latin. Jesus may be referring to this— do not let your "wrong" hand/side, the part of you that comes from the Demiurge and exists in the World of Forms, know what your "correct" side, the redeemed aspect of one's self, is doing. Most likely, this is a return to the idea of individual theology, or the theology of humility: Jesus often counsels those who follow the Way to give anonymously, to pray in private, not to stand on street corners and draw attention to one's spirituality. Those who do so, who wear their religion on their sleeves, are not worthy of the teachings of Jesus. Exclusionist? Perhaps, though remember that the Way is available to anyone. The only people who are excluded are those who choose to exclude themselves.

SIXTY-THREE

Jesus said, "There was a rich person who had a great deal of riches. He said, 'I shall invest my riches so that I may sow, reap, plant, and fill my storehouses with produce, that I may need nothing.' These were the things he was thinking in his mind, but that very night he died. Anyone here with two ears had better listen!"

A parallel can be found in *Luke* 12:16-20:

He made a comparison for them, saying: "Once there was a rich fellow whose land yielded a bumper crop. And he thought to himself, 'What shall I do? I do nothave anywhere to store my crops?' And he said, 'This is what I'll do: I'll tear down my old silos and build bigger ones and store all my grains and good there, and then I will say to my soul, *Soul, you have enough goods stored up for many years: relax; eat, drink, be merry.'*

"But God said to him, 'Fool, this very night you must give up your life. The things you got together, who are they for?' That's how it is with a person who stores up treasures for himself instead of being enriched by God.

The implication is that instead of starting some massive new building project, the man would have been better served giving away any extra riches, letting God provide for him. Jesus counsels those who would follow the Way to invest their worldly endeavours in their own spiritual progress and in helping their neighbors instead of in physical and material concerns.

There is an interesting difference between the parables in *Luke* and *Thomas*. *Luke* starts with the crops; *Thomas* starts with the riches. In both cases, the man is already rich, which intimates that he does not really need the abundance of crops. Of course, one can also look at this Saying in light of the semiotic Gnostic language, in which "riches" represent those material attachments that we all have, and "crops" represent teachings. Taking this interpretation, we can restate the parable thusly:

There was a person with many attachments to the material world. He said, "I shall invest my materials in spiritual teachings, so that I may attain enlightenment." These were the things he was thinking in his mind, but that very night he died.

In this light, the Saying could mean that the Way cannot be bought or sold—those who think they need to spend money on gurus and teachings and courses are making a big mistake. Those who charge for "enlightenment" are false teachers, and those who think they can buy teachings are sadly mistaken.

SIXTY-FOUR

Jesus said, "A man was receiving visitors. When he had prepared the dinner, he sent his slave to invite the visitors. The slave went to the first and said to that one, 'My master calls you.' That one said, 'I have some money for some traders; they are coming to me tonight. I have to go and place orders with them. Please excuse me from dinner.' The slave went to another and said to that one, 'My master has called you.' That one said to the slave, 'I have bought a house, and I have been called away for a day. I shall have no free time.' The slave went to another and said to that one, 'My master invites you.' That one said to the slave, 'My friend is to be married, and I am to make dinner. I shall not be able to come. Please excuse me from dinner.' The slave went to another and said to that one, 'My master invites you.' That one said to the slave, 'I have bought an estate, and I am going to collect the taxes. I shall not be able to come. Please excuse me.' The slave returned and said to his master, 'Those whom you invited to dinner have asked to be excused.' The master said to his slave, 'Go out on the roads and bring back whomever you find to have dinner.'

Buyers and traders [will] not enter the places of my Father."

We find parallels in *Matthew* 22:1-14 and *Luke* 14:15-24. The parable as presented in *Luke* is very similar to this one, the variations minor. *Matthew* tells the parable as an almost different story altogether, where the rich man is a king and the feast is a wedding feast and the invitees kill the servants and the king kills the invitees and, once the "good and bad" are invited instead of the original guests, the king kicks someone out for not dressing correctly.

Is this Saying a commentary on class consciousness, or something even more meaningful? As we will see, each guest represents something different, and taken as a whole the message becomes clear. A masterpiece of metaphor, the Saying reacts to a number of materialistic issues through the medium of the four guests.

The first guest is waiting for some traders to come, so he can put a down payment on some goods and place some orders. The first guest represents buying material things on a personal level.

The second guest bought a house, and represents buying real estate. The implied metaphor would be residential permanence, perhaps with the intention of renting the house.

The third man has to attend a friend's wedding and plan the dinner. The implications are social and familial, the acknowledgement of worldly relationships. The "buying and selling" may represent the wedding gifts or the dowry or simply the fact that guest number three is some kind of wedding planner.

The fourth guest has to collect taxes on an estate that he owns. The implications are governmental— the fact that he owns an estate is inconsequential, but the taxes carry the symbolic weight of this section.

These are not random people doing random things; each of these characters represents a different kind of "buying and selling" that one would find during the period of *Thomas'* composition. It is not as though each person is simply buying and selling— instead, note that each plans to do something with the stuff that they have purchased. Thus, the theme in the previous Saying comes back again. Do not waste your time planning for the future when the Way is concerned: get started now.

Jesus is also, more importantly, telling us that it does not matter if you do not follow the Way for personal reasons, for material reasons, for interpersonal/familial reasons or for reasons set forth by the government—

none of these reasons is a good excuse for ignoring the Way if you feel called to it.

But what about those who do get invited? They are not specifically designated as the poor or homeless, just the first the servant stumbles across. It could be the Jewish High Priest. It could be a Roman Centurion. Could be a leper. Could be a gazillionaire. There is no way for one to know. It is a safe assumption to make, Jesus tells us, that anyone whatsoever may be one of those who has been invited to the feast. As such, it is a good idea to treat every individual person as though he or she is on the list.

Still, it cannot be denied that the essential message of this Saying is the last message: those who spend their time buying and selling are distracted from the Way, and will have a difficult time falling upon the Kingdom of Heaven.

SIXTY-FIVE

He said, "A just person owned a vineyard and rented it to some tenant farmers, so they could work it and he could collect its crop from them. He sent his slave so the farmers would give him the vineyard's crop. They grabbed him, beat him, and almost killed him, and the slave returned and told his master. His master said, 'Perhaps he didn't know them.' He sent another slave, and the farmers beat that one as well. Then the master sent his son and said, 'Perhaps they will be ashamed before my son.' Because the farmers knew that he was the heir to the vineyard, they grabbed him and killed him. He who has ears had better listen!"

Saying 65 is a continuation of the landowner/farmer/rich man parable theme that runs through the last few Sayings. It is also a return to the theme of "growing things," this time grapes. In Saying 40, we defined the grapevine as representative of the World of Forms, and we know that growing things in the context of farming can represent teachings, or the Word— the Logos which fills the Pleroma and redeems mankind through gnosis.

We might call this one, "The Parable of the Jerks." So who are the jerk farmers? The farmers neglect the authority of the landowner, and somehow think that even if they beat up his slaves and kill his son, they will still inherit the land. They are acting on their own authority, disregarding the authority of the landowner, harvesting the teachings of the Logos which are present in the World of Forms for their own ends. To me, this seems to indicate that our farmers are those in positions of authority here on the Earth, especially those who desire power for themselves and do so by controlling sources of information which should be made available to all.

It strikes us that the landowner is pretty even-handed, all things considered, after the first time he sends along a servant and the farmers beat him up. He's willing to give them the benefit of the doubt **twice**, hoping that they only beat up the servants because they thought the servants were there to do some harm to his vines. So, he sends his son along, thinking, "well heck, they've gotta know who he is," but the farmers kill the son regardless, afraid that his continued existence will keep them from keeping their precious, precious grapes.

In the canonical versions, the landowner retaliates by murdering the tenant farmers and giving the vineyard to others. This conclusion, however, does not occur in the Gnostic version— in true "koan" fashion, it is open ended, and contains the code phrase, "He who has ears had better listen," which, in Gnostic literature, usually means that anyone who hears should try to understand on her own— no interpretation forthcoming.

So, if the field is the world, the grapes are the Logos and information about the Way which is trapped in the world—and thus in the clutches of the "farmers," the worldly leaders and Archons—then who are the servants and who is the son? Traditional interpretations hold that the servants are prophets, the son is Jesus, and the landowner is God. Nothing in Gnosticism would run contrary to this idea, though one could just as easily take the son to be the Gnostic himself, the perfected heir to the vineyard, and the servants other seekers on the Way.

The seekers escape harm, but because they are not due to inherit the whole kit and caboodle— they are still 'slaves,' trapped in servitude, and not 'free men' or heirs to their own property. In this case, Jesus could be warning his disciples that the further along the Way one is, the more one attracts the attentions of the worldly rulers and Archons, and the more imperiled one becomes.

SIXTY-SIX

Jesus said, "Show me the stone that the builders rejected: that is the cornerstone."

This is, of course, a famous Saying, also found within the synoptics, directly after the parable which appears in *Thomas* as number 65. The first appearance of this Saying comes from the book of *Psalms*, 118:22, a hymn in praise of God, which states that "The stone the builders rejected has become the capstone."

The Saying itself, about the cornerstone, has more than one Gnostic connotation. At face value, it seems as though Jesus tells us that his "cornerstone" are those who have been rejected by worldly society, the meek and humble and poor. It also foreshadows Jesus's own rejection at the hands of the "Builders" of society, and may serve to equate him with God of *Psalms*, or at least to show his familiarity with that text. However, it helps to recall that in Gnostic myth, the "Builders" are the Demiurge and his archons, the creators of the World of Forms who labored to divide the World of Forms into sections of space and time and created the Earth as a pathetic copy of an image of the true heavenly temple. Their actions are reflected in everything that exists, especially the control mechanisms that tie us to the Demiurge's altar. When one has entered the community of those who follow the Way, however, one has escaped these chains and is "rejected" by the archons. When this occurs, one opens one's self to the Logos. Thus, one could say that the cornerstone is the community of those who follow the Way, who do tend to get rejected by the world's control mechanisms. Such people, found worthless by the archons, are, in Jesus's eyes, perfect enough to be used as the most important foundational component of the Kingdom of Heaven.

SIXTY-SEVEN

Jesus said, "Those who know the All, but need themselves, need the Entirety."

Saying 67, certainly one of the most important in *Thomas*, takes us all the way back to the basis of Western philosophy, established over the doors of the Oracle at Delphi and spread mostly via Socrates to the rest of the world: **Know Thyself.** Jesus agrees, telling us that, in essence, no matter what you know, even if you know everything that exists in the creation, if you do not know yourself, you know nothing.

Of course, in light of the Way, this also has a deeper meaning, directed towards the concept that each individual's divine spark is a fragment of the universal entirety. As each fragment consists of the single consciousness of God, knowing one's self is equal to knowing the Universe and God. If this is indeed the case, then, truly, all answers—so one could assume from the Delphic Oracle inscription—are found within. The quest of the follower of the Way, then, can be framed in terms of actually **having gnosis of one's self** as the best way to know God.

This is not some kind of over-sentimentalised, New-Agey, "we are all Gods," "come to know your inner God" nonsense. Knowing one's self does not mean learning about one's self, or coming to grips with the psychological issues driven into each one of us by living in an insane universe, or coming to some kind of realization about a career path. Knowing one's self, in light of the Way, is the deeper experience of direct enlightenment. It is a mystery, as it should be, and if one does not come to terms with her inner mystery, one will find it very difficult to come to terms with the entirety.

Enlightenment does not grant superpowers, the ability to read minds or materialize things out of thin air. It is not available for sale. The Path is not revealed by channeled Atlantean Warriors or UFOnauts or visions of the Blessed Virgin Mary. Enlightened beings do not perform miracles or intervene on behalf of this or the other organization— even Jesus himself refused to perform miracles for people who asked for them. Most mystical traditions state that getting in touch with one's past lives or performing magic tricks are actually substantial distractions from the path. Zen monks tell you to ignore visions and prophecies you receive when meditating because they are not the goal.

Zen monks do not do card tricks.

The Path is **only** available through humility and compassion, but, most importantly, through **self-examination**.

SIXTY-EIGHT and SIXTY-NINE

Jesus said, "Blessed are you when they hate and persecute you; and no place will be found, wherever you have been persecuted."

Jesus said, "Congratulations to those who have been persecuted in their hearts: they have known the Father in truth. Blessed are the hungry, so that they may satisfy the belly of he who desires."

Here in the United States, some of our more fundamentalist brothers and sisters claim that Christians are currently undergoing "persecution" like never before. The feeling of persecution is a bonding experience that makes one feel special and important, but at this point in Western society, Christians and Wiccans and a number of other faiths that were persecuted in the past really have very little persecution to worry about. Unfortunately, the same cannot be said for some of our Muslim and Jewish and homosexual brothers and sisters, who, in the current manifestation of the Black Iron Prison, actually **do** have valid concerns about wrongful persecution.

A Western Christian who claims that he or she is being "persecuted" by the omission, say of the phrase "under God" from the pledge, or the removal of a Ten Commandments statue from a courtroom, insultingly belittles and denigrates the valid concerns of those people who actually have to fear doing certain things because their fellow citizens or their governments do not agree with their belief systems. Persecution is having to worry that one might be assaulted for wearing a headscarf, not the abolition of all religious imagery from courthouses. Those who actively desire persecution simply enjoy being victims. Unfortunately, the canonical versions of these Sayings, when interpreted this way, simply add fuel to the fire.

During Jesus's time, the issue was unarguably far more pertinent for Christians—who, let us recall, were persecuted far more for refusing to acknowledge the divinity of the emperor than for their actual religious beliefs. Some Gnostics even looked down upon martyrs as foolish. After all, if all is one, and everything is full of the Logos and the Spirit of God, then the term one uses to describe the fullness of God does not have to be restricted to a certain name. Why not, then, claim that the Emperor is "divine," which technically is not a lie, as everything contains divinity, and survive the pogroms? Jesus never really said "seek out persecution and die for me," but his words were twisted by these victimless religious suicide bombers, who had no problem dying for Christ. What he did say, though, is that if you are being persecuted, you may be doing something right.

"Congratulations to those who have been persecuted **in their hearts.**" What exactly does it mean to be persecuted in one's heart? The Saying continues: congratulations to those who choose to go hungry so that those less fortunate can eat. Imagine going without eating and giving one's food to someone less fortunate. In a society based on consumerist control systems, such a concept is absurd!

Why feed the poor, who are obviously too lazy to fend for themselves? Why pay extra taxes to educate somebody else's children? When Alabama's governor, facing a major state budgetary crisis, asked the citizenry to accept a tax hike that would help the less fortunate as doing so was a "Christian Duty," the hike was resoundingly defeated by the overwhelmingly "Christian" community of Alabama. The idea of tax hikes to help the poor? Ludicrous. Insane. Awarding the lazy. Apparently only a few of these people actually took it upon themselves to ask what Jesus would have done.

This, however, is exactly the kind of internal persecution to which Jesus refers: persecution by the control system for doing something that does not submit to said system. One is not persecuted by other people as were the original Christians, but by one's own inner submission to the system in which we reside. Sure, there were plenty of good, decent folks in Alabama who voted against the tax hikes, but it is because they were not persecuted— they felt nothing about ignoring the plight of their state. Societal norms and preconceived notions that whispered 'how will you be able to consume more if you give money to others? We need to be fed." To these people, this is not persecution, but the norm. The control system does not need to persecute those who already submit unquestioningly.

Those who are "persecuted in their hearts," on the other hand, feel the pull of the control system, the persecution within, but are able to overcome it as having been touched by the Way. They might say, "you know, I **really want** that new coat, but I don't need it— I'll give this money to someone who needs a meal." These are the people who, in their own ways, realize the fullness of God in the Universe and, clear-eyed, at least try, however imperfectly, to live a life of generosity, humility and kindness.

SEVENTY

Jesus said, "If you beget what is within you, what you have will save you. If you do not have that within you, what you do not have within you [will] kill you."

What is already within each one of us? The Pleroma, the Fullness of God. Begetting it will bring one salvation. It is a process, in Gnosticism, of giving birth to God's presence in the false world— in Gnostic Christianity, one is not simply born again, one also gives birth to the presence of God in the world, which brings an eventual escape from the insanity and illusion, or salvation. As Valentinus, Gnostic teacher and poet says in his poem "Summer Harvest," the presence of God is **like "Crops rushing forth from the deep/A babe rushing forth from the womb."**

This Pleroma, or fullness, is absolutely present in every aspect of the World of Forms, in no uncertain terms. However, it is hidden, or covered up, or "lacking" due to the illusion created by the Demiurge. To those who have not experienced gnosis, or uncovered that fullness, said fullness does not even exist. This seems silly on the surface, but it is absolutely supported by our culture of empiricism, where nothing is considered 'true' or 'real' unless it is observed by science. So, those who are 'lacking' do so through either ignorance of God or by denying their experiences and keeping the presence of God 'covered up,' or absent.

However, keeping the presence of God within one, instead of bringing it out and letting it interact with the world, can "kill" you. According to our Gnostic semiotic language, we know that death and dying are associated with the "dead" World of Forms, the World of Forms, the realm of the Demiurge which lacks the divine presence because it does not recognize it. Jesus is not telling us that keeping the presence of God within will literally kill you, or that you will suffer some kind of eternal damnation. He tells us that keeping the presence of God within one's self due to the illusion that said presence is not there will keep one chained to the control structures of the dead world.

Some perceive an elitism in Gnosticism, illustrated in statements like this Saying, that imply that those who have not experienced gnosis are somehow 'doomed,' like those folks who say that those who are not Christians are eternally damned to Hell.   Gnosticism, however is not truly elitist. Gnostic eschatology is based on theoretically logical extensions of the Gnostic worldview, which dictates that those who have not experienced gnosis may be reincarnated back into the world until they do. However, no Gnostic would claim to be "the King of Karma."[xxv] There is absolutely no way to know what happens to us after death until we die. It is pretty much speculation based on our myth, which generally indicates that everyone will eventually be saved anyhow.

Many, many people experience gnosis without realizing that they've experienced it. They simply have no language in which to express the experience. Some people experience it during the birth of their child. Some people experience it while watching a spectacular sunset over the Crazy Mountains in Montana. Some people experience it while meditating or praying. For some people, it is smack-you-upside-the-head enlightenment, and for some people it is the contact with God that they get when they take communion or read an enlightening passage from their holy scriptures.

Some people may not know they have experienced it. Some people may spend their entire lives trying to recreate the experience. Some people may feel it as a cool breeze, others as a slow burn.

It is not necessary to practice "Gnosticism" to achieve gnosis, any more than it is necessary to be a physicist to understand how to toss a baseball. Now, Gnostics would certainly say that it helps, but then so would Zen Buddhism, Sufism, devotional Catholicism, Orthodoxy, Southern Baptism, Mormonism, doing the laundry, taking the dog for a walk, staying up late and chatting philosophically with a bunch of stoned friends . . . you get the picture.

The important thing to remember is that all it takes is one flash of gnosis to be "eligible" for salvation. That is all the experience of God that one needs—it is usually all one gets during this short lifetime. The universe, after all, is timeless, a big blob where everything happens all at once. Everyone is saved, and when and where it happens are inconsequential; Gnosticism is just one language that Jesus and his followers and the followers of the Way used to describe this experience and this worldview.

SEVENTY-ONE

Jesus said, "I will destroy [this] house, and no one will be able to rebuild it."

The canonical parallels are Jesus's various declarations that he'll be tearing down the Temple in Jerusalem. The Temple is, of course, the House of God, which holds the Holy of Holies. Why would Jesus want to destroy it? And, is the Temple the same "house" Jesus refers to in this Saying? As usual, the answer is yes and no.

Inasmuch as some Gnostics saw the Temple as a corrupt representative of the Demiurge's world, controlled by priests and built by kings, one could certainly argue that Jesus speaks of the World of Forms, the created world, when he refers to this "house." However, in the *Gospel of Philip*, we find further details as to the meaning or interpretation of the Temple as a symbol:

> At the present time, we have the manifest things of creation. We say, "The strong who are held in high regard are great people. And the weak who are despised are the obscure." Contrast the manifest things of truth: they are weak and despised, while the hidden things are strong and held in high regard. The mysteries of truth are revealed, though in type and image. The bridal chamber, however, remains hidden. It is the Holy in the Holy. The veil at first concealed how God controlled the creation, but when the veil is rent and the things inside are revealed, this house will be left desolate, or rather will be destroyed.

The Temple itself is representative of the "manifest things of Creation." As we know, the Temple, surrounded by a "veil," contains the Holy of Holies. The Temple, as a giant, magnificent stone building located in beautiful downtown Jerusalem, means absolutely nothing without the Holy of Holies contained therein. The "veil" represents the veil of illusion that covers the World of Forms, and the Holy of Holies is the spirit within the body, the Pleroma and fullness of God within the individual and the world.

According to Judaic Law, only the High Priest was ever allowed to enter the Holy of Holies, and only on certain days. What Jesus wants to do, however, in destroying the "Temple," is remove this veil and make the essence within available to all seekers on every day, not just those who are somehow better because they are priests. Of course, instead of thinking of this as "Jesus wants to do away with the High Priest and Holy Days," the Gnostic might think of it instead as "Jesus wants to make **everyone** High Priests and **every** day Holy." Jesus wants everyone to realize that the external appearance of the Temple, and thus the world and the body are nothing compared to what exists within. In doing so, he destroys the Temple, meaning he destroys the illusion of strength presented by the insane delusions of the Universe. By telling us that he wants to destroy this house, Jesus refers not to some kind of physical destruction, but an end to the false power structures that prevent each and every one of us from entering our own Holy of Holies.

The giant, edificial Temple, intimidating and "strong," is nothing — **nothing** — compared to the hidden wonder of the Holy of Holies within its center, beyond its veil. In the same way, the body is nothing compared to the indwelling wonder of the soul. In the same way, the created World of Forms is nothing compared to the indwelling fullness of God. However, because it is easy to confuse that which is external for that which is "strong," it is necessary to destroy the illusion of strength, to bring down the Temple and rend its veil, to reveal the Holy of Holies within.

SEVENTY-TWO

A man said to him, "Speak to my brothers, so that they will divide my father's belongings with me."

He said to the person, "Man, who has made me a divider?"

He turned to his disciples and said to them, "Truly, I'm not a divider, am I?"

Perhaps due to the tone or the pacing of the Saying, we find this it almost humorous. The Gnostics were no strangers to employing humor as a rhetorical device, though much of what they considered "humor" would be funnier to a citizen of the Roman Empire than to our 21st Century ears. The image of the "laughing savior" carries a special relevance in the Gnostic corpus, best illustrated in *The Apocalypse of Peter*:

> The Savior said to me, "He whom you saw on the tree, glad and laughing, this is the living Jesus. But this one into whose hands and feet they drive the nails is his fleshly part, which is the substitute being put to shame, the one who came into being in his likeness. But look at him and me."

Christ laughs for various reasons, but implicit in this image is the sheer joy and wonder and, yes, humor that one finds when following the Way and overcoming the Archonic forces that rule the World of Forms.

The enlightenment of humour appears in any tradition that employs parables as spiritual tools. Humor, by its very nature, serves to remind us that things like "meaning" are transitory. "Getting" a joke is actually an excellent metaphor for achieving gnosis: both require a sort of "a-ha!" moment, and just as a joke loses its humour if you have to explain it, gnosis isn't "gnosis" if you have to explain it.

The Sufis are perhaps the greatest utilizers of humor as a teaching tool leading to enlightenment. Take, for example, the collections of stories about and attributed to "Mulla Nasrudin," the Sufi "wise fool":

Nasrudin found himself without the help of a donkey to assist him in his daily chores. Desperate, without the means to buy one, he started do pray to Allah, to send him a new animal. He prayed for a long time and later, when he was walking down a road, found a man riding a donkey and trotting behind there was a smaller and younger donkey. Nasrudin came closer to the man and the man told him:

"What a shame! I've been traveling for many hours and I and my animals are exhausted and here we have this fine rested man doing nothing!"

And menacing Nasrudin with his sword, the man said:

"Hurry! Put the smaller donkey on your back and carry it along till the next city!"

Nasrudin, afraid, did what the man ordered.

After many hours of walking carrying the donkey on his back, he was exhausted, they arrived in the next city in the afternoon. The man simply ordered the donkey to the ground and went away, without even giving thanks to Nasrudin.

Nasrudin turned his eyes to the sky and said:

"Very well, Allah. I've learned my lesson. Next time I will try to be more specific!"[xxvi]

Sometimes, it can be helpful to think of the Sayings in the *Gospel of Thomas* as jokes. This Saying, in particular, seems to contain a kernel of humor; one can almost picture the glimmer in Jesus's eye as he slyly ridicules both the young man and his disciples.

Of course, the **meaning** of the Saying does not necessitate the humor. Jesus has a message for both the man and for his disciples. To the man, Jesus says, "look, I'm not some kind of arbitrator of possessions, here to enforce ownership laws. I'm not a lawyer who can help you work out your issues." We already know about Jesus's disdain for worldly possessions, but his opinion on traditional Judaic law is also implicit in his reply. He tells his listeners, "Whoa, hold on— I'm not a lawyer, man."

Someone in Jewish society probably would not ask someone to arbitrate legal issues without having gotten the idea from someone that said person was good at arbitration, or studied in the Law. Or, perhaps Jesus's reputation as a wise fellow somehow got back to the asker. It is obvious, though, that someone has been spreading word that Jesus knows all about the Law. The humor, to me, seems to be that Jesus is subtly rebuking his disciples for spreading falsehoods about Jesus, or for misunderstanding his teachings, by phrasing his rebuke in the form of an open-ended question. We picture the disciples looking on sheepishly, like a class of kindergarteners. "Class, I didn't say you could have any more juice, did I?"

Asking this question in an open-ended format actually serves another purpose: it coerces the listener into asking herself, "okay, if Jesus isn't a divider, then he must be a uniter. What does that mean?"

Throughout the Gnostic corpus, and *Thomas* itself, we find the importance of "unity." In Saying 61, for instance, Jesus tells Salome that, "if one is whole, one will be filled with light, but if one is divided, one will be filled with darkness." Jesus comes to teach us about the essential unity of the Universe, and to bring the different spiritual aspects of people together into unities through gnosis.

SEVENTY-THREE

Jesus said, "The harvest is plentiful, but the laborers are few; pray to the Lord to send laborers to the harvest."

As we know from previous Sayings like the Parable of the Seeds, "harvest" and "crops" refer to the Word, the living information contained within the teachings of the Logos. The creation is full of the Word; the Logos is contained within everything but needs to be released through gnosis. Thus, the harvest is plentiful. However, there are not enough workers, which implies that not enough people have access to the crops.

Now, the Gnostics were never big on the concept of proselytization. As says the *Gospel of Philip*, **"A Hebrew makes another Hebrew, and such a person is called 'proselyte'. But a proselyte does not make another proselyte."** The essential idea behind Gnosticism is that one needs to discover the Logos for one's self. Someone who has experienced gnosis cannot duplicate that experience in someone else— it is necessary to let each person figure out gnosis for herself. Of course, making information available should be encouraged. Active proselytizing, however, is frowned upon.

One can "pray to the Lord to send more workers," which presumes that the Logos can work through people who have experienced gnosis in order to harvest itself. Note, however, that the statement entices us to depend upon God to send the workers, not that we all need to go out and recruit the workers ourselves— we should be too busy harvesting for that!

SEVENTY-FOUR

He said, "Lord, there are many around the fountain, but there is nothing in the well."

Is Jesus addressing the Lord? Or, is this one of the disciples addressing Jesus? The meaning remains either way. In Gnostic code, drinking something is the equivalent of learning about the Way—thus, in Saying 13, Thomas becomes "drunk" on Jesus's teachings. Whomever the speaker, his words seem to indicate that many people are thirsty for the truth, but the truth cannot be found.

When we hear "well," we picture a jack–and–jill–type stone well with a wooden bucket and crank. Historically, however, the Saying actually concerns cisterns. We know that Jesus was a master of metaphor, often choosing everyday objects to explain exceptionally profound concepts. Cisterns, as opposed to wells, are intended to capture and hold great quantities of water in dry areas where digging for wells is not always the best option. Cisterns in the Levant were generally carved from rock and supplemented with plaster, and woe betide the village whose cistern began to leak. The cistern would need constant attention and repair to ensure that no cracks formed.

So, we can expand upon this Saying a bit. Why would a cistern be empty? It is possible that it had not rained, but if that was the case, then why would people gather around the cistern? More likely, it is a matter of a cistern, in this case the world, that's fallen into disrepair or neglect due to its imperfection, which means that the knowledge of the Way seeped out of it.

Note also that a dry cistern meant for a desperate situation. The speaker, be he Jesus or a disciple, is literally pleading for the desperate crowd around the reservoir. Truly, as some of us know all too well, seeking for Truth in this deranged universe is a desperate act. The speaker pleads on our behalf, asking God, or the Logos residing in Jesus, to provide Truth for the thirsty crowd.

SEVENTY-FIVE

Jesus said, "There are many standing at the door, but only the single ones will enter the bridal chamber."

The mysterious "bridal chamber" is an image that should be familiar to most Christians, as the Canonical texts mention it regularly. Wedding symbolism played an important role in all stripes of early Christianity. From the miracle at Cana to the parable of the virgins in Matthew, the idea of Christ as the "bridegroom" returns again and again.

However, the concept of marriage as a semiotic device played a far larger role in Gnosticism than in mainstream Christianity. Much of organized Gnosticism was rooted in Greek mystery traditions, which included the concept of hieros gamos, or "divine marriage." In fact, Greek tradition included a purifying "hieros gamos" ritual between Zeus and Hera on or around the middle of February, when many cultures celebrate Valentine's Day as a day honoring love. Note also that Valentinus and the Valentinian Gnostics most likely celebrated the hieros gamos in an actual ritual "bridal chamber." Hieros gamos, as an essential aspect of esoteric teachings, represented the commingling of the masculine and feminine divinity, the Logos and Sophia.

In the language of Gnosticism, what is the bridal suite? First of all, it obviously implies a wedding of some kind, but a wedding between whom? The Gnostic *Exegesis on the Soul* (ES) provides us with a clue. In the ES, the soul is an androgynous virgin who falls into the World of Forms and is subsequently raped by the powers that rule it:

> As long as she was alone with the father, she was virgin and in form androgynous. But when she fell down into a body and came to this life, then she fell into the hands of many robbers. And the wanton creatures passed her from one to another and [...] her. Some made use of her by force, while others did so by seducing her with a gift. In short, they defiled her, and she [...] her virginity.

And in her body she prostituted herself and gave herself to one and all, considering each one she was about to embrace to be her husband.

Our souls, trapped and amazed and boggled by the World of Forms and the rulers of the Black Iron Prison, in essence, prostitute themselves. The *Exegesis* continues, quoting Paul to support its thesis:

Yet the greatest struggle has to do with the prostitution of the soul. From it arises the prostitution of the body as well. Therefore Paul, writing to the Corinthians (1Co 5:9-10), said, "I wrote you in the letter, 'Do not associate with prostitutes,' not at all (meaning) the prostitutes of this world or the greedy or the thieves or the idolaters, since then you would have to go out from the world." - here it is speaking spiritually - "For our struggle is not against flesh and blood - as he said (Ep 6:12) - but against the world rulers of this darkness and the spirits of wickedness."

As long as the soul keeps running about everywhere copulating with whomever she meets and defiling herself, she exists suffering her just deserts. But when she perceives the straits she is in and weeps before the father and repents, then the father will have mercy on her and he will make her womb turn from the external domain and will turn it again inward, so that the soul will regain her proper character.

Note the use of the word "perceives." This reminds us that spiritual perception is an act of gnosis, an actual awakening. Only after this awakening occurs can God send help. In order to redeem the soul, God sends down the Christos, the Logos, the soul's "brother," who becomes her bridegroom within the bridal chamber. This hieros gamos redeems the soul, purifies her through a holy matrimony:

From heaven the father sent her her man, who is her brother, the firstborn. Then the bridegroom came down to the bride. She gave up her former prostitution and cleansed herself of the pollutions of the adulterers, and she was renewed so as to be a bride. She cleansed herself in the bridal chamber; she filled it with perfume; she sat in it waiting for the true bridegroom.

No longer does she run about the market place, copulating with whomever she desires, but she continued to wait for him - (Saying) "When will he come?" - and to fear him, for she did not know what he looked like: she no longer remembers since the time she fell from her father's house. But by the will of the father <...> And she dreamed of him like a woman in love with a man.

But then the bridegroom, according to the father's will, came down to her into the bridal chamber, which was prepared. And he decorated the bridal chamber.

This concept, of the marriage between the Christos and the soul, is underlined in the Valentinian *Tripartite Tractate*, which states that:

The [Church Universal] shares body and essence with the Savior, since it is like a bridal chamber because of its unity and its agreement with him. For, before every place, the Christ came for [the soul's] sake. The calling, however, has the place of those who rejoice at the bridal chamber, and who are glad and happy at the union of the bridegroom and the bride.

The *Tripartite Tractate* discusses the Saviour's marriage to the soul as the process of Universal Redemption. It continues by giving us another clue about the meaning of "a solitary one"— that the Universal Redemption will not occur until the body of the Church Universal has **"been manifested as the whole body, namely the restoration into the Pleroma."** The Pleroma, as we know, is the fullness of God in the Universe, which includes the World of Forms. Both the *Tractate* and the *Gospel of Philip* indicate that an actual ritual "Bridal chamber" existed, which was decorated with mirrors. The mirrors would represent the archetypes, or images, in a mystery that unfortunately no longer survives in its original form.

The *Gospel of Philip* clarifies the concept even further, when it mentions that **"'The Holy of the Holies' is the bridal chamber. Baptism includes the resurrection and the redemption; the redemption (takes place) in the bridal chamber."** The Holy of Holies, the inner sanctum of the Temple, is where the Jewish High Priest communes with God. Remember from our earlier discussion of Saying 71 that Jesus indicates his desire to make every individual into a High Priest, who can access the Holy of Holies? So the communion of God and the High Priest in the Holy of the Holies is also representative, in Gnostic thought, of the communion of the Christos and the Soul in the Bridal Chamber.

Thus, the physical bridal chamber symbolizes the placeless place wherein the soul is redeemed. Though ritual bridal chambers were used, it goes without Saying that they actually represented a kind of internal state. In Saying 49, we concluded that, **"Being "solitary" describes the realization of our**

nature as pluralities of the single universe." Only those who have had this realization can enter the bridal chamber, the Holy of Holies, the physical representation of the placeless place wherein salvation occurs, and commune with God through the medium of the hieros gamos, the marriage of the soul, the bride, to the Christos, the bridegroom.

SEVENTY-SIX

Jesus said, "The Father's kingdom is like a merchant who had a consignment and fell upon a pearl. That merchant was wise; he gave back the consignment and bought the single pearl for himself. So also with you, seek his treasure that does not perish, that is enduring, where no moth comes to eat and no worm destroys."

Yet another commonly used symbol in early Christianity, the pearl appears frequently in Gnostic literature, and a variation of this Saying in particular appears in Matt 13:45-46 (the "Pearl of Great Price").

The most complete, and one of the most astounding versions of the pearl comes from the *Acts of Thomas*, an early adventure story about Thomas's journeys East after the resurrection. The *Acts* includes the hauntingly beautiful "Hymn of the Pearl," essentially a lengthy, symbolic discourse detailing a seeker's travels to "Egypt" to retrieve a "pearl." The pearl, in this case, represents the soul. Since we discussed the bridal chamber as the place wherein soul and saviour meet in the last Saying, it makes sense that the thought which immediately follows concerns the "pearl-as-soul" concept as well.

In this Saying, the Kingdom of Heaven, as a merchant, stumbles upon the pearl as the symbol of the imperishable soul. Knowing full well that his consignment, perhaps, based on the following sentence, clothing or foodstuffs, is susceptible to decay and the imperfection of the World of Forms. The perishable things of this world, things that can be eaten by moths and worms, are worthless in the proverbial grand scheme.

Note that the merchant returns his consignment and must purchase the pearl; it is not given away for free. The merchant is the Kingdom—as the merchant returns his imperfect items to purchase the pearl, so does the Kingdom of Heaven rid itself of its worthless aspects in order to purchase the soul. Money represents a sacrifice in this case; the sacrifice occurs with the descent of God into the world of matter, thus purchasing the salvation of the imperishable soul, which is a fragment of the awareness of God within each one of us, and it is the Most Valuable Thing.

SEVENTY-SEVEN

Jesus said, "I am the light that is over all things. I am the All: from me the All came forth, and the All split open upon me. Split a piece of wood; I am there. Lift up the stone, and you will find me there."

This is a beautiful Saying that brings to mind the "I am" Sayings found in Chapter 8 of John's Gospel. First Jesus identifies himself as the light that is over all things. When one turns on a light, one awakens— Jesus is the light which allows one to see, and to awaken into gnosis. Here Jesus does not refer to the essential Divine Light itself, but to the light which switches on when one has achieved enlightenment.

Continuing, he refers to himself as "the All," everything that exists. Inasmuch as we are sensory organs of the universe, through which a single consciousness travels from moment to moment, everyone is the All itself, which Jesus recognizes here. The act of splitting brings to mind the process of Universal division, whereby the "All," or Entirety, divides itself into an infinite number of parts, which results in the Universe.

Could Jesus be Saying that he represents the end result of this process of division? If so, it follows that every conscious thing is also the end result of the process of division, and that Jesus is indeed present therein. When one splits a piece of wood, or picks up a stone, what does one find? Jesus? Divine light of some kind? The fullness of God? Maybe metaphorically, but for a moment let us think literally. When one splits open a stick or picks up a rock, one usually finds . . . bugs. Creepy little crawlers. Termites, centipedes, dung beetles, ants, worms. Jesus, in this particular instance, says that he, and therefore the All, is present even in the creepy-crawlies that dig through the dirt.

By proxy, divinity is found even in the most disturbing and disgusting aspects of the Universe. One can even find divinity within the corrupted World of Forms of the Demiurge. One way to discover the ultimate divinity in All, and achieve the All itself, is to contemplate the divinity within even the most banal and useless things. As Philip Dick said in his Exegesis, **"Premise: things are inside out...Therefore the right place to look for the almighty is, e.g., in**

the trash in the alley."[xxvii] Or, as a Buddhist Koan has it, **"Question: What is the Buddha? Answer: The Buddha is a shit-stick."**

Even the bugs under the rocks and living in the wood contain the Logos, the light of Jesus, and one can begin at the very bottom, the smallest fragments of the Universe, and work one's way up through Jesus to the All. Of course, this is something that requires action. Jesus does not simply say, "I'm in wood and under stones"— he says that one must **do** something to achieve gnosis. One must actually **split** the wood; one must actually **lift** the stone. Gnosis is an active process that requires action on the part of the seeker.

SEVENTY-EIGHT

Jesus said, "Why have you come out to the field? To see a reed shaken by the wind? And to see a person dressed in soft clothes, [like your] rulers and your powerful ones? They are dressed in soft clothes, and they cannot understand truth."

Addressing those who have come to hear him speak, Jesus asks them to examine the reasons for which they came to hear him. The second part of the Saying addresses the question, in full, of whether one's outward appearance or worldly power actually give her some sort of greater access to the truth. Obviously, Jesus says that there is no greater access to truth for those who wear fine clothing.

Is Jesus himself the reed? Why one reed—reeds grow in big bunches— it seems odd that he would refer to one reed. Does he mean, then, that the truth that he has is greater than the strength of a single reed, sort of in the tradition of the bundle of sticks being stronger than the single stick? Or, is he making some kind of light-hearted rhetorical jibe, along the lines of "Are you even listening to me? Or, did you people come out here on some kind of nature walk?"

The Gnostics, like most religious practitioners, had a basic semiotic understanding of myth and philosophy which would allow them to express ideas and concepts through symbols and signs—in semiotics, signifiers. Knowing this, and knowing that Jesus was a master at forming metaphor, it is important, if one wants to understand these teachings, to try to look behind the signifiers for the signified. When, therefore, Jesus says "seeds" in one Saying, he clues us in that "seeds" is a sign that signifies a particular concept: teachings, or "the Word." This means that when we see "seeds" in one Saying, we are almost certain that this sign signifies teachings in the same way it does in other Sayings.

Although a disparate group of texts survive, from a number of different Gnostic traditions, they were nonetheless collected together. This indicates that though they may bear no compositional relationship to one another—some were written by Valentinians, some by Sethians, etc.—they do bear a relationship to whomever employed the texts. Those who actually practiced "Gnosticism" understood a relationship between the texts, due to this symbolic language which tied them together.

One of the main reasons for the "continuity of signs" has to do with basic mnemonics. When one considers the level of technology available at the time of their compilation, before the introduction of moveable type and standardization of writing and language, it becomes almost absurd to interpret similar signifiers variously referring to an abundance of signified concepts. Imagine being a Pachomian Monk in Alexandria in 158 AD. In order to study religious texts, one would have to painstakingly transcribe them, but one would also rely heavily on one's memory. Complicating signifiers with one another would make this process overly complex.

And, keep in mind, our ability to remember things declines substantially every time a new solid media arises. Greek poets would memorize the *Iliad* and the *Odyssey* in their entireties. Indian priests would memorize vast amounts of the *Mahabharata*, the *Yanas* and the *Vedas*. The only modern parallel would be Muslims who memorize the entire Quran, an amazing feat that is inconceivable to most non-Muslims. Plato even complained that the written alphabet would cause us to lose our capacity for memory. Can it be argued that he was incorrect?

Because of their oral nature, these texts contained "mnemonic devices," which would assist memorization. The most obvious were, of course, rhyme and meter, but there were others. For instance, in the *Iliad* and *Odyssey*, there are repeated formulas, like "Dawn spread out her rosy fingertips," which would cue the reciter to the upcoming segment, or a change in scene.

All of this coupled together leads us to believe that the continuity of signs in the Gnostic texts were certainly used as mnemonic devices.. Whether those who wrote the texts intended this to be the case is moot. Nonetheless, this is why when we see a word like "reed" in a Saying, we can search the rest of the Gnostic literature for another reference, to investigate whether deeper meaning can be found.

One last caveat is that, of course, to those who composed these texts, the meanings that, to us, seem symbolic and mysterious, would have made perfect sense. Just as a computer programmer would likely understand, "I'm going to FTP a compressed file to my desktop and extract it with WinZip," so might a Second Century Gnostic scholar understand the common words and symbols within the writings of Gnostic teachers.

With this in mind, we do indeed find a reference to a "reed being shaken in the wind" in another Gnostic text called *Trimorphic Protonoia*, or "First Thought in Three Forms." Essentially a Creation Myth, the text is written from the point of view of this "First Thought," an androgynous Christos/Sophia/Logos figure. The story unfolds in the same way as most Gnostic myths: God desires to extend itself, does so, in the process the Demiurge accidentally splits off and begins creating without God's help, leading to the imperfect World of Forms. The Christos/Sophia/Logos figure injects divinity into the imperfect creation of the Demiurge. This divinity results in gnosis, and the undoing of the imperfect creation via the destruction of Fate, and a new Aeon of peace and divinity reigns forevermore. The passage concerning us at the moment details the demolition of the Demiurge's false World of Forms and replacement by the perfection of the Kingdom of Heaven (emphasis mine):

> Now I have come the second time in the likeness of a female, and have spoken with them. And I shall tell them of the coming end of the Aeon and teach them of the beginning of the Aeon to come, the one without change, the one in which our appearance will be changed. We shall be purified within those Aeons from which I revealed myself in the Thought of the likeness of my masculinity. I settled among those who are worthy in the Thought of my changeless Aeon. For I shall tell you a mystery of this particular Aeon, and tell you about the forces that are in it. The birth beckons; hour begets hour, day begets day. The months made known the month. Time has gone round succeeding time. This particular Aeon was completed in this fashion, and it was estimated, and it (was) short, for it was a finger that released a finger, and a joint that separated from a joint. Then, when the great Authorities knew that the time of fulfillment had appeared - just as in the pangs of the parturient it (the time) has drawn near, so also had the destruction approached - all together the elements trembled, and the foundations of the underworld and the ceilings of Chaos shook, and a great fire shone within their midst, *and the rocks and the earth were shaken like a reed shaken by the wind.*

So, in this text, we find reeds being shaken by the wind as a signifier for signs that precede the redemption of the World of Forms via the destruction of this false world by the Logos.

Is it possible, then, that Jesus is referring to this concept in Saying 78? If so, maybe the reference to "a reed being shaken" would read like this: "Why have you come out here to see me? For a prophetic sign indicating the end of the imperfect World of Forms?" This would actually mesh with the parallels in the Canon. It would also explain his tone; Jesus tended to repudiate those who came to see him simply because they wanted miracles or prophecies. Is he telling us, in essence, that those who came for "signs and wonders" are just as bad as those who consider external appearances as signs of Truth?

SEVENTY-NINE

A woman in the crowd said to him, "Blessed are the womb that bore you and the breasts that nourished you."

He said, "Blessed are those who have listened to the Word of the Father: and have watched over it in truth. For there will be days when you will say, 'Lucky are the womb that has not conceived and the breasts that have not given milk.'"

If taken literally, this exchange is fairly straightforward. Just as Jesus often counsels those who follow the Way to forget their fathers and mothers and relatives as there are no such distinctions among the seekers, here he could be pointing out to the woman that listening to the Word of the Father is more important than making distinctions based on the circumstances of one's birth in the World of Forms.

This is actually an interesting aspect of Jesus's ministry, even in the Canon, because, as evinced by the time put into compiling genealogies and lists of ancestors by the authors of the Gospels of Matthew and Luke, many early Christians obviously considered "Divine" pedigree very important. If, however, as Jesus says, hearing and understanding the Word of God is more important than acknowledging the import of one's father and mother, then these genealogical lists are in direct violation of Jesus's own teachings on the subject. If Jesus's family includes the whole of humanity, as he often implies, then whether or not he was related to King David may be a doctrinal addition of those who were trying to convince Jewish individuals that Jesus was the Messiah.

Why, however, does he continue by informing the woman that someday she will consider those who are barren the "lucky ones"? Before continuing, we should mention that many interpret the canonical version of this Saying in light of eschatology, the "days" Jesus refers to signifying the tribulation. As we have discussed previously in great detail, apocalypticism is a rare bird in Gnosticism, and, though we do find references to "end times," it was often understood that these "end times" are eternally occurring within the mythological context of the development of the soul and the universe. As such, it is questionable as to whether Jesus refers to the "end times" in this Saying.

He is, however, using the Coptic collective you ("you all") in his reply, so we can be certain that his answer was not just directed at the woman, but at all who surrounded him. Is he endorsing asceticism and condemning childbirth? While possible, perhaps this Saying actually promises comfort during any time of trouble. Instead of reading, "The people who listen to the Word are the lucky ones, because they are properly ascetic and don't procreate," it can be read to mean, "you think my mother is lucky, but the ones who are lucky are the ones who have heard the Word, because life and comfort are theirs, even on days when they wish they hadn't been born."

This one may even have a secondary cosmological interpretation. According to the *Exegesis of the Soul*, the soul itself has a womb, which mystically changes during the redemptive process:

> So when the womb of the soul, by the will of the father, turns itself inward, it is baptized and is immediately cleansed of the external pollution which was pressed upon it, just as garments, when dirty, are put into the water and turned about until their dirt is removed and they become clean. And so the cleansing of the soul is to regain the newness of her former nature and to turn herself back again. That is her baptism.

Perhaps Jesus indicates that the womb, when turned inward (into the soul), is "barren" in the false World of Forms and fruitful within the Kingdom of Heaven.

EIGHTY

Jesus said, "Whoever has come to know the world has discovered the body, and whoever has discovered the body, of that one the world is not worthy."

This Saying is virtually identical to Saying 56: Jesus said, "Whoever has come to know the world has fallen upon a corpse, and whoever has discovered a carcass, of that person the world is not worthy." We refer the reader to the commentary to Saying 56 for a more detailed analysis of these concepts.

We simply note that when one understands the nature of the world, that the World of Forms is, in essence, a "body," but that the Logos/Christos saves that body through the sacrament of the bridal chamber, then one is for all intents and purposes no longer a subject of the rulers of the world.

EIGHTY-ONE

Jesus said, "Whoever has become rich, let him become king, and he who has power, let him abdicate."

LET ONE WHO HAS POWER RENOUNCE IT.

For quite some time, people have been under the delusion that Christianity and temporal power go hand-in-hand, and that Jesus would have been fine and dandy with electioneering and politicking and having God choose candidates for office. This abjection of Christ's message is, of course, part and parcel of a World of Forms in which illusion is considered far more valid than Truth. It is also indicative of the worldly power desired by those who would speak in Jesus's name.

Jesus never really concerned himself with worldly power one way or the other. He never said, "worldly power is bad," or "worldly power is good." He never honestly gave it much import. A simple overview of a few Canonical scenarios proves this beyond the shadow of a doubt:

- Jesus declines to rule the Kingdoms of the Earth when offered them by the devil.
- Jesus makes the statement that one should render to the ruler what belongs to the ruler, and render to God what belongs to God.
- When asked to pay the Temple Tax, Jesus essentially disagrees that it should be an obligation, but decides to pay it just so as not to offend anyone. He tells Peter to cast his nets, and in the first fish he hauls in, he'll discover enough money for the tax for the both of them.
- Jesus says, quite clearly, that his kingdom is **not** of this world.
-

Jesus's general attitude when faced with questions of worldly governance tends to be sighing, rolling his eyes, and saying, "Whatever." The world is under the power of the Rulers of the World, and those who attain worldly power, no matter how noble their initial reasons, attain service in the employ of those Rulers.

LET HE WHO HAS POWER ABDICATE.

Jesus opposes the constructs of worldly power. Those in worldly power, no matter who they be, are trapped in the network of illusions cast by the World of Forms, the "Black Iron Prison." The false deities and powers that rule this creation, be they actual or metaphorical or mythological, whether the Demiurge or the Devil or Mammon, have one goal: survival. To survive, they must be acknowledged. To be acknowledged, they must distract those who seek the truth from the Way.

Earthly power and politics are indeed a distraction. Whether one supports "Left" or "Right," one's support is a distraction. Whether one thinks "Nation A" is in the right, or "Nation B," one looks in the wrong direction. A wise man once cautioned that, in the end, evil tries to take one's attention away from the good. In the end, the evil, even at its most banal, is always loud and terrifying and attention-grabbing and horrible and shocking. Evil likes to make a bang. But, when one has stripped away the noise made by the terrible things, and looked underneath, the good perseveres.

As individuals and seekers, it is often not in our power to ultimately change the evils of the world. Even attempting such changes often gets one tangled up in the Black Iron Prison's twisted machinations. What we can influence, and change, is on an individual level, and on the level of compassion for others who are in need of compassion, and even those who are not. Voting for the candidate of your choice is all well and good, but loving and supporting your friends and neighbors has a far greater impact of the well-being of the world. Paying your taxes (or dodging them) may achieve this thing or that thing, but taking a moment to breathe in silence and gaze within is a far more powerful achievement.

This Saying, of course, begs a few questions. If everyone in power abdicates that power, does that not result in pure anarchism? The answer is yes, in a sense. Pure anarchism requires the elimination of positions of worldly power in favor of the brother/sisterhood of compassionate individuals. When positions of worldly power are eliminated, the whole Black Iron Prison which requires the erosion of the soul crumbles like the walls of Jericho. This, my friends, is the Kingdom of Heaven.

Absurd, some will say, and roll out all of the same tired old critiques of idealism and anarchism that thousands have before. Is it so absurd, however, to appeal to humanity's inherent goodness? Or, is it more absurd to spend one's entire life in a system which allows one the privilege of being able to afford to eat, to build a roof over one's head, to take a meagre two weeks worth of personal time per year, to retire once one is too far along in years to really enjoy a retirement? Is it more absurd to counsel those in power to step down than it is to cast a vote in a broken system for someone owned by corporations who is slightly less evil than someone else who is owned by the same corporations? Is it more absurd to encourage change on an individual level, or to expect a massive bureaucracy to change for the better based on the opinions of less than two-thirds of the voting public? Again, which is more absurd, hoping beyond hope for the triumph of compassionate living, or following an exploitative system based on externalities with nary an effective protest? Jesus realized this, and in this Saying, counsels those with Earthly power to give it up.

THOSE WHO HAVE POWER SHOULD STEP DOWN.

Implied in his statement, however, is an essential and important idea that has far-reaching ramifications. As we know by now, self-discovery is at the heart of Gnosticism. Knowing one's self, and knowing God on a personal, individual level is essential to the discovery of truth. Without this internal realization, this awakening of the self, one's experience is based on externalities and can fall prey to the Black Iron Prison— one's experience cannot be one hundred percent genuine if it is not based on one's own discoveries. For this reason, Jesus never calls for an overthrow of any sort of governmental power, nor does he counsel attempting to establish change through the petitioning of political leaders. Instead, he counsels those who already have power to take it upon themselves to renounce that power. He calls for them to step down. This is because, according to the basic tenets of Gnostic thought, true change must come from within, otherwise that change is completely invalid.

As an example, let us say that many folks on the Left believe that their candidate is too centrist, even too far too the "Right." With this in mind, many of them campaign to "send a message" to said candidate that he should drift back towards the Left, where they would like him to be. Now, suppose he receives millions of signatures from individuals who want him to move Left, and his campaign managers advise him that maybe he should look into it. Can we ever be sure that he will be doing anything other than paying lip service to a major constituency? And, if all he does is pay lip service, can we ever be certain that he would not betray this constituency should he win the office of President?

However, suppose his heart changes based on **his own experiences**? Would we be more convinced by the actions of someone who has decided to change because of millions of signatures, or someone who has decided to change based on honest compassion? Of course, there are plenty of traps involved in this scenario. For instance, one could argue that many tyrants, who never pay attention to focus groups and constituencies, fit this description of "one whose heart has changed." Unfortunately, this leads to an infinite regression, wherein one goes back and forth and back and forth, until one is completely enmeshed in the Black Iron Prison. There is no way to analyze the world of politics without falling into the hole of illusion and distraction.

When one strips away the externalities, we readily acknowledge that both "parties" in current American politics are two different sides of the same evil coin, and that voting is a symbolic act that is usually at least twice-removed from the actual decisions that make policy. Politics are really a no-win situation for all parties involved. No one can, and no one should, attempt to change other peoples' minds about politics. No die-hard "leftist" will ever change the mind of a die-hard "rightie." It simply cannot be done, nor should it. Politics simply serve to feed the spiraling abyss of the World of Forms, and to take our focus away on the matters that are truly important.

There is also a cosmological implication here, courtesy of Gnostic thought. In Gnostic mythology, the ultimate power in the World of Forms is held by the Demiurge, Yaldabaoth, and his minions, the Archons. These "beings" essentially took control over the World of Forms via a sort of coup of ignorance— they believed that they were the ultimate power, so they made themselves the ultimate power. They are like guests in a house who forget that they are guests and assume that they are the owners of the house (who are away on business). They then begin to fortify the house against the protests of the owners, and begin ordering around the servants. As long as the servants acknowledge the power of guests, the guests stay in power. If, however, the guests abdicate their power and leave the house, the owners can return without a problem and begin to repair the damage caused by the guests.

Of course, this is not to say that those who choose to follow the Way "should" or "shouldn't" do this or that thing. The point is that one is counseled do what one needs to do to better his or her soul, and then the souls of those directly around him or her. If one wants to vote, one should vote. If one wants to protest, one should protest. However, these things must be done based on internal awareness and self-analysis, or they are simply distractions. We **are** involved in the illusion; we certainly cannot help but have feelings and opinions about it. We cannot help but cry out against injustice, and speak against those who perpetuate the cycles of externality and evil and violence. However, a true follower of the Way would not attempt directly to affect political policy. A true follower of the Way will eventually come to the realization that running for political office means absolutely nothing, that those who are in power are some of the most powerless denizens of the world in which we live.

Fundamentalists of any stripe who desire worldly power miss the point entirely. However, those who call for "liberal" members of a religion to speak out against their fundamentalist brethren also miss the point entirely. There can be no change, there can be no coercion when religion and politics mix. There is only a meandering history which tends to correct its own errors through the medium of the Logos/Christos, the goodness which pulses in the background of society.

What can one do, then? All one can do is try to better one's self, and if one desires to lead, one can only lead by example. Wasting one's time with "fruitless polemics"[xxviii] distracts one from the path. One can only tend one's own garden, and hope that enough people experience a realization that the World of Forms is a prison, and a false one as that.

So, what does the first part of the Saying mean? Well, we know that when Jesus refers to "riches" or "treasure" in previous Sayings, he's talking about the aspects of the soul which assist one in following the Way. The one who "has riches" is, by definition, the one who is humble, compassionate and generous. These are the qualities of those who should truly reign, but who are they, and how would they reign? Would they? This is an ironic way to underline the central antagonism-towards-power argument.

EIGHTY-TWO

Jesus said, "Whoever is close to me is close to the fire, and whoever is far from me is far from the Kingdom."

The Gnostic concept of fire represents the divinity inherent within all aspects of the World of Forms. This divinity is hidden, and we call it the Pleroma, or "fullness" doctrine, in which the Logos/Sophia redeems the imperfect World of Forms by activation of the divine fire with which fills it. Of course, that whoever is near Jesus is near this divine fire would be patently obvious once this concept is understood.

Jesus and his disciples lived during a time which appreciated the importance of literal fire far more deeply than we do today. Fire represented many things: safety, light, warmth and civilization. In a large crowd, those nearest to the fire, be it a fireplace or a cooking stove or a campfire, would be in a far more desirable position than those further back away from it.

We picture Jesus sitting around a campfire in the wilderness of the Levant with a crowd of his disciples, perhaps discussing the Pleroma doctrine. A disciple makes an off-hand comment that a place near the campfire is quite welcome for the heat it provides, and for the protection it gives against the dangers of the wilderness. Said disciple continues that he is glad to be near the fire, instead of in the back of the crowd where the warmth of the fire does not reach.

Jesus sees a teaching opportunity, and replies, "hey, **anyone** who sticks with me (the Logos) is close to the campfire. Anyone who sticks with me is safe from the terrors of the darkness and the wilderness of the World of Forms."

But, asks the disciple, what about those who are not close to you in this way?

The original Coptic does not specifically say that the "Kingdom" in question is the Kingdom of the Father as it does in other Sayings— it just says Kingdom. "Heck, they're so far away from the fire that they're not even anywhere near civilization's kingdoms. That's how far away they are."

This also ties into Jesus's teachings about the poor, downtrodden and unlucky, those who are "civilization's" outcasts. Even those who are physically away from the fire are safe from the dangers of the World of Forms if they are close to the Logos.

EIGHTY-THREE

Jesus said, "Images are revealed to people, but the light within them is hidden in the image of the Father's light. He will be disclosed, and his image is hidden away by his light."

The Platonic concept of images appears frequently the Gnostic corpus, which even contains an excerpt discussing the concept from Plato's *Republic*. It is doubtless possible, though certainly not provable, given Plato's perennial popularity, that the historical Jesus was versed in Platonic philosophy; Plato was pretty much the *de facto* scholarship of the time. It would be almost absurd for an educated person of the Roman Empire, especially one who is said to have spent time in Egypt, to escape the influence of Platonism. The similarities between Platonism and Christianity, and the influence the former had on the latter, are well-documented.

According to said thought, the World of Forms, or created world, consists of various levels of images of the ultimate reality, and the further one descends into images, the further one gets from the Truth. Thus, a painting of a flower is less "real" than an actual flower, which is less real than the human concept or mentation of a flower based on the experience of many flowers, which is less real than "FLOWER," an eternal Ideal which exists in the ineffable *potentia* of the universe.

In Gnostic cosmo-conception, the World of Forms, as an image, or reflection, of the ultimate reality, is defective. To understand this concept, picture the Universe as a still pond, in which the sun is reflected. Now imagine that an intelligent fish, swimming around in the pond, looks up and sees the reflection of the sun, which is distorted by ripples on the surface of the pond, and determines that the distorted reflection **is** the sun. The fish establishes a religion in which he points to the image and demands that the other fish worship it instead of the actual sun which is beyond the surface of the pond. Now suppose another fish hears a voice coming from above the pond. "Hey, that other guy's all wet," says the voice. With great effort, the second fish leaps out of the pond, breaking through the image, and perceiving reality itself.

In Gnostic mythology, we might say that the sun is the ultimate reality and the first fish is the Demiurge, the confused or insane aspect of reality who confuses the image with the Thing itself and establishes a system based on images instead of reality. The system it establishes is the Black Iron Prison, that which keeps the other fish from leaping out of the pond, and keeps them subservient to the first fish. The voice is the Logos or Sophia which breaks through sensory experience into the World of Forms. The second fish is, of course, someone who has experienced gnosis or "enlightenment."

Now, to apply the metaphor to this Saying, say that the light of the sun reaches even into the very depths of the pond. The sun's light is blinding— so blinding, in fact, that the more one tries to look at it, the harder it is to see. Thus, a bottom-dwelling fish who tries to see the true sun is so blinded by the light of that sun that he continues to believe that the image of the sun is the sun itself.

The Gnostic text called *The Concept of our Greater Power* elaborates on this:

> [The Demiurge's] eyes were not able to endure my light. After the spirits and the waters moved, the remainder came into being: the whole aeon of the creation, and their . The fire came forth from them and the Power came in the midst of the powers. And the powers desired to see my image. And the soul became its replica.

> This is the work that came into being. See what it is like, that before it comes into being it does not see, because the aeon of the flesh came to be in the great bodies.

As the Demiurgic aspects of the World of Forms, be they an actual "Demiurge" or simply our inner psychological traits which act accordingly, are blinded by the Light of the Father, they become confused and unable to properly discern God. Since we are stuck in the limited World of Forms, even the **actual** light of God which exists here is an image when perceived by the senses of the World of Forms. Only through the medium of gnosis, which transcends the senses, can one truly perceive that which exists beyond the images.

Thus, even Jesus had to establish images of God to assist the seekers on the Way. In the *First Apocalypse of James*, Jesus explains that **"I have brought forth the image of him so that the sons of Him-who-is might know what things are theirs and what things are alien (to them)."** Truth can only exist within the imperfect world in images. Thus, the concept is, at its heart, a concept of semiotics. *The Gospel of Philip* states this almost explicitly: **"Truth did**

not come into the world naked, but it came in types and images. The world will not receive truth in any other way."

The problem of image versus reality cuts to the deepest core of ontological discussion, and gets worrisome when one considers that our culture is in the habit of confusing image with reality, the significator with the signified, cop movies with cops, news reports about politicians with the effect of policies on the ground level. Indeed, many post-modernist thinkers have considered these ideas, most notably Jean Baudrillard in *Simulacra and Simulacrum*— a must read for anyone interested in Gnosticism.

Consider the following, which was noted by Baudrillard in said work: when one is asked to picture the concept of "police," the average, "law abiding" citizen who does not have much personal experience with police conceptualizes based on movies and television shows. After one hundred episodes, Sipowicz, an image of a policeman, becomes more **real** than an actual policeman. When one who conceptualizes police bases his or her interaction with **real** police on the image of Sipowicz, expects the real police to act as Sipowicz acts, one is in for a world of trouble.

Another concern is the development of virtual reality. For instance, suppose ten years from now someone invents a program whereby one can put on a pair of goggles and "visit" the pyramids of Egypt. The experience is essentially identical to the senses of the virtual traveler. Now, instead of having to take a vacation, one can sit and travel the world in the comfort of one's home.

Will it still be important for the average person, in this case, to work to preserve the pyramids? Will the average person still care about conserving the environment when one can experience an identical, "better" version of the environment in one's living room? I submit that it would not, that the development of "virtual reality" programs will be a serious blow to the continued existence of what we call "reality" itself.

For an even worse scenario, consider media saturation and politics. Chances are, few if any of the readers of this text have never actually met any presidential candidate on a more than perfunctory basis. We have never sat down with them, never had tea and discussed their innermost feelings and desires with them. We only experience our politicians through the medium of television, newspapers and the internet. As such, when we say we support one of these individuals, we really do not— we support the mental signifier that we have built based on images, not based on reality. In our era, this affects the candidates themselves— when appearing in public, they are coached into focusing on "image," into becoming signs that build what they hope are desirable images within the perception of the citizens, even though the signs point to empty significants, or worse, signify nothing at all.

This has been going on for so long that our current political system for most people is no longer based in reality— rather, it exists completely as image. This is why voter turnout is so low, why people are apathetic, why people will settle for trusting what an obviously evil regime. People have become passive observers of false signs because the Black Iron Prison has them convinced that signs and images are reality and truth. To the average citizen, the politics of the world are no more "real" than "The West Wing," a fictional television account of American politics. Even participating by voting is a passive act, akin to voting in a television show, voting someone off of Survivor Island or voting for one's favorite American Idol. Voting is sign without substance, and debating whether Democrats or Republicans are better is like debating whether one television sitcom or the other was funnier.

The Gnostics saw a similar replacement of reality by images during the Roman Empire. In more than one sense, they were the semioticians and deconstructionists of their day, serving similar functions, denying any concept based on the limitations of images in their search for the Truth. Just as they fulfilled this function outside of the official capacity of government and politics at the time of the Empire, so must those of us who continue the tradition unceasingly look within and question, question, question exactly what is real and what is simply an image of an image of an image.

Although by now this is something of an old canard, the similarities and parallelisms between the Roman Empire and the current manifestation of the Black Iron Prison, not limited to the United States though arguably strongest here, are almost profound— witness the deification of Ronald Reagan, our own, homegrown Caesar. The image of Ronald Reagan on a ten dollar bill, seriously submitted as a possibility for future currency printings, is a suitable reminder of Jesus's admonition to render unto Caesar that which is Caesar's, to give images to that which has become an image.

EIGHTY-FOUR

Jesus said, "When you see your likeness, you rejoice. But when you see your images that came into being before you and that neither die nor become visible, how much you will have to bear!"

Another Saying focusing on images, 84 explains the concept further by contrasting the difference between one's "likeness," which may refer to the status of the World of Forms as a "likeness" of the Kingdom of Heaven, and one's true Image, that upon which the illusion is based. Remember, everything except God itself is an image of some kind— one can easily become confused between so many images. The difference between the Earthly image and the Divine image is disturbing in its profoundity.

Note that only a single likeness exists in the World of Forms, but the precreative self consists of images. These are the collective images of the fragmented universe, the perceptions of the consciousness which manifests itself as a plurality in each illusory individual. As a resident of the World of Forms, one can only "see" a single image. But, when one experiences gnosis, one can see the entire plurality of these images.

A wonderful elaboration on this idea is the concept expressed in Chapter 11 of the *Bhagavad-Gita*, the conversation between Krisna and Arjuna. After a lengthy discussion on spiritual matters, during which Arjuna understands Krisna as just his chariot driver (Krisna's "Earthly Image"), Arjuna asks to see Krisna as he truly is, his actual form:

As you say yourself to be, O Supreme Lord,

So it is.

I desire to see your form, O Supreme Vision.

If you deem it capable of being seen by me, O Lord, Then Lord of Yoga, show to me your eternal self.

Krisna agrees, and Arjuna, disturbed, to say the least, freaks out. Essentially, when faced with the glory of the Ultimate Reality, he panics and changes his mind:

> I am delighted, having seen what was not previously seen,
>
> But my mind trembles with fear.
>
> Show me that other (human) form of yours, O Lord;
>
> Be gracious, Refuge of the World. (11:45)[xxix]

Arjuna's enlightenment– his experience of gnosis, if you will— describes quite well the difference between the experience of the image of the self and the image of the Ultimate Self. After all, if Krisna is everything, is he not also Arjuna?

EIGHTY-FIVE

Jesus said, "Adam came from great power and great richness, but he was not worthy of you. For had he been worthy, [he would] not [have tasted] death."

First it was John the Baptist in Saying 46, and now Jesus tells those who follow the Way that they have one up on Adam himself, the very first man. Adam did indeed come from a "great power"— or, at least, his soul did. According to many Gnostic myths, the Demiurge created Adam's body from lifeless clay. Not until the great power of Sophia and the Logos entered into Adam did he gain his soul. The *Gospel of Philip* says that **"The soul of Adam came into being by means of a breath;"** this breath (pneuma) signifies the Holy Spirit, Sophia herself.

It is also possible that by "power and riches," Jesus refers to the power of the false creator and the riches of Eden, which Gnostic mythology maintains was more of a Brave New World type paradise, in which humankind's base and physical needs were met abundantly, but our freedom and self-awareness were severely restricted by the law of the Demiurge. Gnostic myth has it that the Demiurge stole divine power from Sophia, and hid it in the Tree, thus his command that they should not eat the fruit. The serpent, actually Sophia/the Logos in disguise, convinced Eve and Adam to eat the fruit in the first act of rebellion against false authority. Eating the fruit allowed them to consume the divine spark and establish a connection with the higher realms of God.

In order to coalesce with what we know about Gnostic myth, we must conclude that Jesus refers here to the "created" Adam, who was an image of the Eternal Adam, in the same sense that we are all images of the Eternal Adam, an image of God itself. The follower of the Way, however, as stated in Saying 1, will not even taste death because the experience of gnosis essentially negates the value of the lower self.

Gnostic myth abounds with confusing concepts and a veritable bestiary of cosmic beings, which include angels, Aeons, archons, the Demiurge, Sophia, the Logos, the Christos, etc. These stories and myths and beings probably become the hugest stumbling block for those interested in pursuing the Gnostic

Way— who is the real God? Does the Demiurge **actually** exist in some alternate dimension? Is there **actually** a female Being called Sophia who dips into our universe on occasion? Did the events in Eden **actually** occur as stated in Gnostic mythology? Who could possibly believe all of this weirdness, or even begin to unravel it?

The answer can only be understood in terms of "myth." Myth, as used by the Gnostics, is not an historical record of literal events, nor is it a collection of stories used to explain natural phenomenon. **Myth is, instead, a common language designed to express inexpressible ideas.** The "events" described in mythology are attempts to describe an inexpressible Mystery, and to the Gnostics, mythology is a way to participate in this Mystery.

Many modern Gnostics take the events described in the mythology as pure, physical reality. There **is** a Demiurge who rules the world, in the same sense that there **is** a physical page on which these words are printed. He has "helpers," the Archons, who some modern Gnostics claim are the aliens who regularly abduct humans!

There are some vague truths based in physical reality that are basic to all Gnostic myths. The World of Forms is a kind of illusion, for example. Another, higher realm exists. Each of us has a spark of divinity within us. Certain events "activate" that spark and allow us to see through the veil of illusion. The mysterious interaction of these elements, however, cannot be explained in human language, so myth serves to bridge the gaps in perception. A symbology, or story-system, is created in order to initiate the student into an understanding of these concepts. The imperfect creation is caused by the Demiurge and his assistants. The spark of divinity is activated by the Logos/Sophia. The energies and powers and forms that mysteriously compose the worlds above and below are angels, Aeons, Archons. Gnostics were encouraged by their teachers to create their own myths using this symbolic language— individual interpretation of myth was all that counted. In this way, Gnostic myths are almost like long, complex Zen koans— often confusing and obscure, but designed to further the student's progress along the Way.

Still, it should not be assumed that just because myths are a language that these mythic concepts do not have a life of their own apart from the internal world. Anyone who has felt a divine warmth or the fluttering of wings during Confirmation can attest to this. Personally, I like the idea that Yaldabaoth actually exists somehow, that there are Archons who rule the World of Forms who are at war with the Powers of The God, led by the Christos and Sophia. It explains, to me, humanity's propensity for abject horror, like that seen at Abu Ghraib. It also explains our propensity for utter goodness and wonder.

These are mythic concepts, so the **physicality** of these concepts is utterly moot. Whether Adam and Eve and the Serpent actually existed in a place called Eden has no bearing on an understanding of the universe, but the myth surrounding these characters gives one a profound understanding thereof. .

Some Gnostics, however, no doubt do not place value on the myth of, say, Yaldabaoth, or perhaps they understand him as "Satan," or believe in a literal Eden, which, according to Gnostic thought, is just fine. It is a Mystery, and needs to remain a mystery in order to allow each **individual** to come to his or her **own** understanding of Being and, more importantly, Self. Declaring an objective reality based on myth is extremely dangerous, because it confuses the signifier and the signified. Anxiously awaiting the rapture makes as much sense as fleeing in terror from a tiger on T.V., or believing the promises of a politician's campaign ads.

So, to return to the Saying, the lower, or created aspect of the Mythic Adam, who represents the lower or created aspect of the Self, tasted death— the lower Adam perished when he ate from the apple, leaving only the Higher Adam behind. Jesus tells us, you are better than this lower Adam— he died, but, as followers of the Way, you will not.

EIGHTY-SIX

Jesus said, "[Foxes have] their dens and birds have their nests, but human beings have no place to lay their heads and rest."

Creatures of the earth and the skies— of the natural world— have places in which they can rest and attain peace while in that world. Unfortunately, the human being (or "Son of Man") who has overcome h/er attachment to the things of this illusory world, does not have the luxury of resting. Resting, or "repose," doesn't come for the enlightened until he or she has actually escaped the illusion in full and attained the resurrection (see Saying 51).

The animals actively participate in the illusion. The dens of foxes and nests of birds are constructs which exist as full-fledged objects in the World of Forms. Nature is indeed an aspect of the World of Forms. It has to be, because the Demiurge created the entirety of our insane "sector." It should be remembered, however, that according to Gnostic myth, this insane World of Forms is modeled on, and shares attributes of, the perfected realms. Sophia and the Logos snuck in almost immediately after the World of Forms was created, and injected it with divinity.

So we have the "nature" created by the Archons, which is in fact the concept of "Enslaved Nature" as something to be controlled or exploited, something seperate from us instead of something in which we should be participating. Then, we have "Redeemed Nature," saved by Wisdom (Sophia) and Word (Logos), which is quite simply the divine realm stripped of the layers of the control system. Since the process of gnosis is the process of awakening from the control systems, part of the process of gnosis is understanding Nature as something that has been raped by the Archonic systems of the World of Forms. Gnosis doesn't just happen to people, it happens to the whole of creation.

This is not to say that the foxes and birds and natural aspects of the World of Forms are bad things, just that those who participate in the illusion, as do the animals, have homes within that same illusion, and can exist in peace within the World of Forms. Those followers of the Way, however, knowing full well that they are within the confines of the Black Iron Prison, constantly strive, internally, and have no "place" in the World of Forms. The Way involves almost constant awareness, and real mental agitation. In a sense, what Jesus is Saying here is that "ignorance is bliss." Of course, ignorance is also an attribute of animals, and not enlightened humans.

EIGHTY-SEVEN

Jesus said, "How wretched is the body that depends on a body, and how wretched is the soul that depends on these two."

We know from previous Sayings that the term "body" generally indicates the World of Forms, the "dead corpse" that resulted from the Demiurge's mistaken approach to creation. Depending, therefore, on the "body" means depending on the corpse-world.

Now, depending upon the corpse world creates misery, even as a participant within the World of Forms. In other words, depending upon reality when reality itself may be a false illusion is silly. Nothing at all is certain— one of those ubiquitous meteors could plummet into us at this very moment. Conversely, one could be offered a million dollars by an unknown relative. Depending too much on worldly 'certainties' is not always the best idea.

However, when the soul itself depends upon one's dependence upon the world, one is in for some real trouble. This part of the Saying, which really reads that it is a wretched soul indeed that depends upon a body that depends upon a body, could apply to those aspiritual folks who refuse to believe in any sort of great mystery or deeper meaning to life, those teleological criminals who simply place all of their chips on the universe's existence as a purposeless nothingness, a pseudo-hierarchical machine with no more intrinsic value than an electric turkey carver.

As says honorary Gnostic Ran Prieur in his "most-hated" essay, "Science the Destroyer":

> The death-based or "mechanistic" view is a religion, the dominant religion of our time. It is far stronger than Christianity, which has totally adopted the machine model, but just tacked souls on top and personified the objectively true detached perspective as an omnipotent sky father deity named "God," manipulating the world from a safe distance just like the scientists.[xxx]

This especially applies to those materialistic nihilists who find religion and spirituality "stupid" or "primitive" or "superstitions," those who literally **do not care** whether or not their lives have some import in the proverbial grand scheme. Or, worse, those who cling to a pseudo-hierarchical image of spirituality that has no mystery or substance behind it.

Someone whose "body" depends upon the body can usually change. Someone whose very soul depends upon their love of the corpse-world has far more difficulty so doing. Imagine visiting a town where everyone eats wax fruit. Consuming so much wax cuts their average lifespan in half— they all die of digestive difficulties around the age of forty. Now imagine that a wandering traveler has a sack full of real fruit. Our traveler comes across Waxy, one of the denizens of WaxFruitVille, eating a wax pear. He gives Waxy a real pear, and after tasting it, our wax pear eater is so utterly amazed that he asks for more, so our traveler (a kind soul) shows him how to plant the seeds and grow his own pear tree. Our friend Waxy represents the "body that depends upon the body."

Now, suppose Waxy offers a real pear to someone who manufactures wax pears. No matter how delicious the real pear is, the manufacturer believes that his well being depends upon his ability to continue making wax pears, which he eats and sells, so he denies that the real pear is truly delicious—and maybe even has Waxy killed. He has doomed himself to an early death because of a false premise— that models of pears are somehow better than real pears, and the saddest part is that he never even had to make wax pears to survive. All he had to do was learn how to grow real pears like Waxy. The wax pear manufacturer is the one whose soul depends on his body's love of the body. In this case, the "body," or corpse-world, is the false system which makes one think there is a desperate need to manufacture wax pears instead of growing real ones, even in the face of all of the evidence.

EIGHTY-EIGHT

Jesus said, "The angels and the prophets will come to you and give you what they have that belongs to you. You, in turn, give them what you have, and say to yourselves, 'When will they come and take what belongs to them?'"

Saying 88 is difficult, in its entirety, to interpret with certainty. The angels, "messengers"— the Coptic uses the Greek word "angelos"— and prophets, evidently fulfilling the same tasks they perform in canonical monotheism, will eventually "return" some "things" that belong to the follower of the Way. In Gnostic mythology, angels can "work" for either God or the Demiurge— in this case, it seems pretty likely that they work for God. Let us assume for the sake of context that the prophets mentioned here are representatives of the Logos, as they have direct communion with God. Angels also carry the message of the Logos to the follower of the Way.

This process of returning fits in with the Gnostic concept of the timeless eschaton— based on what we learned from the other Sayings about the semiotics of Gnostic eschatology, we conclude that the process alluded to Saying 88 is something that occurs outside of the slice of space/time in which we reside, and essentially happens every moment of every day.

So what do these angels and messengers "have"? Most likely they have knowledge of the true self— the angels have this knowledge as they are the conduit through which information flows from God to the Gnostic, and the prophets are the traditional interpreters of this knowledge. This is the knowledge that they "give" to us. According to most Gnostic myth, each of us has a "Holy Guardian Angel," our twin self. This is related to the concept of "Divine Twinship" which runs throughout Thomas literature. According to this tradition, Thomas was Jesus's twin brother. In a sense, Jesus was Thomas's Guardian Angel.

Now, the questions arise from the idea that we have something to give to them. What could we possibly have to give to the angels and prophets that they would require? We give them what we are here to collect: experience and information. When seen in this light, the Saying becomes a bit more clear.

Existence is a conversation between the individual and God. Moving forward with the idea posited here that each individual consciousness is, in effect, a "sensory organ" of God, one can picture what is being described in this Saying in terms of the biological process whereby sensation travels through the nervous system to the brain. If one wants to look at something, the brain—God, referred to in various Gnostic texts as 'Nous,' or mind— sends a signal—the Logos—through the nervous system—the angels—to the various parts of one's biology which allow one to turn the head, focus the eyes and look. Once one has looked and gathered this information, one "sends it back" to the brain through the medium of the nervous system. The brain converses with reality through the sensory process. In this way, God constantly communicates with its parts, which are those of us who possess this lovely thing we call consciousness.

The problem, of course, is that due to the World of Forms's imperfection, some synaptic paths are misfiring, or simply refuse to work at all. The disconnect between God and its parts drove one of its aspects insane. The insane aspect is the one which currently controls or directs the World of Forms.

This is a difficult river to cross for some people, but again, the process of mentation provides an apt analogy. Imagine someone with brain damage, who hallucinates that each individual part of his body exists independently. In other words, when his hand moves, he thinks it is some sort of independent "thing" that is outside of his control. When he sees something, he does not believe that his eyes are doing the seeing, but instead that some kind of irrational outside force is "seeing" for him. Now imagine that this person also suffers from a split personality, and the other personality is perfectly sane. When the insane side is in control, it is completely aware of the sane side, but sees it as some kind of external influence that needs to be suppressed. During moments of lucidity, however, when the sane side is in control, the hallucinations cease, and the person has the sensory capacity to understand himself as a complete whole. While sane, the person can actually work towards healing the insane side.

When we speak about angels and prophets, we speak about the aspects of the sane part of the Universe which help us to realize that this is all a whole. "Oh, this thing is my **hand**, it's part of my body." With this knowledge, the universe can work on the process of healing itself. These angels and prophets travel back and forth between God and his parts at all times, just as the brain constantly sends and receives signals from the sensory organs.

However, we are currently stuck within the insane aspect of the World of Forms. The aspect of the universe in which we reside is an hallucination, an illusion of separation where no separation exists. The conversation between God and the individual occurs eternally, but for most individuals the conversation consists of fantasy and gobbldygook.

This pathway or conversation is corrected in the follower of the Way. The individual understands the language of God; the sensory organ functions as it is intended. The angels and prophets are like the sentences and grammar, and they communicate information from the sane aspect of God. The conscious individual the communicates information back. Gradually, slowly but surely, as more and more synaptic pathways are repaired, as more and more people learn the semiotics of reality, God begins to become more sane.

The last question in the Saying wonders when this final healing will occur. It suggests that the follower of the Way constantly ask, "when are we going to be whole? When are we cured?" It makes sense— these questions help maintain the presence of the sane side of God within the insane side. The conversation between God and its healthy parts must continue at all times and in all places, until, eventually, the insane side of God disappears entirely and the final healing occurs.

EIGHTY-NINE

Jesus said, "Why do you wash the outside of the cup? Don't you understand that the one who created the inside is also the one who created the outside?"

The "outside of the cup" refers to external appearance. It can also refer to that which is "outside" of the realm of God, or the World of Forms. So, Jesus's advice here is to concern one's self with the interior realms, another "know thyself" reference, and another admonition that external appearance is pretty insignificant in the long run.

A bit of confusion exists; if the Demiurge created external appearances with the World of Forms, why does Jesus say that the one who created the inside also created the outside? This is a sort of Gnostic conundrum. It reminds us that even though we exist in a defective part of the universe that was created by the Demiurge, we need to remember that even this defective part was "created" by God as part of its desire to learn about itself.

NINETY

Jesus said, "Come to me, for my yoke is just and my lordship is gentle, and you will find repose for yourselves."

One should never doubt that following any kind of spiritual path can be WORK, and hard work, at that. The Way of Jesus does not require physically difficult work in the Zen sense, sometimes days and weeks of sitting, nor does it require work in the legalistic sense of certain Christian sects, wherein unless one follows a certain number of precepts and canons, one misses out on resurrection and will not be allowed the privilege of laboring for one of the 144,000 "chosen." In the context of Jesus's environment, which had more religious teachers and zealots and magicians and Sons of God than Los Angeles, this could be seen as a reply to someone asking, "why should we follow you? What makes you better than that guy over there?" Jesus replies, "look, it's foolish to think that following a Way doesn't require work. I'll tell you straight up that you'll have to work as hard as an oxen tilling a field. However, the yoke I'll put on you won't hurt you, and eventually you'll be able to take it off and find rest."

The work entailed of anyone who follows the Way is a constant attention to the experience of the Way. Instead of mere intellectualism, it requires of us that our **spiritual** muscles remain tensed at all times. It requires that we consider the Way before each and every decision we make. Even more importantly, it allows us the openness—the "gentle yoke"—to decide what kind of spiritual methodology works best for us. This is because when one walks the Way, one seeks to cultivate the presence of Jesus, as the Logos/Sophia, within one's self. When this occurs, one contains, in essence, the inner quality of Jesus. Thus, one must yoke one's self!

There is, of course, another side to the coin. Although physical work is an effective method for instruction in the discipline required for following the Way, it is not necessary for everyone. Every one has heard the typical platitudes about how any path that offers you an easy way to God may not be a True path. There are, however, sects and schools which offer extremely difficult paths to enlightenment which, when viewed in certain terms, are as far from the Path that you can get. Some sects require exceptional periods of what can be excruciatingly difficult work, not to mention substantial monetary donations— which, of course, represent work one has performed in the "real" world. Yet, where is the actual spiritual value of these sects? Is it not within the individual who practices? What good the physical work, the paying vast sums of money to a wealthy organization if their teaching does not allow one to cultivate one's own inner knowledge? What good is it to hear someone say "you are benefiting from this work that you do," without realizing the benefit for oneself? **Anyone** can tell someone that she is on the proper path to enlightenment; some so-called teachers can even get you to do work for them in exchange for the occasional pat on the head or pop-psychological "realization." If not accompanied by true exertion and concern on one's own part, then who benefits?

Whether someone pays more or works harder in the physical world should have little bearing on their actual spiritual development. In fact, it is indeed possible, though rare, to attain enlightenment/gnosis with no work at all— Zen teachings, for example, are full of stories of simple individuals who become enlightened upon hearing the caw of a crow, or spilling water from a bucket. In the aforementioned paths that **require** difficult work, the possibility always exists that someone who works harder or pays more will be given greater spiritual "ranking" than one who does not work hard or does not pay much. In reality, such distinctions should not be made.

A similar story can be found in Matthew 20:1-16, in which workers who worked all day receive the same wages as those who worked for only an hour. These distinctions don't matter; the INNER qualities truly have bearing on one's enlightenment, and thus Jesus tells us that his lordship is just, and thus some who do very little work will reach enlightenment before some who work with difficulty for their entire lives.

NINETY-ONE

They said to him, "Tell us who you are so that we may believe you."

He said to them, "You read the face of the sky and earth, and he was in your presence then, but now that he is before you, you do not know how to read him."

Gnosticism is the most formalized Western religious philosophy that comes to almost identical conclusions as the most in-depth teachers of Zen Buddhism. The differences are mainly cultural, semiotic and doctrinal; the goals and methods by which they are attained are virtually identical—experientially, of course; ritualistically they vary immensely. A Zen monk might recognize the Sayings in Thomas as koans. A Gnostic might recognize *kensho*, sudden enlightenment, as gnosis. Zen "sitting meditation" and Gnostic "repose prayer" require the same concentration of thought and elimination of the illusion of reality through stillness. We cannot, of course, claim any sort of definite historical connexion between the two traditions; trying to prove such connexions is a fool's game. Rather, the similarities are incredibly noteworthy on more than just cursory levels, and Gnosticism is the Western way to describe the experiences of Zen and vice-versa. That said, Saying 91 can be looked at in terms of the concept of "Buddha-nature," a key concept in Zen.

Much of Zen meditation is geared towards contemplating Buddha-nature. The most basic of the Zen koans, Joshu's dog, is found in many of the more prominent teachings of Zen Buddhism:

> A monk asked Joshu, "Has the dog Buddha nature or not?" Joshu said, "Mu (No-thing)."

Without working through this koan, many students of Zen are not allowed to continue down the path by their teachers. The essentiality of discovering "Buddha nature" is pivotal to one's quest for enlightenment:

In modern-Western manifestations of the Zen Buddhist tradition, it is considered insufficient simply to understand Buddha-nature intellectually. Rather it must be experienced and felt directly, in one's entire mind and body together. Enlightenment in a certain sense consists of a direct experience of one's authentic identity, which is traditionally described as nyata, the ultimate reality of Buddha-nature.[xxxi]

In Gnostic Christianity, one finds the disciples investigating, in an almost identical fashion, the nature of the Christ: Christ-nature. Saying 91 shines a spotlight on this procedure, and on Jesus's instructions for discovering the Christ-nature: the answer appears in examining and meditating on the "present moment." The term "present moment" also occurs very frequently in the literature of Zen. Just as in Zen, meditation allows one to enter the "present moment"— the world devoid of illusion— in order to discover the meaning of "Buddha-nature" through enlightenment, so in Gnosticism, prayer/experience allows one to enter the "present moment"— the world devoid of illusion— in order to discover the meaning of "Christ-nature" through gnosis.

Just as Jesus tells the disciples in Saying 91 that they he cannot be recognized when he stands right in front of them, so Zen implies that one cannot recognize the Buddha when he stands right before them. And, just as Zen tells us that once we meet the Buddha we must kill him, so Christian Gnosticism requires us to crucify Jesus once we discover his true nature.

NINETY-TWO

Jesus said, "Seek and you will find. In the past, however, I did not tell you the things about which you asked me then. Now I am willing to tell them, but you are not after them."

Saying 92 continues the thought-stream of the preceding Saying. When read together, the flow between the two becomes obvious:

> [The disciples] said to him, "Tell us who you are so that we may believe in you."

> He said to them, "You examine the face of heaven and earth, but you have not come to know the one who is in your presence, and you do not know how to examine the present moment. Seek and you will find.

> "In the past, however, I did not tell you the things about which you asked me then. Now I am willing to tell them, but you are not seeking them."

If it seems like a rebuke, it probably is, but it also instructs the seeker that though the path can become rather obscure, there is great importance in constant seeking. In fact, constant seeking is the best way to examine the present moment.

The curious may wonder, what exactly is sought after? Is it some kind of abstract mystical state? Is it the Christ-nature? And, how does one seek? Apparently this is not an external process that simply means scrying the "face of heaven and earth;" what, then, is this process of seeking? Without answering these questions, "seek and you will find" is almost meaningless.

The "seeking" process, however, occurs so frequently within Gnostic and Christian literature that, along with a nifty metaphor for leading a "spiritual life," it probably also has a concrete semiotic meaning within Gnostic language that varied little from setting to setting. For instance, Jesus's teachings on "seeking" in Thomas are found in Sayings 2, 24, 38, 60, and 76. Note the semiotic similarities in each Saying from Thomas on the subject of seeking. This is not, however, limited to Thomas, but a concept that runs throughout the tradition. We find a clue within the *Apocryphon of James*:

> "Verily, I say unto you, none will be saved unless they believe in my cross. But those who have believed in my cross, theirs is the kingdom of God. Therefore, become seekers for death, like the dead who seek for life; for that which they seek is revealed to them. And what is there to trouble them? As for you, when you examine death, it will teach you election. Verily, I say unto you, none of those who fear death will be saved; for the kingdom belongs to those who put themselves to death. Become better than I; make yourselves like the son of the Holy Spirit!"

This is a really profound paragraph! "Become seekers for death," Jesus tells us, because unless one **puts one's self to death**, one cannot find the kingdom. He then goes on to encourage the listener to become better than he is! ("If you meet the Buddha on the road, kill him.") In this paragraph, Jesus equates seeking death with examining death— scrutinizing it. Yet, we come to realize that this scrutiny is an **internal** process, just as in Saying 91 the counsel is not to investigate the sky and earth, but to scrutinize the present moment.

The Gnostic magickal text called *Allogenes* contains another interesting occurrence of the concept:

> "If you seek with a perfect seeking, then you shall know the Good that is in you; then you will know yourself as well, (as) one who derives from God who truly pre-exists.

The common interpretation of the admonition to seek and find conjures images of an external search for truth— the disciples asking questions of Jesus, or the lone seeker marching through the Himalayas in search of the wise guru on the mountaintop. This, however, is not the case. Seeking is the process of knowing one's **self**, not knowing the truth of another. The perfect seeking is the one which reveals the Good that is **in you**. **This** is the kind of seeking that will result in gnosis. "Seeking," in a Gnostic sense, is an intense **internal** process— finding the Christ within and killing him.

NINETY-THREE

"Don't give what is holy to dogs, for they might throw them upon the dung heap. Don't throw pearls [to] pigs, or they might [make them worthless]."

This Saying emphasizes a need for discernment. One has to know what gets what, as evinced by the following passage from the *Gospel of Philip*:

> There was a householder who had every conceivable thing, be it son or slave or cattle or dog or pig or corn or barley or chaff or grass or [...] or meat and acorn. Now he was a sensible fellow, and he knew what the food of each one was. He served the children bread [...]. He served the slaves [...] and meal. And he threw barley and chaff and grass to the cattle. He threw bones to the dogs, and to the pigs he threw acorns and slop. Compare the disciple of God: if he is a sensible fellow, he understands what discipleship is all about. The bodily forms will not deceive him, but he will look at the condition of the soul of each one and speak with him. There are many animals in the world which are in a human form. When he identifies them, to the swine he will throw acorns, to the cattle he will throw barley and chaff and grass, to the dogs he will throw bones. To the slaves he will give only the elementary lessons, to the children he will give the complete instruction.

Cultural support for slavery aside, this passage contains an interesting message that relates to how one "tells" if one has experienced gnosis. Just as the householder could say, "okay, that pig there gets this here slop, an' them there dawgs get these here bones," so the follower of the Way should be able to discern that which is not good for the spirit and avoid tossing the spirit in its direction. So in life we encounter many situations that require discernment. This is by no means a requirement to avoid contact or discussion with those who are not on the Way, just to be extremely careful to what one chooses to expose one's soul.

Many cultural taboos stigmatized dogs and pigs during the era of *Thomas*'s composition. We tend to think of Scooby and Piglet when we think of dogs and pigs. In many Semitic cultures, however, dogs are considered so unclean that one must perform a ritual cleansing upon any canine contact. Pigs, as well we know, are forbidden in the Jewish faith. And, as we know from Saying 76, the "pearl" represents the inner soul/spirit/divine quality of Gnostic enlightenment. When Jesus warns against tossing pearls to swine, he very emphatically states that one should not toss one's very soul to the absolute essence of uncleanliness.

In some ways, this is also kind of a no-brainer. Who in his or her right mind would toss a pearl to pigs or something really nice to some dogs to begin with? Is it even reasonable? Jesus was a master of metaphor— we cannot help but note that exposing the soul to that which isn't "clean" requires a level of deception by the illusion. It is almost as though in giving this advice, he does not speak to those who have already achieved gnosis, as they should know one way or the other. In this regard, we find another enlightening passage in *Philip*:

> When the pearl is cast down into the mud, it becomes greatly despised, nor if it is anointed with balsam oil will it become more precious. But it always has value in the eyes of its owner. Compare the Sons of God: wherever they may be, they still have value in the eyes of their Father.

NINETY-FOUR

Jesus [said], "One who seeks will find, and for he who is called in, it will be opened."

"Knock and it shall be opened": an exceptionally familiar admonition, though the Coptic twists it about a bit to open the door for one "who is called in." A question we might ask ourselves at this point is, to where are we called? A door has to lead somewhere, right? One possibility is illustrated in Saying 75:

Jesus said, "There are many standing at the door, but those who are alone will enter the bridal suite."

This idea is also backed up in *Authoritative Teaching*, a discourse on the nature of the soul presented as a metaphor in which the soul is the bride:

But the soul - she who has tasted these things - realized that sweet passions are transitory…. Afterwards she despises this life, because it is transitory. And she looks for those foods that will take her into life, and leaves behind her those deceitful foods. And she learns about her light, as she goes about stripping off this world, while her true garment clothes her within, (and) her bridal clothing is placed upon her in beauty of mind, not in pride of flesh. And she learns about her depth and runs into her fold, while her shepherd stands at the door. In return for all the shame and scorn, then, that she received in this world, she receives ten thousand times the grace and glory.

That the door leads to the bridal suite, the Gnostic inner Holy of Holies wherein the self and the divine Logos come together, makes perfect metaphorical sense. To enter a bridal suite, not only must one knock, one must also be expected and invited. One must also be alone. This points to the fact that one cannot pass through the door to gnosis with anyone else. Others can walk the path with you, and even show you where the door might be, but one must go through by one's self. Perhaps the door at which the follower of Jesus's Way knocks is a sort of "Doorless Door." If one seeks the Door in earnest, one will be expected and invited into the bridal chamber after having knocked.

NINETY-FIVE

"If you have money, don't lend it at interest. Rather, give [it] to someone from whom you won't get it back."

The temptation exists to give this Saying a cursory glance and come away with nothing more than the surface wisdom, which is certainly profound and carries Jesus's familiar admonition to charity. However, a deeper investigation into the implications of the idea of giving money away without charging interest reveals this idea as incredibly radical.

There are a number of points that can be made about this Saying that sound trite and clichéd: money is just money, do not cling to material things, be nice to people, etc. etc. etc. There is also the eschatological argument of which many canonical Christians are fond, which essentially concludes that lending at interest is silly because we will all be taken up in the Rapture in the near future. Although these explanations all have merit, they miss sight of perhaps the best reason of all to give money away.

The practice of charging interest typically occurs institutionally. In other words, when one lends money to someone and charges interest, one is probably a moneylender by trade, or works at a bank. If one lends to friends, chances are one would not ask for payment with interest, and also will be more lenient with the time it takes friends to pay one back. As far as family is concerned, most family members lend to one another with little to no concern for repayment. So, what Jesus tells us through his admonitions against usury is that we should treat every individual as though he or she is family!

For most people, especially those institutions which charge interest, giving money away carries with it a basic mistrust of individuals. This is yet another example of the inherent evil of objectification; lending at interest works under the assumption that one will be able to profit off of someone's inability or unwillingness to pay back the loan. This is really pretty twisted when one thinks about it. What Jesus says in this Saying is that it is healthier for your soul just to give the money away— it becomes a matter of faith in the essentially good nature of humankind, and a slap in the face of the illusory worldly institutions that rely on usury to make a living. It also comes naturally with a healthy detachment from material goods.

The caveat still exists, however; Jesus has already warned us against selfish charity. The idea that one should not do what one hates, found in Saying 6, reminds us that engaging in charity to further one's own ends is more insidious than not giving at all. Rather, the best reason to give away money without expecting repayment is because one considers everyone equally deserving of everything.

NINETY-SIX

Jesus [said], "The Father's Kingdom is comparable to a woman. She took a little leaven, [hid] it in dough, and made it into large loaves of bread. He who has ears had better listen!"

The difference between the Canonical parallels and Saying 96 are worth noting. Take, for example, the passage from Luke 13:20-21:

> And again, he said, "What shall I compare the kingdom of God to? It's like yeast, which a woman took and mixed in with three sacks of flour till it all rose."

Now note the passage from Matthew 13:33:

> Another metaphor he spoke to them: "The kingdom of the skies is like yeast which a woman took and mixed in with three sacks of flour till it all rose.

See the difference? In the Canon, Jesus compares the kingdom of God to the leaven, whereas in Thomas, the kingdom is like the woman! This is a pretty major distinction; why might this be the case?

We find a possible clue in the Valentinian *Testimony of Truth*, which opens as follows (emphasis mine):

> I will speak to those who know to hear not with the ears of the body but with the ears of the mind. For many have sought after the truth and have not been able to find it; because there has taken hold of them the old leaven of the Pharisees and the scribes of the Law. **And the leaven is the errant desire of the angels and the demons and the stars.**

This passage suggests that the truth cannot be known or activated by those who depend upon the "old," or inactive leaven of the Pharisees— it must come through the "ears of the mind." As the Law was perceived as the pre-Christian way to come to know and understand God, the new Way, or leaven, is gnosis, the realization of that tiny spark of Christ-nature that exists within each one of us. It requires action on the part of the individual to activate this leaven and allow it to rise within us.

Note the contrast in the original language between the teensy-tiny amount of leaven used by the woman and the massive amounts of bread it produced. This illustrates that only a mere glimpse of gnosis is required to awaken one to the nature of the entire universal Truth.

NINETY-SEVEN

Jesus said, "The [Father's] kingdom is like a woman who was carrying a [jar] full of meal. While she was walking along [a] distant road, the handle of the jar broke and the meal spilled behind her [along] the road. She didn't know it; didn't she realize there was trouble? When she reached her house, she put the jar down and discovered that it was empty."

We can picture Jesus laughing and looking around at his audience as he describes the woman's predicament. As in Saying 96, the Kingdom ("paradise") is being compared to the woman as opposed to the jar. The "jar," or the breakable vessel in general, such as a bottle, is a common enough symbol in Gnostic teachings of various cultures, including Sufism and Zen, and usually relates to one's concept of the material world. For example, a Zen koan with many variants states that "a goose is trapped in a jar. How can you free it without breaking the jar?"

There are many possible interpretations of this Saying. Perhaps the woman represents the progress of the Kingdom within each one of us. As we progress along the Way, we begin to lose focus on the World of Forms— even unknowingly, we begin to place the overtly material aspects of ourselves behind us. More likely, due to semiotic continuity which tells us that meal or seeds are "teachings"—living information, remember— the parable illustrates that the further one progresses down the path, the easier it is to lose the living information that we need to nourish our spiritual side. Is this good, or bad? It depends on whether or not one is able to free the goose.

In "The *Gospel of Truth*," we find the following passage, a more cosmological view of the jar-as-symbol:

> Having filled the deficiency, [the Father] abolished the form - the form of it is the world, that in which he served. - For the place where there is envy and strife is deficient, but the place where (there is) Unity is perfect. Since the deficiency came into being because the Father was

not known, therefore, when the Father is known, from that moment on, the deficiency will no longer exist. As in the case of the ignorance of a person, when he comes to have knowledge, his ignorance vanishes of itself, as the darkness vanishes when the light appears, so also the deficiency vanishes in the perfection. So from that moment on, the form is not apparent, but it will vanish in the fusion of Unity, for now their works lie scattered. In time, Unity will perfect the spaces. It is within Unity that each one will attain himself; within knowledge, he will purify himself from multiplicity into Unity, consuming matter within himself like fire, and darkness by light, death by life.

If indeed these things have happened to each one of us, then we must see to it above all that the house will be holy and silent for the Unity - as in the case of some people who moved out of dwellings having jars that in spots were not good. They would break them, and the master of the house would not suffer loss. Rather, is glad, because in place of the bad jars (there are) full ones which are made perfect.

All signs point to the parable admonishing us to pay strict attention, but also illustrating the inevitability of the degradation and loss of spiritual teachings and living information while within the World of Forms. Still, the passage from the *Gospel of Truth* points out that even in the worse case, all is not lost. Taking the jar as symbolic of the imperfect World of Forms, or one's concept of it, it follows that, as illustrated in the above excerpt, the weak jar which breaks and empties will be replaced by perfect, full jars when "the consummation of consummations has taken place." In this sense, the woman in the parable is indeed the "Kingdom," present within us, but the imperfect concept thereof that we have due to residing in an imperfect universe.

As a final aside, the Gnostic writings at Nag Hammadi, which Philip Dick believed contained actual entities composed of living information, were found stored in earthen jars. I provide this bit of synchronicity for the interested reader.

NINETY-EIGHT

Jesus said, "The Father's kingdom is like a person who wanted to kill a powerful man. While still at home he drew his sword and thrust it into the wall to find out inwardly whether his hand would be steady. Then he slew the powerful one."

It might seem out of place for Jesus to compare the Kingdom to an assassin. Is Jesus not the "turn the other cheek" guy, after all? Upon reflection, however, it makes good rhetorical sense on a number of levels. Assassination, a far more resonant issue during Jesus's time, was a fairly common occurrence, and a theme with which his audience would have been familiar. In fact, messages utilizing violent imagery were commonplace in Jesus's teachings. Take Saying 16, for instance, where Jesus tells us he has come to bring fire, sword and war.

Jesus realizes that sometimes a good rhetorical jolt is the best way to slap some sense into someone. Some people are more likely to listen, pay attention to and— perhaps most importantly— remember something that seems odd or offensive. When teachers mix the offensive with the holy, it gives us reason to pause and reflect: what is holiness? What is offensive? Can they be one and the same? If all has been emanated by God, then isn't even the offensive beautiful? One could consider the poetry of Rimbaud, or even Saying 77, in which Jesus tells us that if we lift a rock, we can find him underneath where the soil is rotten and the centipedes make their homes.

So, we can compare the Kingdom of Heaven to a murderer if we need to make a point, but, again, we need to look at the semiotics presented in the Saying if we really want to get to its heart. The sword, as a metaphor, typically represents the intellect, reason, the sharp edge of the Mind's Judgment, as explained in the *Gospel of Truth*: **"For this is the judgment which has come from above and which has judged every person, a drawn two-edged sword cutting on this side and that."**

The assassin represents the coming of the Logos. We know that the assassin is not powerful in the worldly sense— he has to act in secret, alone, without an army or powerful group to back him up. Generally speaking, he also has only one chance to make his move once he faces his target. If he screws up, sometimes even if he succeeds, he faces immediate executions.

The "powerful man," in this case, is a symbol common in Gnostic mythology that signifies the "rulers of this world," the false powers and systems in which we can be trapped and distracted. We can especially apply this, these days, to the political realm, and our bad habit of becoming so enmeshed within politics that we become willing to give ourselves over to the System.

Instead, Jesus counsels, we should consider "killing" said systems. Again, this is not a literal call for violence. Rather, it is intended to illustrate to us that, as the Systems of this world are so much more powerful than any one of us within the World of Forms, confronting them takes forethought and reason, steadfastness of thought and judgment. Just as the assassin is dangerous for what he represents—violent change within a system— so the seeker of the Way is also dangerous to the System at large.

NINETY-NINE

The disciples said to him, "Your brothers and your mother are standing outside."

He said to them, "Those here who do the will of my Father are my brothers and my mother. They are the ones who will enter my Father's kingdom."

Interestingly, "father" does not appear in this Saying. According to the *Gospel of Philip*, **"When we were Hebrews, we were orphans and had only our mother, but when we became Christians, we had both father and mother."** We will be addressing these concepts in full in Saying 101.

ONE HUNDRED

They showed Jesus a coin and said to him, "Caesar's people demand taxes from us."

He said to them, "Give Caesar what belongs to Caesar, give God what belongs to God, and give me what is mine."

Once again, I point the reader to the works of Jacques Ellul, this time in *Anarchy and Christianity,* in which he discusses the canonical version of this parable (emphasis mine).

It was evidently a Roman coin. One of the skillful means of integration used by the Romans was to circulate their own money throughout the empire. This became the basic coinage against which all others were measured. The Herodians replied to Jesus: "Caesar's." Now we need to realize that in the Roman world an individual mark on an object denoted ownership, like cattle brands in the American West in the 19th century.

The mark was the only way in which ownership could be recognized. In the composite structure of the Roman empire it applied to all goods. People all had their own marks, whether a seal, stamp, or painted sign. The head of Caesar on this coin was more than a decoration or a mark of honor. It signified that all the money in circulation in the empire belonged to Caesar. This was very important. Those who held the coins were very precarious owners. They never really owned the bronze or silver pieces. Whenever an emperor died, the likeness was changed. Caesar was the sole proprietor.

Jesus, then, had a very simple answer: "Render to Caesar that which is Caesar's." You find his likeness on the coin. The coin, then, belongs to him. Give it back to him when he demands it. With this answer Jesus does not say that taxes are lawful. He does not counsel obedience to the Romans. He simply faces up to the evidence. But what really belongs to Caesar? The excellent example used by Jesus makes this plain: Whatever bears his mark! Here is the basis and limit of his power. But where is this mark? On coins, on public monuments, and on certain altars. That is all. Render to Caesar. You can pay the tax. **Doing so is without importance or significance, for all money belongs to Caesar, and if he wanted he could simply confiscate it. Paying or not paying taxes is not a basic question; it is not even a true political question.**

On the other hand, whatever does not bear Caesar's mark does not belong to him. It all belongs to God. This is where the real conscientious objection arises. Caesar has no right whatever to the rest. First we have life. Caesar has no right of life and death. Caesar has no right to plunge people into war. Caesar has no right to devastate and ruin a country. Caesar's domain is very limited. We may oppose most of his pretensions in the name of God. Jesus challenges the Herodians, then, for they can have no objections to what he says. They, too, were Jews, and since the text tells us that those who put the question were Pharisees as well as Herodians, we can be certain that some of them were devout Jews. Hence they could not contest the statement of Jesus that all the rest is God's. At the same time Jesus was replying indirectly to the Zealots who wanted to transform the struggle for the liberation of Israel into a political struggle. He reminded them what was the limit as well as the basis of the struggle.

Although Ellul definitely explains the "gist" of this parable from an anarchistic perspective, the Thomas version adds "give me what is mine" to all of the canonical versions. Is Jesus placing himself higher than Caesar and **God**? Yes and no. The "God" to whom Jesus refers in this case is arguably the Demiurgic power that controls the created World of Forms.

Remember that the Demiurge "exists" on two levels. He can be considered a separate spiritual entity or power of some kind, but also as the limited concept each of us has of a god— the collection of symbols and signs we envision when we try to speak for "God" or impose upon reality our idea of what God should be. In a sense, then, these images that we have of "God" are indeed parallel to the image of Caesar on the coins in question, and those things on which "God's" face is stamped belong not to the true God, but to the insane streak of the universe. When fundamentalists of any stripe declare that they are speaking on God's behalf, they barter with the coinage of a false deity.

The Christos, however, as the inner Logos or Divine Human, is found indelibly stamped within each of those who follow his Way. Once one has experienced enlightenment, one "belongs" to the Christos— not in the sense of ownership, but in the sense that one belongs to the family discussed in the previous Saying.

Paying taxes is a HUGE concern for many people of conscience, especially to an evil government that uses these taxes to fund a hideous war machine. Should one pay? If so, does one not contribute to the evil committed by the government? If one refuses to pay, however, there are often severe repercussions. Is tax protest worth going to jail for? The short answer seems to be, "it's up to you."

As Ellul shows us, Jesus likely never intended to tacitly support paying taxes because he approved of so doing. He was more likely telling the listeners that paying taxes makes no real difference in the big picture. After all, any government will take "taxes" from one, if not financially then in freedom, whether or not one protests and withholds payment. But, Jesus tells us, look whose face is on the money. In our case Washington, Franklin, Jefferson et al. grace our coinage. And, they symbolize an America that does not even exist anymore. So, go ahead and pay. May as well— all such payment is a symbolic, valueless exchange of paper and metal and, in these days of funds transfer, numbers in a locationless "account." Chances are, one's money doesn't even exist! Money, such an ephemeral thing, only works because everyone says it does. Imagine if everybody woke up one day and said, "wait, exchanging paper bills and metal coins makes as much sense, realistically, as exchanging leaves and rocks."

This is most certainly blackmail. One can be all for paying lots and lots of taxes if the money goes to things like education and food for the poor and health care and etc. One can certainly wish that the part of one's income that funds torturing inmates in Iraqi prisons could be used somewhere else. One can be quite peeved that attempts at protest could result in jail time, and most certainly a bureaucratic nightmare. But hey, this is not really our money. Once one pays one's taxes, the government takes on any responsibility for what it does with said money. They own the cash to begin with— they just give it to all of us to hold for a while. Money and credit cards are the same damned things— the government can take all of their money back any time they want.

So, if one wants to protest taxes, fine, but be warned that on such a small scale it probably will not make much difference, and one will have to put up with increased government intrusion into one's life. If one wants to pay them, this is fine, too, but keep in mind that such payments amount to blackmail by the System. These issues are all absurd anyhow, like "gentlemen's" gambling with someone else's poker chips—the chips still must be returned at the end of the game.

The late Bill Hicks, one of the greatest modern philosophers who happened to ply his ideas in the form of stand-up comedy, closed pretty much every show with a variation of the following, which really applies here. Of course, Bill was murdered by the insane universe for speaking the truth, just like Phil Dick and so many others, but we can bet that he gave Jesus what was his.

I'm gonna share with you a vision that I had, cause I love you. And you feel it. You know all that money we spend on nuclear weapons and defense each year, trillions of dollars, correct? Instead — just play with this — if we spent that money feeding and clothing the poor of the world — and it would pay for it many times over, not one human being excluded — we can explore space together, both inner and outer, forever in peace.

ONE HUNDRED and ONE

"Whoever does not hate [father] and mother as I do cannot be my [disciple], and whoever does [not] love [father and] mother as I do cannot be my [disciple]. For my mother gave me my body, but my true mother gave me Life."

Saying 101 is an extension and development of the statements found in Saying 55 and Saying 99. This is a pretty shocking statement in a culture to which "Honor Thy Father and Mother" is one of the ten Big Rules. As mentioned in Saying 55, refusing to honor one's father and mother meant far more than it does today:

Here is the pertinent commandment in context (Exodus 20:12):
"Honor your father and your mother, so that you may live long in the land the LORD your God is giving you." Ol' Yaldabaoth/Yahweh seems to be encouraging honor of father and mother not because they gave one life and are due respect, but so that the Holy Land stays in the hands of the "chosen people." By telling his students to hate father and mother and thereby lose their inheritances, Jesus also informs them that this commandment does not apply, another indication that the literal covenant between the false Creator and the Jewish people should be considered null and void.

Although Jesus uses "hate," an incredibly strong word, a better interpretation would be "detach yourself from." Remember, this was not a nuclear-family society; for many people, families were essentially microtribes with the parents at the head. The parents were the leaders, teachers—both secular and religious, providers. In less cosmopolitan areas, one lived near one's parents—or husband's parents—one's whole life. Detaching from them took more than simply moving to another state, it was a demolition of the most immediate power structure in a person's life, which is essentially the point behind this Saying: divorcing one's self from immediate power structures, which comprise the framework of the Black Iron Prison.

Jesus continues to tell us that we must also love our fathers and mothers. This is quite a conundrum, and why the term "divorce" or "detach from" makes things clearer. One can, and, according to Jesus, should, break away from the power structures of the world but **continue to love them**. This is not a worldly love— after all, the mother and father simply provided the body. Instead, this is the compassion that one has for all of one's fellows who are still caught within these structures. It is extremely difficult to apply this philosophy in today's exceptionally divisive culture, especially when the servants of the Rulers of Darkness are in power like never before. One still must show compassion for those "fathers and mothers" of iniquity who are driving the world into deepening darkness.

The mother that Jesus "hates" is not Mary, it is the system in which Mary resides when he makes this statement. The mother who gave Jesus his body was the world. Jesus tells us, once again, to detach one's self from the world and instead love that which resides therein. Who is the "true mother" that gave Jesus life? The True Mother is Sophia, the Aeonic power of Wisdom that descends from the Pleroma and "empowers" the Logos. Wisdom gives life to the Word. On Christmas Day, Jesus's mother, the world and the power structures therein, gave him his body, but his True mother gave him life in the Kingdom of Heaven when it descended into him during his baptism.

ONE HUNDRED and TWO

Jesus said, "Woe to the Pharisees! They are like a dog sleeping in the oxen manger: the dog neither eats nor permits the oxen to eat."

Jesus applies an ancient fable to the "Pharisees," those false teachers who, as mentioned in Saying 39, believe in religious elitism and exclusivity. This story in particular shows up in the tales of Aesop as follows:

> A Dog lay in a manger, and by his growling and snapping prevented the oxen from eating the hay which had been placed for them. "What a selfish Dog!" said one of them to his companions; "he cannot eat the hay himself, and yet refuses to allow those to eat who can."

Remember that, according to our Gnostic semiotic dictionary, grain—hay in the manger, as an example—generally symbolizes those teachings that assist one's advance down the Path of enlightenment, the Logos, the living information which reveals the Kingdom to the sincere seeker. This is another reason why it was so important that Jesus was actually born in a manger— grain represents the teaching and Jesus himself, as the Logos, is the grain that nourishes the world.

This is an interesting Saying in the context of the current religious climate in much of the world, where religious fundamentalists claim that they, and they alone have perfected the Path, and anyone who does not follow their Path is condemned to eternal damnation. Unfortunately, this approach has serious detrimental effects. First of all, someone sincerely interested in following a Path takes a look at these self-righteous fundamentalists and thinks, "yeah, right." Many times, however, said seeker decides to abandon **all** such Paths. Most anti-religionists chose to be so based on negative experiences with ultra-zealous fundamentalists.

Trying to force people to change their minds has pretty much always been a bad approach to life. The best way to lead is by example. If someone is pressured into joining this or that group with threats of damnation or promises of exclusive benefits, then has their mind truly and sincerely changed? What good is that for the teacher or the taught? The best way to get people interested in what one is teaching is not by forcing them read what one writes, but by making ideas one finds important available to those who are already interested in seeking, and letting those ideas stand on their own merit.

Presuming to judge others and sentence them to eternal damnation for following a different Path contradicts Jesus's teachings and his actions. Absolutists and strict legalists who condemn vast swaths of people to eternal hellfire, or slaughter people who disagree with them, or even just treat "unbelievers" a bit differently, are not really "doing unto their neighbors," are they? Reading Jesus's message, we tend to see more about compassion and acceptance than condemnation and hatred.

Anyone who follows any spiritual path whatsoever, even the most fundamentalist ones, can achieve enlightenment provided the path they follow is one of compassion and humility, like Jesus and the Buddha and Muhammad were known to have said. The Gnostic Way does not deal in the mind-changing business or eternal-damnation game.

ONE HUNDRED and THREE

Jesus said, "Blessed are those who know where the thieves are going to enter. So that they can rise, gather their kingdom, and take up arms before the thieves arrive."

This Saying continues upon themes first discussed in Sayings 21 and 35 concerning attentiveness, the nearly constant state of tension required of the seeker. We know by now what is symbolized by "robbers," "brigands," etc. in Gnostic literature.   Remember that in the *Exegesis of the Soul*, the feminine soul who resides with God falls into the World of Forms and is subsequently raped by brigands and robbers:

> But when she fell down into a body and came to this life, then she fell into the hands of many robbers. And the wanton creatures passed her from one to another and [made use of] her. Some made use of her by force, while others did so by seducing her with a gift. In short, they defiled her, and she [lost] her virginity.

In the Commentary to Saying 35, we find that ". . . in Gnostic symbology, the robbers are those who focus on and concern themselves with the things of this world. They are the aspects of the Cosmos, both human and abstract, which attach the student to the world and open h/er up to distraction from the Path."

It is indeed interesting, and a bit scary, to really investigate this concept of the Archons and their various powers as thieves, brigands or robbers. They really, literally desire to **steal** something from you, something you have— the Pearl of the Soul, the spark of true divinity that resides within each of us. Metaphorically or mythologically, the Archons in their various incarnations, be they psychological states of sub/un/consciousness or interdimensional UFOnauts, aim to take, by force or by deceit and subtlety, that part of each of us that can connect to the divine through the Logos. Note that in this parable, the counsel we receive is that we should know where the bandits will break in. This suggests that the strategy of the servants of the rulers is to attack where they are least expected. This makes sense, when considered in the context of

Jacques Ellul's admonition that those who are the most propagandized are those who believe they are the least propagandized.

Those who are the most highly and rabidly ideological are the most vulnerable to manipulation via their own ideology. It is important not to be attached to one's material possessions, but it is even more important to constantly question one's own assumptions and ideas about the nature of Being and one's place within it. This is the nature of true detachment, which has nothing to do with how much stuff one owns or how much time one spends watching television.

For this reason, it is important to constantly question, question, question. One must constantly be on one's guard against the machinations of the Archons and their servants, who literally feed on fear, but who also require ignorance in order to maintain their existences as "objects of worship." To maintain this ignorance, they must create structures within society that perpetuate fear and veneration, but the structures must be ideological black holes that trap the psyches of those who venture too far past the event horizon. The Archons sit like ant lions at the bottoms of the ideological black holes, waiting for the average ontonaut to cross that point of no return. If, however, someone is educated on the tactics of the Archons and their servants, and trusts nothing that emerges from the mouths of ideologues without verifying for one's self, then one knows where the bandits plan to enter, and can essentially rally the troops to fight them off.

This is not to say that all ideologies are bad, just that each paradigm is worth twenty cents (ha ha ha). The problem arises when one embraces an ideology without experience or compassion. This attentiveness required of the seeker does not just mean paying attention to one's own actions, but also to the effects that one's actions will have on other beings with whom we share the World of Forms. As the Gnostics knew thousands of years ago, it is a matter of experience as opposed to belief. Embracing any ideology is all well and good, but one cannot build walls of protection by **believing** that they exist— one must temper those walls with **direct experience of the Holy** through the medium of compassion.

One's best bet of all is to find allies—"friends/imperial resources/kingdom" in the above Saying— people one loves and respects. There is a great reason for this that often gets overlooked. Our friends and loved ones, the people with whom we interact and with whom we "gel," provide us with the most direct experiences we can have. It is all well and good to rail against the neocons or environmental decay or filthy liberals, but none of those things can **really** be experienced in the powerful way that we connect with those around us. The bandits' most devious, treacherous and downright effective way to get us is by convincing us that fake things are real, that we can experience, with value, their intricate structural webs.

ONE HUNDRED and FOUR

They said to Jesus, "Come, pray today, and fast."

Jesus said, "What sin have I committed, or how have I been undone? Rather, when the groom leaves the bridal suite, then let people fast and pray."

Sayings 6 and 14 provide context for Jesus's rebuke to the disciples in this case. This Saying seems to imply that Jesus was without sin. We know from Saying 75 that the bridal suite is the inner Holy of Holies, that placeless place in which the Logos meets the divine spark through gnosis, and Jesus seems to say that sin is not possible while this suite is occupied. For the Gnostic, however, the suite is permanently occupied, so Jesus may be implying that while he is present as the Logos, sin is not possible for the Gnostic, and while he is present in the world, there is no need to pray and fast.

This Saying is also interesting for the questions it brings up about the nature of Jesus. At one time, you couldn't throw a rock in theological circles without hitting someone who was discussing whether Jesus sinned, laughed, spent money, experienced fatigue or ate and digested food like everybody else. Theologians through the ages have scratched their heads and scratched quills on parchment trying to find the answer to a very specific question: in essence, did Jesus shit?

Pardon the coarseness, but this is a good context within which to discuss Christology because it turns our preconceptions on their ears. Was Jesus himself coarse? Did he cuss and tell dirty jokes? Did he wipe his ass with his left hand after a bad bout of diarrhea? Did Jesus, while sitting around after a meal discussing the Kingdom of Heaven with the disciples, break a loud and stinky fart and laugh about it? Did he get sick and cough up phlegm?

This seems silly to think about, but it is a valid question, because, if he was the Son of God, why would he do disgusting stuff like that? If Jesus shit like the rest of us, then was he truly Perfect? And, if not, then was he not also susceptible to sin? Was Jesus fully God, with all that that implies? Or, was he just a schlub like us who realized his own divinity and was "possessed" by God?

All kinds of heretical groups sprang up around these questions almost immediately after Jesus's lifetime.

Valentinus, the most famous of the Gnostic teachers addressed this very question of Jesus's nature in these vulgar terms exactly. Unfortunately, only a fragment of the argument survives:

> He was continent, enduring all things. Jesus digested divinity: he ate and drank in a special way without excreting his solids. He had such a great capacity for continence that the nourishment within him was not corrupted, for he did not experience corruption.

Make of this what you will.

Philip Dick used to say that the manifestation of God in the world always began in the lowest place, the detritus in the trash, the gutter of experience. This fits in with our understanding of Jesus as divinity which has temporarily manifested itself within gross material— what an amazing sacrifice God made on behalf of those of us stranded down here! Similarly, St. Francis of Assisi, the son of a wealthy trader, decided to toss away his riches for the sake of caring for lepers. We find similar sentiments in Saying 77, where Jesus discusses how one can find him when one splits a piece of wood or looks under a rock. One can find divinity even within the slimy, gunk-covered beetles and centipedes that live under rocks. Think of the World of Forms as a giant Mandelbrot fractal. The smaller, filthier things that creep and crawl around the edges of the fractal are still self-similar to the divinity at its roots, but they all lead back to that divinity.

When it comes down to it, the Gnostics Way is more interested in Jesus's teachings, not whether he parted his hair to the left or right or had a relationship with Mary Magdalene. But, he was fully human, a human who was possessed by that which is fully Divine, and said human occasionally had to empty his bowels. Really, not only do we think that Jesus shat, but we should celebrate that fact! It means that nothing is too gross to be redeemed— no aspect of the World of Forms is so filthy or low that it won't someday receive salvation, and the bridal suite is contained within all of gross matter, waiting to be occupied by the Logos.

ONE HUNDRED and FIVE

Jesus said, "Whoever knows the father and the mother will be called a son of a harlot."

"Knowing" in this context is gnosis, and the father and mother the typical Gnostic mythological figures: the father is God and the mother is its feminine aspect, be it Barbelo (on a highest level) or Sophia. We can state this with near certainty because Jesus refers to **the** father and **the** mother— the singular. For more on the semiotic values of father and mother, see Sayings 55, 99 and 101. This is most certainly another warning that those who walk along the Way can expect hostility and persecution at the hands of those who are not on said path.

There is another level, though: the level illustrated by the term "harlot" ("whore," "bitch," etc.— could also be prostitute, tramp, lady of the night, "working girl," whatever one prefers). In Gnostic mythological semiotics, the whore represents the occluded feminine divinity within the World of Forms and the soul. An almost epic poem found at Nag Hammadi called *Thunder, Perfect Mind* consists of the Divine Feminine listing her various aspects and qualities. The poem plays with dialectic; the qualities recited are always opposites, the point being, of course, that nothing can exist without its opposite and that the Ultimate Reality manifests itself within all aspects of being. The poem includes the following passage:

> For I am the first and the last.
>
> I am the honored one and the scorned one.
>
> I am the whore and the holy one.
>
> I am the wife and the virgin.
>
> I am and the daughter.
>
> I am the members of my mother.
>
> I am the barren one
>
> and many are her sons.
>
> I am she whose wedding is great,

and I have not taken a husband.

"Thunder, Perfect Mind" is an exceptionally striking piece of religious literature. It is a good indication that in Gnostic religious language, "whore" carries a meaning opposite to that which it carries in the cultural/societal sense.

The "Sacred Prostitute" is also a common theme in ancient Mediterranean culture. Oftimes prostitutes who had dedicated their lives to this or that deity would live in temples, and during certain festivals would have intercourse with congregants. Any offspring produced from these unions was considered a son or daughter of the deity in question. So, one might see the reference to "Son of a Whore" as a reference to this practice, wherein the son of a whore is the son of a god!

Also, we can refer once again to that old favorite, the *Exegesis on the Soul*, which describes the fallen soul in the following terms:

And in her body she prostituted herself and gave herself to one and all, considering each one she was about to embrace to be her husband. When she had given herself to wanton, unfaithful adulterers, so that they might make use of her, then she sighed deeply and repented. But even when she turns her face from those adulterers, she runs to others and they compel her to live with them and render service to them upon their bed, as if they were her masters.

In referring to those who know the father and mother as children of whores, Jesus is also illustrating, in Gnostic semiotic code, the transition one's soul makes via gnosis, from its fallen state to its perfected state— as well we know, children are used to symbolize those who have achieved perfection via communion with the divine and have become "innocent," or entered a state of relative perfection. So, in this context, being called a son of a whore isn't really all that bad. Jesus is telling the seeker that a proper response to such a slur might be, "hey, cool, thanks, I appreciate that."

ONE-HUNDRED and SIX

Jesus said, "When you make the two into one, you will become children of Man, and when you say, 'Mountain, move from here!' it will move."

     This is a variation on themes from previous Sayings, especially 22, 28 and 48. The idea of moving mountains with faith can be found in various spiritual traditions. It appears in the Canonical Gospels in *Mark* 11:20-25 and *Matthew* 17:19-20, and appears in Paul's *First Epistle to the Corinthians* 13:2. It also appears in the collection of Sayings attributed to Jesus in the Muslim faith. It is very possible that Gnosticism and Islam may have influenced one another.

     Making the two into one, or the inner like the outer, has already been covered in great detail. We recall that it refers to a divine oneness that occurs when one has experienced gnosis, often referred to in Gnostic literature as a state of solitude, or solitariness. This oneness extends throughout the placeless place that exists beyond the world of division, in which all events occur simultaneously.

     This is not meant to refer to sentimentalist New Age "we are all one with the universe mmmmmmm" schools of thought. Instead, this refers to a specific spiritual state in which one recognizes the essential nature of being and identifies one's place therein, recognizes how everything is connected less in a silly New Age way and more in the fashion of Douglas Adam's Total Perspective Vortex—though stunningly less fatal:

> The Total Perspective Vortex derives its picture of the whole Universe on the principle of extrapolated matter analyses.

> To explain—since every piece of matter in the Universe is in some way affected by every other piece of matter in the Universe, it is in theory possible to extrapolate the whole of creation—every sun, every planet, their orbits, their composition, and their economic and social history from, say, one small piece of fairy cake.

The man who invented the Total Perspective Vortex did so basically in order to annoy his wife.

Trin Tragula—for that was his name—was a dreamer, a thinker, a speculative philosopher or, as his wife would have it, an idiot.

And she would nag him incessantly about the utterly inordinate amount of time he spent staring out into space, or mulling over the mechanics of safety pins, or doing spectrographic analyses of pieces of fairy cake.

"Have some sense of proportion!" she would say, sometimes as often as thirty-eight times in a single day.

And so he built the Total Perspective Vortex—just to show her.

And into one end, he plugged the whole of reality as extrapolated from a piece of fairy cake, and into the other, he plugged his wife: so that when he turned it on she saw in one instant the whole infinity of creation and herself in relation to it.

To Trin Tragula's horror, the shock completely annihilated her brain, but to his satisfaction he realized that he had proved conclusively that if life is going to exist in a Universe of this size, then one thing it cannot afford to have is a sense of proportion.xxxii

Trin Tragula, a Sufi "wise fool" if ever there was one, may have utilized strict physical mechanics to develop his Vortex, but the follower of Jesus's Way does so purely through meditation on the divine light of the Logos and the union of the Logos with the Soul. When one has this realization, one "moves the mountain" because the Mountain itself moves the Mountain. A Zen master once said, when referring to enlightenment, that "When I heard the sound of the bell ringing, there was no bell and no I, just the ringing." In this way, one can say that there is no mountain and no I, just the movement.

Or, it could be that Jesus is simply using hyperbole to illustrate the power of gnosis. This is a pretty powerful image, and the mountain carries a plethora of symbolic connotations. In this sense, Jesus is Saying that once one has experienced gnosis, one can move the world, shake things up a bit.

ONE HUNDRED and SEVEN

Jesus said, "The kingdom is like a shepherd who had a hundred sheep. One of them, the largest, went astray. He left the ninety- nine and looked for the one until he found it. Having been troubled, he said to the sheep, 'I love you more than the ninety- nine.'"

This is a pretty familiar parable from Matthew 18:12-14 and Luke 15:3-7, with slight differences. In Saying 107, the sheep in question is the **largest**, instead of just another sheep. Also, in the canonical versions, the sheep represents the sinner, whereas in *Thomas* the shepherd is like paradise and the sheep represents the Gnostic seeker.

Saying 107 is unique in *Thomas* because we actually have an exposition of this parable in another Gnostic text, the Valentinian *Gospel of Truth:*

> [Jesus] is the shepherd who left behind the ninety-nine sheep which had not strayed and went in search of that one which was lost. He rejoiced when he had found it. For ninety-nine is a number of the left hand, which holds it. The moment he finds the one, however, the whole number is transferred to the right hand. Thus it is with him who lacks the one, that is, the entire right hand which attracts that in which it is deficient, seizes it from the left side and transfers it to the right. In this way, then, the number becomes one hundred. This number signifies the Father.

The numbers 99 and 100 relate to a complicated form of hand counting employed during the Roman era. Those who counted using this method could count from 1 to 99 on their left hand, using both fingers and individual joints, but had to switch to the right hand to begin counting at 100.

As well know our left-handed friends, the left hand signified uncleanliness in many ancient cultures—the Latin word for "Left" is sinister. So, we have our shepherd, looking over his sheep, counting up to 99 on his left hand. When he would have switched to the right hand for that final sheep, he finds that it is missing. In essence, his flock is "unclean," as they are still on his left hand. The *Gospel of Truth* also states that 100 "signifies the Father;" most likely this is another reference to the "perfect" nature of the number 100, which is a return to completeness, the process through which the entire World of Forms is currently undergoing.

How to explain the apparent difference in the parable and its exposition in the *Gospel of Truth* concerning what the shepherd symbolizes? Jesus claims that the shepherd represents the "Kingdom," Gnostic code for the perfected state. The *Gospel of Truth* indicates that Jesus himself, as the divine Logos/Christos, is the shepherd. This may be what it seems to be, a difference based simply on interpretation by a later expositor, but it also indicates the concept of God as existing simultaneously as a power and a placeless place with its own consistent morphology.

If indeed God is infinite, which is one of the basic assumptions of Gnosticism, then God **is** the "Kingdom," and the Palm Tree Garden, as Philip K. Dick called paradise, is a "living" entity that extends to the World of Forms through the Logos. Most readers will agree that it does no good to think of God as some giant enthroned bearded man in the clouds, but it is still exceptionally difficult to avoid anthropomorphization. It therefore helps to think of God as all possible points in all possible layers of space-time, which, to our limited brains, is more like a place than like an entity. The God, as perfection, is far more similar to a mountain meadow at the base of a glacial flow with a clear-blue pool than some white-haired, bearded guy in a dress. And, in essence, mythological stories and expositions are attempts at trying to map God's topography —more of a morphography, of course, since a topography usually deals in two dimensions.

So, the shepherd represents the Logos/Kingdom, as a manifestation of a placeless place— perhaps the self-same meadow wherein the sheep graze. He counts over the sheep, which always represent those under the watchful gaze of the Logos and the divine perfection, and notices that the largest one is missing, which means that the flock is imperfect, represented by the left-hand count. When he discovers that it is missing, that shepherd drops everything he is doing and focuses intently on the search for the missing sheep. When one has experienced gnosis, one can feel this intense focus, this seeking, as though a satellite in orbit is focusing a pink beam of light over the face of the planet, looking for you in particular.

Now, the translations indicate that the sheep is the "biggest," but the Coptic word being used is **noch**, which can also mean "the greatest" as in "Great Leader." We find it used this way in Saying 12, when the disciples ask

Jesus who will be their leader (lit. "Who is he who will become great up over us?"). Based on this use of the word, the sheep in question is not the fattest, but instead represents the bellwether, or leader of the flock. This would be an even more important reason for the shepherd to concern himself if it went missing—without the bellwether, the rest of the flock might get lost, too! The bellwether in this case may represent the seeker, who, in seeking, leads.

Regardless, the missing one is the Most Important Sheep, and on finding it, the shepherd, having worked so diligently to locate it, embraces it and assures it that it is loved and needed. The sheep in question, as the seeker, is bathed in the love of the placeless place represented by the Logos and regarded as the most necessary component of the flock. As the *Gospel of Truth* concludes in its exposition on this parable:

> He labored even on the Sabbath for the sheep which he found fallen into the pit. He saved the life of that sheep, bringing it up from the pit in order that you may understand fully what that Sabbath is, you who possess full understanding. It is a day in which it is not fitting that salvation be idle, so that you may speak of that heavenly day which has no night and of the sun which does not set because it is perfect. Say then in your heart that you are this perfect day and that in you dwells the light which does not fail.

ONE HUNDRED and EIGHT

Jesus said, "Whoever drinks from my mouth will be along my Way; I myself shall become that person, and the hidden things will be revealed to him."

The concept of drinking from Jesus's mouth can also be found in Saying 13:

> Thomas said to him, "Master, my mouth will not allow me to say what you are like."

> Jesus said, "I am not your master. Because you have drunk, you have become intoxicated from the bubbling spring that I have measured out."

"Drinking from one's mouth," not a particularly pleasing concept to our modern sensibilities, almost assuredly refers to taking in the Logos, as living information, and transmitted via teachings. As says the *Gospel of Truth*:

> For each one loves truth because truth is the mouth of the Father. His tongue is the Holy Spirit, who joins him to truth attaching him to the mouth of the Father by his tongue at the time he shall receive the Holy Spirit.

The Logos then crossbonds throughout the person who has drunk fro the mouth of Jesus, literally becoming the bearer of the Logos who can then transmit the information along via the understanding given through gnosis; in effect, Jesus as the Logos does indeed become the enlightened person, and vice-versa.

The whole concept is expressed perfectly by Philip K. Dick in his "Tractates Cryptica Scriptura":

> I term the Immortal one a plasmate, because it is a form of energy; it is living information. It replicates itself - not through information or in information-- but as information

23. The plasmate can crossbond with a human, creating what I call a homoplasmate. This annexes the mortal human permanently to the plasmate. We know this as the "birth from above" or "birth from the Spirit." It was initiated by Christ, but the Empire destroyed all the homoplasmates before they could replicate.

24. In dormant seed form, the plasmate slumbered in the buried library of codices at Chenoboskion [Nag Hammadi] until 1945 C.E. This is what Jesus meant when he spoke elliptically of the "mustard seed" which, he said, "would grow into a tree large enough for the birds to roost in." He foresaw not only his own death but that of all homoplasmates. He foresaw the codices unearthed, read, and the plasmate seeking out new human hosts to crossbond with; but he foresaw the absence of the plasmate for almost two thousand years.

25. As living information, the plasmate travels up to the optic nerve of a human to the pineal body. It uses the human brain as a female host in which to replicate itself into its active form. This is an interspecies symbiosis. The Hermatic alchemists knew of it in theory from ancient texts, but could not duplicate it, since they could not locate the dormant, buried plasmate. Bruno suspected that the plasmate had been destroyed by the Empire; for hinting at this he was burned. "The Empire never ended."xxxiii

Some find these ideas hard to swallow (pardon the pun)— enlightened humans are mutant crossbreeds who play host to an invasive intelligent force? Does this plasmate, as Dick believed, take the form of the Holy Spirit and travel **"up the optic nerve of a human to the pineal body[, using] the human brain as a female host in which to replicate itself into its active form. This is an interspecies symbiosis."**

Of course, Dick believed that the plasmate resided specifically in ancient texts which were hidden during a period in which the Black Iron Prison, manifesting as the Roman Empire, was destroying homoplasmates. The plasmate is active again thanks to the discovery of the Gnostic collection at Nag Hammadi in 1945. From our current context, it makes more sense that the plasmate was still working during this period, but wounded. We also find that the plasmate can be transferred via information in general, not specifically written language— more like we are already bonded with an inactive portion of the plasmate that can be activated either by exposure to another plasmate or by the experience of gnosis. To top it all off, the plasmate is also transmittable via the practices of the Eucharistic mystery tradition, given through the priest who distributes information about the Logos through the medium of the consecrated bread, wine and water.

There is something to be said for the idea that the plasmate exists as living information, somehow outside of the realms of physicality, and is transferred through the medium of what we refer to as gnosis. Historically, there is a definite geographical course for this kind of gnosticism from Egypt to Rome to Eastern Europe through Manichaeism, to the Bogomils to Italy, which is where Albigensian-style Catharism got its start. During the Albigensian period, the Cathar movement traveled over the Pyranees into Spain, where, by 1218, an organized faction had settled in the city of Leon and were persecuted by a Spanish prelate called Lucas of Tuy, who wrote a book called "The Other Life, Against the Errors of the Albigensians" and destroyed the local Cathar chapel, driving them underground once again.

Later that century, a rabbi by the name of Moses de Leon composed or discovered the *Sepher ha-Zohar*, arguably the most important work of the mystical Jewish tradition known as the Qabbalah. Qabbalah spread throughout Europe after the expulsion of the Jews from Spain, once again by the Inquisition. In the other direction, the ideas contained therein were "carried" by the Sufis. Moorish Spain was a veritable hotbed of Sufism during this era, and finding all of these traditions together in one place, indeed, in one city, causes one to wonder.

One could readily argue that the ideas contained in gnosticism survived in Europe, albeit in somewhat bastardized forms, within the Qabbalah and the "occultist" Hermetic movements inspired by it, including mystical alchemy—all different forms, all basically containing the same living information, staying alive in drips and drabs but eventually culminating in the much-maligned but essential Theosophical Society. The various fragments of Gnostic teaching that were discovered before Nag Hammadi were made public and interpreted for the first time in English by G.R.S. Mead, personal secretary to H.P. Blavatsky, founder of Theosophy. Mead would not likely have been involved in transmitting this information without the desire of the various Occult Lodges, Western Kabbalists and Theosophists who were already "seeded" to accept these new tidbits of information.

Of course, the current revival, heralded by Philip K. Dick, a sort of modern John the Baptist, was confirmed by the publication of the Nag Hammadi cache, which contains enough of the living information to "infect" the population on an increasingly large scale. The plasmates currently reside not only in the Nag Hammadi, but in the almost viral explosion of Gnostic-related items found in pop culture of late.

This is good and bad, of course, because, like Thomas says, a city on a high hill is easily defended but difficult to hide; just ask the Cathars at Montsegur. Now that the plasmates are once again being spread throughout society, the Rulers of the World know it and are redoubling their efforts to squelch the ideas contained in Gnosticism. This time their efforts are more subtle, and more pernicious. Instead of simply killing off the Gnostics, the Archons are assuming the forms taken by the plasmates, becoming counterfeit deliverers of "salvation," confusing and muddling the minds of the already-occluded by distracting them from the Way.

The vagaries and speculative aspects of this theory aside, most find it either extremely illustrative of the divine process, or extremely creepy. One can think of it as a metaphor if one prefers, or in terms of memetics— it works that way, too. However, taken as a metaphor or literally, it explains quite a bit, and Saying 108 encompasses either interpretation.

ONE HUNDRED and NINE

Jesus said, "The Kingdom is like a person who had a hidden treasure in his field but did not know it. And [when] he died he left it to his [son]. The son [did] not know about it either. He took over the field and sold it. The buyer went plowing, [discovered] the treasure, and began to lend money at interest to whomever he loved."

Once again we find variations on themes that have already been discussed. Note that neither the father or the son know—have gnosis of—the treasure in the field. The field also appears in Saying 21. We have a father and son ignorant of this great treasure; the son sells the field to some lucky fellow who discovers the treasure and becomes a moneylender.

The father and son must not have taken terribly good care of their field to begin with. A similar parable found in the *Midrash* tells the story of a father who leaves a field to his sons and tells them there is a great treasure hidden within it. When the father dies, the sons set to work and dig up the field. They find no treasure, but the work they did turns the soil and they profit greatly from the more fertile field. We can probably assume that neither the father nor the son in our parable bothered to work the field and reveal the treasure. The father dies, and the son sells it. "Treasure," as money/jewels/pearls generally denotes teachings concerning the Logos and the pearl, the Living Information we discussed in the previous statement.

We could easily jump to the conclusion that the lucky man who found the treasure is meant to signify the seeker. In fact, the man who buys the field and discovers the treasure immediately turns around and abuses his luck by becoming one of the most despicable citizens of the Empire: a moneylender. Jesus tends to revile moneylenders. Saying 95 specifically abjures the reader not to lend money: **"If you have money, don't lend it at interest. Rather, give [it] to someone from whom you won't get it back."** And, let's not forget who Jesus kicked out of the Temple.

One can easily stumble upon some kind of crazy and insightful and enriching esoteric teaching, and then turn around and kill one's soul by using it to make a **quick** buck. Moneylending is essentially selling one's own money to further one's own finances at the expense of others who, by virtue of coming to a moneylender in the first place, are in great need. Just as our jerk of a landbuyer enriches himself with wisdom and then lends with interest to his own needy family and friends, so people who claim to have some kind of hidden knowledge, whether or not personally "enlightened" by said knowledge, take advantage of people in need by requiring them to buy it.

Those who charge for spiritual information tend to be sham artists. They tie knowledge to money, and imply that anyone can become enlightened who can afford to do so. This damages potential seekers, because it forbids them the opportunity to make up their own minds, a process that requires work and introspection, not something that can be bought for any amount of cash. The only **real** information is free and comes more from within than without. Sadly, our culture tends to reinforce the idea that anything can be bought, and so we have every other chicanery-laden flim-flam fest available in the New Age section of the local Barnes and Noble.

In truth, Jesus does not want us to be like **any** of the individuals in the story. Neither the father nor the son were completely aware of what they already had, so they ended up losing it. The buyer, on the other hand, took advantage of what he had been given to cheat other people. All three are pretty reprehensible.

ONE HUNDRED and TEN

Jesus said, "Let one who has found the world, and has become wealthy, renounce the world."

This really complements the previous Saying, in which our friend the land speculator finds a treasure in his yard and becomes a moneylender. This is what Jesus has been teaching all along: the world, as a corpse-world, is an illusion, as are the Systems which exist within the corpse-world. Power, politics, money— these things are pointless distractions and merit very little in the way of actual attention. Republican vs. Democrat, Capitalism vs. Communism, Israel vs. Palestine, rich vs. poor, left vs. right, Islam vs. Christianity, these are all moot. Ideologues enmeshed in dichotomic and falsely hierarchical systems spend a lot of time making things uncomfortable for a lot of people with very little in the way of healthy results that improve everyone's well-being. The realization one has, as a seeker, that one exists within this framework can be described as "finding the world," which does lead to a certain wealth— the wealth of gnosis, the teachings/information represented by the treasure in Saying 109.

So what exactly does this renunciation of the world entail? The Servants of the Rulers of the World, those residents of the World of Forms who impose their structures upon other individuals, have created an intricate and attractive framework which enmeshes all of us. Obviously, unless one becomes a hermit in a cave, and even then it can be difficult, one who lives within the constraints of the system cannot help but be caught up within it. After all, one must eat and sleep someplace warm. The very act of being born into this World of Forms entails, for most individuals, barring the occasional bodhisattva, being involuntarily thrust into these systems against one's will. For most of us, the only **physical** escape is death, and unless one has done some serious work on one's self while here, most Mystery systems agree that one runs a very serious risk of getting tossed back into this realm for another try (and another, and another, and another . . .). Gnosticism generally allows for reincarnation; not even suicide can help you, because all one does is end the program early. One then has to start again from the beginning.

If one is trapped in a system against one's will, the only way to find peace is to find peace for one's self. Stumbling across the world and coming to the realization that the World of Forms is a construct in which we are trapped, one of our options is to renounce the World of Forms, to live our lives with the realization that, as nothing is permanent but the Immortal aspects of consciousness, these are the things that deserve the highest investment. Anything else is mere utilitarianism.

This is a return to the Black Iron Prison metaphor: you are imprisoned for a crime you did not commit. You have no way to escape. You can decorate your cell in any way you choose; you can rail against the Authorities but will never overturn them; you can enmesh yourself in prison politics and join a gang; you can chart the routines of the guards and the schedules by which it is determined when you get to go out into the yard for exercise. You can even make friends with the guards and wardens and work for the Authorities, thereby making your physical lot in life more comfortable and bearable. If any of this makes you feel better, well, great— go for it. In the end, however, you are still imprisoned; accepting this fact without renouncing the whole kit and caboodle will enmesh you even further in the system that tossed you away for life for a crime you did not commit in the first place. Then, when you are eventually released, you are tossed right back in— after all, you never renounced the System the first time, so why should another go-round be any different?

Or, in terms of popular culture, in the first Matrix movie, Cypher, one of the human rebels, turns traitor and agrees to work for the Agents in return for replacement in the Matrix, in which he is promised an ideal physical existence of bodily pleasures, his memories of his rebel days erased. One finds it difficult to blame him; the "Real" world in the Matrix was not exactly a fun place. Nonetheless, as viewers, we find his actions pretty much reprehensible. His renunciation of the world was incomplete; he turned it on its ear. Still, why begrudge him his decision? Is an illusory life of luxury not far better than a life of poverty in the so-called "Real"? The answer to the Seeker can only be a resounding **no**, because accepting the illusion also amounts to accepting the fact that one is under the control of the Authorities. With the Real, no matter one's personal circumstances, one is at least Free to create one's own Zion. Within the System, the World of Forms, the Black Iron Prison, one does not have control over even the smallest aspects of one's existence.

This renunciation is a single, continuous aspect of enlightenment, a constant repulsion of the illusions of the Authorities and their ability to control your inner being. It is casting off the fetters of control. This is not to say that one is physically free of the influence of the Authorities— by virtue of existing in their world, we often have to play by their rules. Instead, this is the happiness and joy that comes with realizing one's existence for oneself. No matter how bad things are in this life, one's renunciation of the world allows one to look upon every single occurrence as something to be celebrated and a cause for joy. When the Cathars at Montsegur were led to the stake by the Inquisition, they went joyfully, singing, unaffected by the soldiers of the Inquisition and unruled by the System which they had renounced. So, too, does the follower of the Way face the individual vortexes of life that he or she encounters in day-to-day life.

There are a lot of similarities between what the Gnostic Jesus taught and Cynicism, the original Cynicism of Diogenes, not the trendy cynicism of postmodernists and teen-angst movies. Both philosophies are based on the act of eternally questioning, even being willing to question one's own conclusions. The Mysteries were the celebration of humankind's ability to overcome complacency, a skill which many seem to have lost. Thus, the act of renunciation declared by Jesus and other teachers isn't a simple statement of purpose. It's an eternal act that needs to be applied to every aspect of life, because the very second we take back our renunciation, we are right back where we began.

ONE HUNDRED and ELEVEN

Jesus said, "The heavens and the earth will roll up in your presence, and whoever is living from the living one will not see death."

Does not Jesus say, "Those who have found themselves, of them the world is not worthy"?

We picture a massive animated fog bank rolling up like a sleeping bag. There must be some old Popeye cartoon with that image. This image is interesting because it seems to indicate that the World of Forms is layered. How shocking would that be? One moment we are standing around, minding your own business, perhaps dickering over the price of a nice cut of London broil, and BLAM! The corners of the horizon lift off of this plane of existence and begin rolling up into the other levels of reality!

This sounds eschatological on the surface. Jesus seems to be talking about the "end times," when God picks up the corners of the tablecloth like a dime store magician and yanks away, and those who are "living from the living one" will not "see death," whereas those poor saps who have not been born again fall off of the sides of the card table like silverware and fine china, plummeting to their doom and making a rather nasty mess on the floor. As we have come to understand, however, just as reality itself exists in layers, so do the Sayings we have been analyzing, and we must roll the literal layer off to reveal the underlying Reality.

We find a major clue in Saying 11: **"This sky will pass away, and she who is above her will pass away, and the dead are not alive, and the living will not die."** As mentioned in the commentary to that Saying:

"Dead" and "living" are often used by Gnostics to refer to the two states of human awareness. When a Gnostic says dead, he or she usually means "asleep," "unaware," "without gnosis." Someone who is living, on the other hand, is someone who has a personal acquaintance with God, someone who is awake. So, of course the "dead," or those who are as of yet unenlightened, will not "live"— and neither will the "living" die.

This indicates that the Saying is once again encoded. If the living ones are awake, then they will not die, which translates to something along the lines of "Whoever has been enlightened by the Logos won't ever lose that enlightenment."

What, then, does it mean that the heavens and earth are rolling up? This is actually a pretty good description of what happens once one has communed with the Logos and begins to understand that the World of Forms is filled with God as Pleroma. Although it is almost impossible to describe the experience, most people who have attained gnosis feel as though a veil has been lifted from their eyes. The world, on which they thought they had a pretty decent handle, is literally destroyed, lifted away and rolled up. This is not a literal description of the end times; instead, this is a pretty sharp description of psychospiritual processes within the seeker. This is what happens when one realizes that the World of Forms consists of images and systems— the World of Forms itself "lifts up," revealing the underlying nature of things.

We also have a comment on the Saying by a later editor: "Does not Jesus say, "Those who have found themselves, of them the world is not worthy"?" We've discussed this idea in its entirety in Saying 56, which states that "Whoever has come to know the world has discovered a carcass, and whoever has discovered a carcass, of that person the world is not worthy." Again, we see the connections between the living and the dead, the corpse-world and the Immortal underlying perfection which one discovers when those heavens roll on up within. This individual, however, reminds us that in order to transcend the world, one must find one's self, the living one mentioned in the first part of the Saying.

It all ties together rather nicely, and when looked at on the level of inner meaning instead of outward appearance, has an amazingly consistent internal logic.   Taking things literally is, as has been stated previously, a dangerous game to play, because doing so means playing in the sandbox of images. The Gnostic texts are very clear that descriptions of the End Times and the resurrection are metaphors for recurring internal processes within the psyche.

ONE HUNDRED and TWELVE

Jesus said, "Woe to the flesh that depends on the soul.
Woe to the soul that depends on the flesh."

Saying 112 is a return to themes encountered directly in Saying 29 and Saying 87. Jesus points out the false dichotomy of soul vs. the flesh. One is damned if one's body depends upon one's soul, if one's existence within the world of illusion is predicated on and controlled by the world of the soul. One is also damned, and even moreso, if one uses aspects of the illusion to predicate one's spirituality.

This is a warning— sure, we are forced to reside in this illusory manifestation, but using this to justify extremism will certainly bring trouble. Just look at our global culture's stock of religious fanatics of all stripes, who stick so fiercely to legalism and writ and attempts at being holy that they injure others in the process, whether willingly or not. On the other hand, look at those scientific industrialist technocrat materialist types who believe that this world is the be-all-end-all, who actively proselytize against religion and spirituality. Neither extreme is appropriate, but according to this Saying, it is better to at least believe in **something**. Jesus teaches an almost identical concept as the Middle Way taught by Gautama Buddha, the idea that extremes might work for some people but enlightenment is better achieved by balancing the material with the spiritual.

Looked at another way, the Saying may have an additional level of meaning. If we take "depends" to mean something like "hangs from," or "is suspended by," we see evidence of Gnostic cosmology, which sees the body as hanging from the soul, or in Gnostic code, the world of illusion hanging from the Pleroma as an image/emanation. If so, then of course the body that depends on the soul is "woeful," not in the sense that it is being punished, but in the sense that it is removed from the source. In this way, the soul that depends on the body is indeed worse, because it is an image of an image— a false creation by the body that appears real and can be used to manipulate others.

ONE HUNDRED and THIRTEEN

His disciples said to him, "When will the kingdom come?"

"It will not come by watching for it. It will not be said, 'Look, here!' or 'Look, that one!' Rather, the Father's kingdom is spreading out upon the earth, and people don't see her."

And now we come full circle. There are quite a few good arguments one could make about the order of the Sayings in Thomas. Saying 113 essentially rounds out Thomas is its relation to Saying 3. Sayings 1 and 2 serve essentially as introductions to the text; 1A tells you who said and collected the teachings, and 1B and 2 tell you how and why one should go about investigating and studying what has been written:

> (A) These are the secret Sayings that Jesus, who lives, spoke, and Didymos Judas Thomas wrote down.

> (B) 1. And he said, "Whoever falls onto the meaning of these words will not taste death."

> 2. Jesus said, He or she who seeks should not stop seeking until he or she finds what he or she is seeking. When they find what they are seeking, they will be troubled. When they are troubled, they will be amazed, and will become king over the All."

The actual wisdom teachings divorced from the instructional introduction begin with Saying 3, and end with Saying 113. Saying 3 states that:

> Jesus said, "If your leaders say to you, 'Look, the (Father's) kingdom is in the sky,' then the birds of the sky will precede you. If they say to you, 'It is in the sea,' then the fish will precede you. Rather, the (Father's) kingdom is within you and it is outside you.

When you know yourselves, then you will be known, and you will understand that you are children of the living Father. But if you do not know yourselves, then you live in poverty, and you are the poverty."

This is really an introduction of the entire body of the teachings that follow— almost every single Saying can be considered a corollary to Saying 3.

In the same way, Saying 113 summarizes everything just learned. This is a pretty common literary device, and there is no reason to assume that it was not done purposefully by the compiler of these Sayings. In essence, *Thomas* concludes with the disciples asking Jesus, "well, this is all well and good, but when is this stuff going to happen?" Jesus replies, "You can't just look for it. It's not something that appears to the eye. Instead, it's spreading out over the earth, but people don't see it." The Coptic word used for "spread" here, *porshe*, relates to the word *presh*, which translates to "something that is spread," such as a mattress or a cloak or a coverlet— something which is already whole that covers another object through the medium of someone doing the spreading. Jesus indicates a process which occurs in that remarkable timeless fashion that cannot be expressed using our limited verb tenses— the kingdom has been/is/will be eternally spread/ing out "across" the World of Forms through the medium of the Logos, within the body of the Pleroma.

Funnily enough, even within the canonical Gospels Jesus repudiates people who try to figure out when the "Kingdom will come" within an historical context. In *Luke* 17, Jesus makes his famous remark to the Pharisees that the **"kingdom of God is within you."** In his first letter to the Thessalonians, Paul reminds them that **"the day of the Lord will come like a thief in the night."** In *Matthew* 24, Jesus tells us that **". . . you don't know on what day your Lord will come. But understand this: If the owner of the house had known at what time of night the thief was coming, he would have kept watch and would not have let his house be broken into. So you also must be ready, because the Son of Man will come at an hour when you do not expect him."** All of those who are ready for the rapture and for the end times and who pour over prophecy and try to tie it to historical events are essentially wasting their time and confusing people, and ignoring the words of Jesus that are found right there in the canon.

Everything we have learned in Thomas, as introduced in Saying 3 and summed up in Saying 113, explains why we should not be looking to a future "end times" within history. Doing so places the Kingdom of Heaven within the confines of the illusion, an act that causes the soul to depend upon the flesh. When one divorces the process of gnosis and redemption from its eternal nature and tries to stick it within history, one commits a, perhaps the, Demiurgic act.

Gnosis, redemption, resurrection, anastasis, the Logos, the Pleroma, eschatology, everything we have been taught has been/is/will be occurring within each of us every second of every day while we are stuck within the World of Forms. It has been/is/will be occurring within the World of Forms itself as a gradual process, spreading throughout the corruption of the Black Iron Prison through the medium of God. Saying 3 teaches us that this is something that happens inside us and outside us; Sayings 4-112 (and 114) teach us how to understand this concept and apply it to life in the Black Iron Prison through the process of coming to know one's self via the medium of living information which grants one gnosis, and Saying 113 reminds us that all of this is happening to us RIGHT NOW!

This very second!

It's happening to you as you read this!

You're trapped in the illusory world, the corpse-world, and you're subject to the fancies of the Servants of the Rulers of the Prison!

But, you're also being resurrected, you're being assisted from within by a cosmic underground of trained escape artists and divine powers and you are part of the eternal process of the redemption of the ENTIRE UNIVERSE!

The Universe is being saved by you and within you— you're a superhero!

So, what are you going to do about it?

ONE HUNDRED and FOURTEEN

Simon Peter said to them, "Make Mariam leave us, for females don't deserve life."

Jesus said, "Look, I will guide her to make her male, so that she too may become a living spirit resembling you males. For every female who makes herself male will enter the kingdom of Heaven."

As mentioned earlier, many scholars believe that this Saying was added to Thomas later, which may be true, but not really a necessary distinction, except among the PC crowd who might want to whitewash this Saying since it sounds so anti-feminist. This Saying is perhaps out of order; since we know that the Sayings run somewhat thematically, we might place this Saying before Saying 22, which states that:

> "When you make the two into one, and when you make the inner like the outer and the outer like the inner, and the upper like the lower, and when you make male and female into a single one, so that the male will not be male nor the female be female, when you make eyes in place of an eye, a hand in place of a hand, a foot in place of a foot, an image in place of an image, then you will enter the kingdom."

This is such an interesting Saying on a bunch of different levels. Let us begin with the most obvious button-pusher, the apparent misogyny implicit in the idea that "every female who makes herself male" etc. We know very well from almost every single primary and secondary source that the Gnostics were about as far as possible from misogynistic as an organization could be during the early days of Christianity. They considered women equal to men. They allowed women to join the clergy, even to become bishops, according to some. They absolved Eve of the "sin" of eating the fruit from the Tree in Eden, making her into the *de facto* primary Gnostic saviour. They allowed for a coequal feminine counterpart of God, known by various sects as Barbelo, whose descended aspect, Sophia, is given as much import as the Logos in Gnostic mythology —after all, the Word without Wisdom seems pretty useless. Declaring a misogynistic bent based on a single Saying does not make a whole lot of sense.

We can always pull out the old platitudes that God has no gender, that the Early Christians lived in a more misogynistic culture than we so we should accept, say, Paul's misogyny, or, on the other hand, we can take the radical Wiccan theme and declare that all religion MUST be traced back to GODDESS worship and start producing "female" translations of the I Ching where we change all masculine references to feminine references.

Or, we can stop being so bloody literal-minded and realize that speaking in terms of gender hierarchy within mystical religious traditions has absolutely nothing to do with the battle of the sexes! As soon as we plug **human** gender into the mix and give abstract spiritual concepts **human** penises and vaginas, we are immediately drawing those concepts into limited illusion and making the mistake of the Demiurge— the creation of illusory constructs based on our limited understanding of what happens in the realm of God. Whether a power is named as male or female within the context of myth was almost **never** an issue within spiritual culture until literalists took over and made it one.

Character A from myth is described as female, character B male. A does something evil to B, or B does something evil to A. In mythic language, this is where it stops! There is literally no need whatsoever to claim that all women are evil because of what Eve did, nor is there any need to claim that the Gnostics were somehow more enlightened specifically because the afforded equal mythic status to the female. This is not an hierarchical matter.

So why even describe these things in terms of gender? This is a good question, and we can think of the matter in terms of expressive vs. receptive. The Logos is described as "masculine" because the Word is expressive— uttered, spoken. Sophia, as Wisdom, is receptive. Wisdom absorbs, listens, gestates. The Soul is described as "feminine" for the same reason. The Soul is receptive, absorbent, "takes in" the Logos as the bride "takes in" the bridegroom. This is code, not literal, and does not imply that something is better than something else.

The process of Being within the cosmos is a constant back and forth between the expressive and the receptive—a game of catch, as it were. The Logos enters the Soul, the Soul receives and gestates the Logos, the Soul is transformed into an expressive Spirit which gives itself to Sophia, who gestates it, and in turn gives it, through expression, to the Divine. This is how every "female" who makes herself "male" will enter into the divine— every Soul who becomes an expressive Spirit through the medium of the Logos will "resemble males." The Demiurge and his servants who exist without understanding this are essentially juggling, or tossing the ball against a wall. The fact remains that these are internal processes that have nothing to do with the gender of the disciples.

Now that the technical aspects have been discussed, let us take a look at crotchety old Peter. In many of his Gnostic portrayals, we see him as quite jealous of Mary Magdalene. In the *Pistis Sophia* , the disciples, including Mary and her sister Martha, are gathered together listening to the resurrected Christ and having a conversation with him about various subjects. Mary proves one of the more brilliant disciples, and provides long and enlightened discourse on the nature of Being. After a while, Peter interrupts with, **"My Lord, we are not able to suffer this woman who takes the opportunity from us, and does not allow anyone of us to speak, but she speaks many times."**

In the *Gospel According to Mary*, after Mary gives a discourse on secrets given to her by Christ, we find the following exchange:

Peter answered and spoke concerning these same things.

4) He questioned them about the Savior: Did He really speak privately with a woman and not openly to us? Are we to turn about and all listen to her? Did He prefer her to us?

5) Then Mary wept and said to Peter, My brother Peter, what do you think? Do you think that I have thought this up myself in my heart, or that I am lying about the Savior?

6) Levi answered and said to Peter, Peter you have always been hot tempered.

7) Now I see you contending against the woman like the adversaries.

8) But if the Savior made her worthy, who are you indeed to reject her? Surely the Savior knows her very well.

9) That is why He loved her more than us. Rather let us be ashamed and put on the perfect Man, and separate as He commanded us and preach the gospel, not laying down any other rule or other law beyond what the Savior said.

Is Peter just simply envious? Or can we find a deeper meaning?

Looking at the matter from the standpoint of Gnostic code, Peter represents, in these cases, just what represented in the Canonical tradition, the Worldly Church. Levi all but tells Peter that he is acting like the Archons, railing against women like the legalists. Mary represents the Gnostic who comes to know the inner teachings of the Logos, and Peter represents the exoteric Church and the teachings as interpreted by illusion and culture.

It is **extremely** important to recognize in this context that Peter is by no means a reviled, unenlightened, hopeless case. He is, after all, right there with the disciples, just as important as the rest and certainly enlightened. In the *Pistis Sophia*, after his outburst, he is allowed his own chance to give an exposition on Gnostic thought, which is every bit as important and valid as the interpretations of teaching given by Mary. Peter's error in these cases is not that he is **wrong**, it is that he tries to impose his illusory hierarchical structure on someone else instead of just waiting his turn and sharing his own gnosis. The Gnostics who used the "Peter as Church" code in no way condemned the Worldly Church for their teachings, which can certainly lead one to gnosis; they condemned the Worldly Church because it, like Peter, often relies too much on cultural and legal dogma and try to impose that cultural and legal dogma onto others.

So, in this final Saying, Jesus does not condemn Peter, but instead speaks to him in his own language, addressing him as an **individual** with individual concerns. It is possible, according to this Saying, to express the ideas contained within Gnosticism in any context, even to those involved in the literalist churches. It does not take the value away from the Worldly Church; rather, it opens the door to all who are receptive ("female") that they might become expressive ("male") and thereby enter the kingdom of Heaven, that wonderful kingdom that spreads out all around us, but that people just do not see.

ENDNOTES

---

[i] Mead, G.R.S. trans. *Pistis Sophia* Chap. 61.

[ii] Suzuki, D.T. *Zen Buddhism; Selected Writings of D.T. Suzuki.* p. 84.

[iii] Remember that when we refer to Gnostic "code," we're referring to a semiotic system that made perfect sense to those who composed and would have studied the original Gnostic teachings. It is "code" to us because we are not familiar with the concepts in the same way that "I'm going to download the zipped file onto my hard drive" might be considered code to someone unfamiliar with computers.

[iv] Ellul, Jacques. *Anarchy and Christianity.*

[v] Layton, Bentley ed. *The Gnostic Scriptures.*

[vi] Gandhi, M.K. *An Autobiography: The Story of My Experiments with Truth.*

[vii] As an oblique aside, this brings to mind the prophecy of the witches in Macbeth— that he cannotbe harmed by anyone "born of woman." Macbeth's confidence that he couldn't be harmed was shattered when his enemy, Macduff, revealed that he'd been "untimely ripped" from his mother's womb.

[viii] Pagels, Elaine. *The Gnostic Gospels.*

[ix] Ibid.

[x] As a matter of fact, I'll be referring to Dick so frequently that to locate specific sources in his wealth of writings would be tedious for both you and me. If you're interested in exploring Dick's Gnostic concepts in further detail, I suggest *In Pursuit of VALIS: Selections from the Exegesis*, as well as the semi-fictional *VALIS* trilogy, which outlines his Gnostic philosophy in great detail.

[xi] Ellul, Jacques. *The Presence of the Kingdom.* pp 55-56.

[xii] What, did you expect me to do all of your work for you?

[xiii] Boy, that Jesus guy sure does like nekkid people, don't he?

[xiv] "The Answer to Life, The Universe and Everything." Wikipedia Online Encyclopedia. Page last modified April 7, 2005.

http://en.wikipedia.org/wiki/The_Answer_to_Life,_the_Universe,_and_Everything

[xv] See, for instance, *The Jesus Mysteries*, by Timothy Freke and Peter Gandy—certainly one of the more comprehensive and valuable works on the subject.

[xvi] For the importance of the enlightened human as the "Son of God," *vide* Morton Smith's *Jesus the Magician*.

[xvii] Mead, G.R.S. trans. *Corpus Hermeticum.* "The Secret Sermon on the Mountain."

[xviii] Ibid. "Poemandres, the Shepard of Men."

[xix] Enemies.com. Page last modified January 26, 2004. http://www.enemies.com/html/oldtestament/4/10commandment.html

[xx] Parrott, Douglas M. and Wilson, R. McL trans. *The Acts of Peter and the Twelve Apostles.* http://www.webcom.com/gnosis/naghamm/actp.html

http://en.wikipedia.org/wiki/George_Berkeley

[xxii] "Heisenberg Uncertainty Principle." http://zebu.uoregon.edu/~imamura/208/jan27/hup.html

[xxiii] Kazantzakis, Nikos. *The Saviours of God.*

[xxiv] "Sacrifice." JewishEncyclopedia.com. http://www.jewishencyclopedia.com/view.jsp?artid=35&letter=S#3

[xxv] Tip of the hat to Rev. Sam Osborne+, Hagia Sophia Chapel, Ecclesia Gnostica.

[xxvi] Saying found in various collections.

[xxvii] Dick, Phillip K. *In Pursuit of VALIS: Selections from the Exegesis.*

[xxviii] Thanks to Brett Hamil.

[xxix] De Nicolas, Antonio trans. "Baghavad Gita: The Song of Embodied Vision." *Avatara: The Humanization of Philosophy Through the Baghavad Gita.* 1976.

[xxx] Prieur, Ran. "Science the Destroyer." http://ranprieur.com/essays/scidest.html.

[xxxi] "Buddha Nature." The Free Dictionary. http://encyclopedia.thefreedictionary.com/buddha%20nature.

[xxxii] Adams, Douglas. *The Hitchhiker's Guide to the Galaxy.*

[xxxiii] Dick, Philip K. *VALIS.*

ABOUT THE AUTHOR

Bro. Jeremy Puma has been a student of Gnosticism for fourteen years. He is one of the founding members of the Palm Tree Garden Gnostic Community, online at www.palmtreegarden.org, as well as the Gnostic Order of Allogenes, an independent Gnostic ministry. Bro. Puma lives in Seattle, Washington with his wonderful wife Emily and their little dog, too. He can be contacted at eleleth@palmtreegarden.org.

OTHER BOOKS BY JEREMY PUMA

Running Towards the Bomb: Essays on Gnosticism and the End of Civilisation

A collection of essays, originally published on the fantastic planet weblog, concerning the Gnostic philosophy as applied to the End of Civilisation. The collection also touches upon Gnosticism and conspiracy theory, UFOs and other diverse topics, including Scooby Doo!

73 pp.   ISBN 978-1-4116-4523-3

Mysteries of the Gnostic Ascent: A Gnostic Prayer Sequence

A Gnostic Prayer Sequence for individual or group practice based on the Secret Book of John from the Nag Hammadi Library. Includes instructions for a Gnostic chaplet (prayer beads, like a rosary).

56 pp. ISBN 978-1-84728-883-7

The Pirate's Garden: Musings and Manifestoes

The Pirate's Garden features musings and manifestos on life in the modern Gnostic revival, in theory and practice. Including thoughts on Mary Magdalene, Gnostic Myth and Chaos Theory, Overcoming fear, and much, much more, "The Pirate's Garden" is certain to get you thinking in new ways about an ancient tradition!

143 pp. ISBN 978-1-84728-027-5

Brother Tom's Miracle Book of Signs and Wonders: A Gnostic Folk Gospel

"These are some things that our teacher said and that I, Brother Tom, wrote down. The teacher really said all of these things to us." These pages contain a secret message. A Gnostic Folk Gospel from the Palm Tree Garden, based on a reading of the Gospel of Thomas. Illustrated.

Order through your locally-owned bookseller or online at www.lulu.com/eleleth.

www.palmtreegarden.org

3368460

Made in the USA